Behind the effervescent, ever-cheerful image that Doris Day portrayed through dozens of classic Hollywood movies was an extraordinary story of private pain. Her dazzling smile hid a tormented personal life that included a disastrous marriage to a violent psychopath and a terrifying accident that nearly ended her life. And yet for generations of movie-goers Doris Day remained the embodiment of innocent beauty and apple-pie homeliness and even today she exerts a powerful fascination for millions of fans around the world.

Eric Braun, MA (Cantab.), is a theatre and film critic and show-business writer. After service in the Royal Artillery he began his career with Odeon cinemas before entering the film industry. He has written a biography of Deborah Kerr and three books with Beryl Reid.

Doris Day

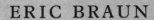

ERIC BRAUN

ORION

An Orion paperback
First published in Great Britain by
George Weidenfeld & Nicolson in 1991
This paperback edition published in 1994 by Orion Books Ltd,
Orion House, 5 Upper St Martin's Lane, London WC2H 9EA

Eighth impression

Revised edition 2004

A CIP catalogue record for this book is
available from the British Library.

ISBN: 0 75281 715 9

Typeset at The Spartan Press Ltd, Lymington, Hants

Printed in England by Clays Ltd, St Ives plc

Some of the illustrations in this book are stills issued to publicize films
made or distributed by the following companies.

Warner Brothers: *My Dream is Yours, Tea For Two, Storm Warning,
I'll See You in My Dreams, April in Paris, Calamity Jane, Young at
Heart*; MGM/Turner Entertainment Company: *Love Me or Leave
Me, Please Don't Eat the Daisies, Glass Bottom Boat*; Paramount: *The
Man Who Knew Too Much*; Universal: *Pillow Talk, Ballad of Josie*;
Twentieth Century-Fox: *Move Over, Darling, Do Not Disturb,
Caprice*.

Photographs have been made available by the National Film Archive,
the Doug McCelland Collection, Weidenfeld & Nicolson Archive,
Martyn Daye for the Doris Day Society, Terry O'Neill, Pierre Patrick,
Leo Fuchs and Marjie Neswitz.

Although every effort has been made to trace the copyright holders
of all photographs, the publishers apologize in advance for any
unintentional omission and will be pleased to make the appropriate
acknowledgements to companies or individuals in subsequent
editions of this book.

CONTENTS

ACKNOWLEDGEMENTS

The road to Carmel and Doris Day was a circuitous one, via Scarsdale, New York, where I went to arrange details of a proposed biography of the late Joan Bennett, femme fatale of the famous Bennett family: actually the gentlest of the film-star daughters of Richard – Constance and Barbara were the others – she was so named because of some of the most prestigious roles she played on the screen. When the deal was finally set up with my publishers Weidenfeld & Nicolson, Joan and her husband, movie-drama critic David Wilde, on the verge of signing the contract, decided she was not well enough to go ahead with the interviews, and, in fact, she sadly died some months later. There I was with a deadline and no subject, when the publishers in London came forward with their most exciting project – Doris Day.

My grateful thanks are due to many people for their generous cooperation and practical help in preparing this book – notable among them Christopher Frayling who, with his colleague, producer Margaret Sharp, persuaded Doris to appear in their 1989 documentary on her life and work, *I Don't Even* Like *Apple Pie*, for BBC Television, for which they went to her home town, Carmel, Central California to do the filming. His perceptive and witty account of their experiences at that time forms an essential pivotal chapter, which he kindly took time to amend and correct, despite the heavy demands of his work as Professor of Cultural History at the Royal College of Art in Kensington Gore. Another academic whose work was of inestimable assistance was my friend David Balhatchet, who managed to combine his studies of Politics, Philosophy and History at Birkbeck College, London University with helping me collate an index as comprehensive, we dare hope, as the subject warrants. His colleague at the University, Alison King, performed miracles of speed and efficiency with her word processor in re-assembling the material, while Marjie Skates of Hayes proved a veritable genie of the typewriter with last-minute rewrites, as did Anne Poole for the index.

International biographer and entertainments writer Michael Thornton deserves a paragraph to himself for his generous support, advice and diligent help in every department, along with my most supportive friend Jim Longridge, Chief Projectionist at the Odeon, Richmond, himself a Doris Day fan from the time he started showing her films, who has supplied works of reference and videos that have been of invaluable assistance.

Doug McClelland, American author of acclaimed biographies on Ronald Reagan, Susan Hayward and Eleanor Parker, among many others, turned over to me his comprehensive DD file and several most useful and rare photographs, besides keeping me posted with up-to-date clippings from across the Atlantic on the lady's current activities. As always, the BFI and Spotlight, London, provided a mass of indispensable material during my months of research in their Archives, along with a wealth of photographs and useful addresses and contacts. Contacts, too and essential information came from author-journalist Hilton Tims of the *Surrey Comet*, ever helpful David Quinlan, Films Editor of the *TV Times*, my agent, Carolyn Whitaker, the BBC's Lyn Fairhurst, writer-publicist Howard Elson, show-business writer and ballet expert Audrey Smith and my long-time friend and colleague Marjorie Cummins.

Martyn and Carol Daye at their headquarters at Ambleside in the Lake District made available their voluminous files on Doris Day and her life's work, amassed during their years of running the Doris Day Society, with its magazine *Simply Doris*, while John Frye, another energetic member who works for the Film Section of the BBC at Ealing Studios, willingly and most helpfully lent me his definitive collection of Day videos.

Of Doris's colleagues most valuable insights into working with her have been provided by Rosemary De Camp, Natasha Parry and Mamie Van Doren, while for their correspondence I am indebted to Doris Day's PRO, Linda Dozoretz, James Garner, Howard Keel, Deborah Kerr, Virginia Mayo, Tony Randall, Ronald Reagan and Doris's butler, or, as she calls him, 'houseman', Sydney Wood, Dagenham's contribution to one of the original British Doris Day Fan Clubs.

I owe a debt of gratitude to Sandra and Gary Barnes – the then management of the Waldegrave Arms, Teddington, who were long-suffering in allowing myself and Swanee to monopolize their most comfortable window-seat and table during opening hours for exhaustive proofreading sessions. Further, they not only fed us excellently, but on occasions made available office amenities left behind in the stress of the moment – a kindness far in excess of the normal call of hospitality!

Last but by no means least, bringing us up to date with this 2004 revision, my thanks go to researcher Stephen Munns, who instigated the splendid idea to update my book in time for Doris's landmark 80th birthday. His knowledge on the subject of Doris Day, gleaned while compiling his website *www.dorisdaytribute.com* and working as a project coordinator for Sony Music, was invaluable – providing me with a wealth of new music, film and photo content. In addition, he helped rally the troops, so to speak, encouraging an array of avid DD supporters worldwide, to step forward and interject their vast and varied expertise. Some of these kind people who, each in their own right, deserve a special thanks are Ken Hallett (Canada), Howard Green (USA), Bill Glynn (USA), Pierre Patrick (USA), Jerry Geohring (USA), Douglas Evans (USA), Paul Brochette (USA) and Alan Moore (Australia) – president of The Australian Doris Day Society.

Eric Braun

PHOTO CREDITS

Section 1

Doris Day, aged three, with her brother Paul (British Film Institute)
Doris as an adolescent (British Film Institute)
With the bandleader Barney Rapp (British Film Institute)
As vocalist to Bob Crosby and his Bobcats (British Film Institute)
With Lee Bowman in the movie *My Dream is Yours* (Weidenfeld & Nicolson Archives)
With Eve Arden in *Tea for Two* (Doug McClelland Collection)
With son Terry (British Film Institute)
On the set of *Storm Warning* (Doug McClelland Collection)
Wedding to Marty Melcher (Weidenfeld & Nicolson Archives)
Recording session with Johnnie Ray and Frankie Laine (Doris Day Society)
With her mother, Alma Kappelhoff (British Film Institute)
With Danny Thomas in *I'll See You in My Dreams* (Weidenfeld & Nicolson Archives)
On the set of *I'll See You in My Dreams* (National Film Archive)

A lunchbox for Terry (Weidenfeld & Nicolson Archives)

With Ray Bolger and Claude Dauphin in *April in Paris* (Doug McClelland Collection)

A 'kooky moment' from *My Dream is Yours* (National Film Archive)

As *Calamity Jane* (Weidenfeld & Nicolson Archives)

With Frank Sinatra in *Young at Heart* (Doug McClelland Collection)

As Thirties' singing star, Ruth Etting with James Cagney, in *Love Me or Leave Me* (Doug McClelland Collection)

In *Love Me or Leave Me* with director Charles Vidor (National Film Archive)

Directed by Alfred Hitchcock in *The Man Who Knew Too Much* (National Film Archive)

With James Stewart in *The Man Who Knew Too Much* (Doug McClelland Collection)

Section 2

As the virtuous advertising executive Carol Templeton in *Lover Come Back*, photo by Leo Fuchs (Leo Fuchs)

With Cary Grant, taken during the filming of *That Touch of Mink*, photo by Leo Fuchs (Leo Fuchs)

With Rex Harrison in *Midnight Lace* (Doug McClelland Collection)

With James Garner, Casey Adams and Fred Clark in *Move Over, Darling* (Doug McClelland Collection)

A bizarre moment in *Move Over, Darling* (Doug McClelland Collection)

Doris admiring the roses in the garden of her previous [Beverley Hills] home in LA, photo by Leo Fuchs (Leo Fuchs)

Doris being kissed by her co-star and friend Rock

Hudson, in their second comedy movie, *Lover Come Back* – photo by Leo Fuchs (Leo Fuchs)

Doris having fun trying hats in a Beverly Hills milliners, photo by Leo Fuchs (Leo Fuchs)

With Rod Taylor in *The Glass Bottom Boat* (Doug McClelland Collection)

Waiting to be called for *The Doris Day Show* (Doris Day Society)

With mother Alma (National Film Archive)

With Perry Como on *The Doris Mary Anne Kappelhoff Special* (Doris Day Society)

Doris cycling – her favourite form of relaxation, captured awheel by Kent Gavin for the *Daily Mail* (Doris Day Society)

At home in verdant Carmel, photo by Terry O'Neill (Doris Day Society)

Photo call with Rock Hudson for *Doris Day's Best Friends* (Doris Day Society)

With Clint Eastwood at the Golden Globe Awards ceremony (Doris Day Society)

With Pierre Patrick, the producer of musical *My Doris Day* at her home in Carmel (Pierre Patrick/Patty Carver)

PROLOGUE TO 2004 EDITION

———— ✹ ————

The timing of this revision to Eric Braun's *Doris Day* biography (originally a top-ten bestseller) is not by chance, but its release coincides with the year that the unique, sparkling, ever-youthful Miss Day celebrates her 80th birthday.

Although the Doris of today is so far removed from her showbiz heyday of the 'Fifties and 'Sixties, she still remains that very vibrant and sunny character, much as people will remember her being during the career which is so well documented throughout Eric's book. It's just that her days of being in make-up, on film sets or at Columbia's recording studios are now replaced with eventful days surrounded by and caring for her many four-legged friends, who live with her on her vast and picturesque estate in Carmel.

Her concerns are no longer learning lines or lyrics but lobbying tirelessly for the sake of suffering animals, defending their rights to the hilt (something she does out of sheer passion and sincere conviction).

She achieves this through her two animal charities, the Doris Day Animal League *www.ddal.org* and the Doris Day Animal Foundation *www.ddaf.org* for which she writes regular columns in their joint magazine *Animal Guardian*, spreading the word about the next topical crusade. Her efforts were even acknowledged by the American Society for the Prevention of Cruelty to Animals, which, in 1993, honoured her with their award for the *Significant Contribution to the Welfare of Animals*.

As people grow older their focus of attention tends to change, and for Doris it has meant that she has been happy to distance herself from the spotlight. Her publicist, almost as a matter of course, gracefully declines the many television and film requests which still find their way to her.

Since her last television interviews given to British chat-show hosts Gloria Hunniford and Des O'Connor in 1994, she has made but a few sporadic guest appearances on radio shows in the USA, a medium with which she still seems comfortable. A regular spot, for example, would be an annual telephone chat on her birthday with a Philadelphia radio DJ, answering questions submitted by ardent fans. This, however, could never come close to quenching the thirst music and film lovers worldwide still have for her.

This obvious void has been only partially filled by the constant flurry of activity from the many companies she worked with during her acting and singing days. Over the last decade alone nearly all of her studio albums have been digitally remastered and reissued on CD by Sony Music in England (something with which I have been involved), and more recently by Collectables in the USA. The same can also, thankfully, be said for most of her movie roles, which have found their way onto VHS format, and which are now gradually being reissued on DVD.

The truth is that none of this would be possible if Doris Day's appeal hadn't transcended generations – but it has! The perfect testimony to this was in 1998, when the American television network A&E Biography aired *It's Magic,* their two-hour tribute to her life and career, which was an instant hit and their most successful until chat-show queen Oprah Winfrey was profiled.

Even Hollywood has begun to reflect on her legacy with cult film producer Baz Luhrmann having used her Latin song 'Perhaps, Perhaps, Perhaps' on the trendy soundtrack to his movie *Strictly Ballroom*. (Incidentally, this song was remixed in the spring of 2003 by a club DJ who works for independent dance label Pure Groove Music in London.) Furthermore, another Day recording, 'High Hopes', found its way in 1998 into the popular animated movie *Antz*, again raising her profile, this time for a younger audience. Most significantly, attempts have been made to resurrect the classic Hudson/Day genre of 'comedy movie', with the release in 2003 of the movie *Down with Love* starring Ewan McGregor and Renée Zellweger.

Bringing us up to date in 2004, Sony Music in England plan to salute her legacy of song by issuing a very special three-CD boxed set, embracing three themes which reflect her: soundtracks, golden greats and classic collaborations.

As for the future, Warner Brothers has just given its blessing to Broadway giant Randy Skinner, whose musical credits include *42nd Street* and Rodgers and Hammerstein's *State Fair*, to create and direct a new music and dance explosion of *Calamity Jane*. The musical, which was made famous by Doris in the 1953 film adaptation, was recently voted into the Top 25 of British television audiences' *100 Greatest Musicals*, proving the timing couldn't be better for the stage version. Pierre Patrick, the associate producer, tells me it will have its New York Premiere in 2005, with a special benefit performance for Doris's Animal League charity.

Rumours are also about town that some of today's biggest and brightest stars are queuing to play Doris's immortal role of Calamity, with a distinct possibility that the making of the show will become the subject of a hot new reality-TV programme in the USA.

For further up-to-date information concerning Doris Day, visit my tribute website at *www.dorisdaytribute.com*.

Stephen Munns

INTRODUCTION

'Desperately Seeking Doris . . .'

My first sight of Doris Day on screen was in the trailer for *It's Magic*. I had read the enthusiastic blurb in *Picturegoer*, one of several movie magazines which proliferated at that time, and to which I occasionally contributed articles: 'Dawn of a Bright New Day!' was the headline, and one of the quotes from the new star which I found rather appealing was, 'Are you afraid of the dark?' 'That depends who's in it!' she said. Nevertheless, I decided to give the film a miss: as assistant manager for Odeons on leaving the army, I had suffered from rather a surfeit of Grables, and this new girl, so pleasantly singing the title song up there, reminded me too much of Betty, all Technicolored platinum blonde, ruby lips and ribbons and bows – with just a dash of Frances Langford in the melodious voice. The plot, too – a poor working girl, decked out in expensive clothes, provided by someone else so she could impersonate a rich socialite enjoying a cruise on a luxury liner – hadn't we been through something like that with Alice Faye, equally blonde and cuddly, in *Weekend in Havana*? So, no DD for the time being, although she was under contract to Warners and they had a good track record with glamorous women stars.

It was, indirectly, MGM, their greatest rivals among

Hollywood studios, which provided the catalyst for my belated appreciation of Doris Day. In 1936 stage actress Gladys George had a stage hit called *In Person*, which Paramount purchased for Mae West: she made it over in her own highly inimitable way and it came to the screen under the title of *Go West Young Man*. Gladys George, deprived of her opportunity of piloting herself into screen stardom in her own vehicle, was offered a consolation prize as the lead in a Western-type role in a film called *Valiant Is The Word For Carrie*, and the result was an MGM contract, under which her first assignment was to star with Spencer Tracy, no less, in a World War One drama, *They Gave Him A Gun*, followed by the perennial *Madame X* in 1937. A crazy comedy, then all the go in film entertainment, *Love Is A Headache* with Franchot Tone followed, but Louis B. Mayer, the Czar of the MGM hierarchy, decided that, at thirty-eight, her blonde, hard-boiled image was not the stuff of which enduring stardom is made, and she was demoted to supporting Norma Shearer's *Marie Antoinette*, as Madame Dubarry, on the receiving end of the Queen's quip, obliged by the King to receive her hated rival at court, 'Ah, Madame, even royalty enjoys an occasional roll in the gutter!'

From then on Gladys, much in demand for character parts, moved to Warners, where James Cagney died memorably in her arms in *The Roaring 'Twenties* in 1939. By 1951 she was cast to play Doris Day's alcoholic ex-Broadway star mother in *Lullaby Of Broadway*, which I, as a confirmed Gladys George fan since *Carrie*, went to see on the strength of a trailer featuring her wonderfully hoarse rendering of 'It's Only A Shanty In Old Shanty Town'. From the moment of 'daughter' Doris's entrance in top hat and tails, to sing 'Just One Of Those Things', that's the way it was with me – I fell hook, line and sinker. From then on she joined my own charmed circle of hitherto exclusively Thirties top ten favourite cinema stars; Constance Bennett and sister Joan; Myrna Loy, Kay Francis, *King Kong*'s Fay Wray, our own Gracie Fields, Marlene Dietrich, Joan Crawford, Greta Garbo and, of course – Gladys George! From then on it was a case of move over, Garbo.

Lullaby Of Broadway was Doris's eighth movie and from then on I quickly went in search for the missing seven, often cycling to the outskirts of London, and, on one memorable occasion, to Southsea, to catch up with the second, *My Dream Is Yours*, showing, uniquely, with Constance Bennett's own production *Smart Woman*, with Brian Aherne, on a double bill. That was, indeed, a red-letter day in my filmgoing life, and a red-letter day in my literary life was when I was asked to write a new biography of Doris Day. Her following had remained vast and loyal since she withdrew from the roar of the crowd and the smell of the greasepaint, and a new BBC documentary at the beginning of the year had evoked tremendous response.

Almost a lifetime of following her movies and dreaming to her records formed a solid background to my research; seemingly all that remained was to write to the lady herself and ask if she could squeeze in the time to see me. My letter to Carmel was posted well before Christmas 1989: in the New Year I started exhaustive research in the British Film Institute Archives and waited. And waited. In May 1990 my letter was returned – not known! That was, in itself, a wry laugh. I was advised I had one letter wrong in the PO box number – through such tiny errors can kingdoms topple. However, I obtained the address of Doris's Press Agent, Linda Dozoretz of McMullen and Dozoretz of Sunset Boulevard, Los Angeles, and readdressed the letter care of her.

There was nothing for it but to carry on researching and wait. My friend, author-journalist Michael Thornton heard out my woes and went into a brown study. On 29 May there appeared an item in the *Evening Standard*'s London Life page – Mr Pepys's Diary, headed 'Desperately Seeking Doris', accompanied by a glowing photograph of the lady of Carmel with one of her most adored pets, Biggest – so called because he was the largest, I believe. The story reported my perplexity and that of my dog Swanee, custodian of my Answerphone.

The next morning I had a call from a stranger in the Lake District – one Martyn Daye, head of the Doris Day Society. He and his wife Carol had just returned from a holiday with 'Do Do' – their pet name for her – in Carmel and happened upon Mr Pepys. We arranged that we would travel to their home in Ambleside to spend a few days exploring the labyrinthine archives of the Society, located in their house. The morning I left for the Lake District it arrived, a letter from Doris, posted in Carmel on 4 July. A letter of much warmth and charm, explaining that she was so busy with her animal rescue work, plus managing a very large home which formed the centre of her activities, with lots of her own pets so there would not be enough time to see me before the end of the year, but finishing, 'Thank you very much for asking me and I shall sincerely look forward to meeting you one of these days. My warmest regards, Doris.' She added a characteristic PS 'I loved the photograph of Swanee and Fluffy. I have a dog named Buster who looks very much like Swanee and a cat named Punky who looks exactly like Fluffy. Aren't they all wonderful!!!'

In the meantime, there were the rewarding trips to the Lake District and to other people associated with Doris, especially John Frye in Maidenhead, another bastion of the Doris Day Appreciation Society, who kindly provided virtually all the DD videos I did not already have – some twenty-eight packed into the panniers of my bicycle which gave up the ghost with a puncture in Windsor and led to a demeaning haul on the train home.

Of over thirty letters to associates who worked with Doris in her film days, there were a couple of surprising results. Virginia Mayo sent an attractive signed photograph of herself – and nothing else. After a visit to Richard Harris's superb portrayal of Pirandello's *Henry IV* at Wyndham's Theatre, I sent a couple of letters to his dressing-room which evoked the remarkable response, via a young lady assistant, that he could only answer questions about working with Miss Day in the film *Caprice* with her written permission. To counterbalance these curious responses there was an immediate and most helpful reply from the delightful Rosemary De Camp, who twice 'mothered' Doris in the movies. Her testimonial is included in the section on *By The Light Of The Silvery Moon* and *On Moonlight Bay*; likewise the letter from Mamie Van Doren on the subject of Doris Day's treatment of her in the film *Teacher's Pet*. She also enclosed a photograph which showed she has changed little of her raunchy appeal since she was *The Girl Who Invented Rock and Roll*. To these ladies and everyone else who helped to shed light on the subject of our star I am deeply obliged.

I

❀

Renaissance, 1989

Saturday, 4 March 1989, marked an occasion for jubila-
tion, not only for members of the flourishing and ubiquitous Doris Day Society, but for everyone in the
British Isles with access to a television set. Everyone,
that is, either mature enough to have grown up during
the peak Day years for movies, from 1948–1968, or
young enough in heart to recall what now seems to have
been an age of innocence reflected in her early musicals
which, although reflecting the then current need for
escapism in the wake of World War Two, also mirrored
the glamour of a Hollywood where boy not only met,
and eventually won, girl, but girl became an overnight
sensation. These situations, invariably derided as clichés,
had, in fact, occurred in show-business circles at least as
far back as the turn of the century, so this was the cinema
holding up a rose-tinted mirror to life, a life transformed
into instant sunshine by the Doris Day persona of the
radiant 'Girl Next Door'. Myrna Loy once said in a film
'I think life should be more like the movies'; in a way it
was, transmogrified into something shiny and bright, a
sure-fire palliative for the world-weary audiences.

So, on this red – or should this be pink – letter day in
1989 BBC TV heralded a short season of Doris Day
films with a brand-new documentary called *I Don't Even*

Like *Apple Pie* in which, interviewed by Christopher Frayling, she disposed of a few myths, confirmed a few others, and, with the help of film clips, illustrated the burgeoning of her fame and talents through three stages; the band singer into film star of *It's Magic* (and it was) and sixteen other Warner Brothers productions, most, bar two dramas, with music and terpsichory; the independent star of top-grossing films which began with her great biographical musical, *Love Me or Leave Me*; and the final peak phase of popularity inaugurated by producer Ross Hunter with the sophisticated and glitzy comedy *Pillow Talk* with Rock Hudson, culminating in *With Six You Get Eggroll* in 1968. That, for the majority of British viewers, marked the last of Doris Day, film star: the five years of TV sit-coms, *The Doris Day Show* to which her late manager-husband Martin Melcher had committed her before his sudden death, although all were top-rated in the USA were, for some obscure reason, only minimally and regionally shown in Britain. Her talk show *Doris Day's Best Friends* on Cable's Christian Broadcast Network in 1985/6, was filmed around her home in Carmel, featuring her abiding concern and work her Pet Foundation, and although her friends included Rock Hudson in his last deeply disturbing appearance on television, the late Leslie Halliwell, responsible for hiring subjects for screening in Britain, told Martyn Daye, President of the Doris Day Society, that the quality of production did not warrant their purchase for showing in Britain.

I Don't Even Like *Apple Pie* started with a clip from her third film *It's A Great Feeling* in which nearly every star on the Warner roster puts in an appearance: Doris, as the studio commissary waitress Judy Adams, trembling on the brink of her big break, is nonetheless demonstrating the independent spirit which was to be the guiding force for most of her screen roles by declaring passionately 'Maybe I can't act and maybe I can't sing, but I want to find out for myself, Mr Dennis Morgan, and, if you don't mind I'll buy my own ticket to the Hollywood Bowl!' The camera then reveals today's Doris, stating, 'I wasn't the typical glamour girl, and the ladies and the girls thought – if she can make it, so can I.' She concedes, 'Maybe they could': more likely, maybe they couldn't. Frayling, defining her as one of the most popular and influential movie stars of all time, points out that, despite the fact that in a twenty-year career of thirty-nine movies she played a wide range of parts, from musicals, thrillers and melodramas to sophisticated comedies, people still tend to remember her from that role created in her early films, that of the 'All-American Girl Next Door', the 'Perpetual Virgin' and 'Miss Goody Twoshoes', rather than the independent and resolute heroine she was, on film and in her life.

She denies categorically all those early tags and later protests she doesn't even like apple pie – she prefers peaches! Be that as it may, she certainly glows with *bonhomie* (maybe bonnefemmie is more apposite) and what could well pass for perpetual youth. Good humour and spontaneity were what first endeared her to the public; as she sits in her chair by a window she appears relaxed in answering most of Christopher Frayling's questions – the only time her *sangfroid* seems on the point of deserting her is over the question of Mamie Van Doren's statements in her autobiography that Doris on the set of *Teacher's Pet* behaved like a temperamental film star and would not speak to her. Momentarily the Day's sunshine leaves her voice as she says, 'She is not well. This lady is making that up, and that's too bad. I feel sorry for her to say something like that. That is *not* true – I don't behave like that!' When her interlocutor goes on to muse whether the difference between the dumb blonde played by Van Doren and Doris as the career woman was done deliberately to point the difference between her role image and that played by such sex symbols as Monroe or Jayne Mansfield, the immediate reaction is 'But I'm not either of them; I couldn't possibly do that!' But instantly the thunder-clouds disperse and with a laugh she says, 'Well, maybe I could, maybe I could', concluding cheerfully, 'No – I don't think so; you are what you are.'

She talked glowingly of some of her leading men, notably Rock Hudson, Clark Gable, Gordon MacRae and James Garner and the interview ends with her statement of her total dedication to the animals in her life, her sadness over the thousands of those put down daily by euthanasia, campaigning for universal sterilization of all but carefully chosen breed pets, over which President Reagan explained it would have to be a State law – and, 'How do you go about that, Christopher? It's so hard.' So many people, she points out, work for the elderly and the children, not enough for the animals, which is what made her decide to go in that direction, although she does work for pets for the elderly – and loves children. She also loves people – especially animal people, but it's the genus animalia which claims the major portion of her heart. Of her Pet Foundation she says, 'If we find a dog on the street and it's homeless, we take it in: we never put a dog down unless it's very ill – we keep them as long as we have to. They have a right to live out their lives, because their lives aren't that long anyway, so they go into the foster homes of which we have many wonderful ones in Los Angeles.' She feels an empathy for the animals which impels her to do everything she can for them 'until the day I die'.

Regarding 'Que Sera Sera', widely regarded as the

theme song for her life, she defines her philosophy as, 'the way we live our lives is what shapes our lives'. Her last words are directed to the people who through the years have written her letters saying that when they feel depressed her films have cheered them up. Tearfully she blows a kiss and says, 'I really love them'. This is no actress-orientated 'Farewell for now and 'till we meet again the number of my next record is . . .': Doris Day is the most unactressy of stars; the truth of the emotion that shines through her work must account for her enduring popularity with all ages, classes and nationalities, so many years after her films were seen in the cinema. Television repeats and constant airings of her recordings – in Japan she has again become Number One in what used to be known as the Hit Parade – cannot entirely account for the ageless quality of her appeal, captured so poignantly in Christopher Frayling's straight-to-the-heart documentary.

The quality of the work is all the more praiseworthy considering it was made, like his other interviews for television and radio with legendary film names, during his 'free time' – or research time – during his more than demanding full-time work as Professor of Cultural History at London's Royal College of Art. The story behind the filming is as fascinating (at least to Doris Day fans, which must account for almost 'Anyone Who had a Heart', in the memorable words of Miss Cilla Black) as the finished product. I sought him out after class – the title 'Teacher's Pet' leapt to mind, to be quelled instantly – to find out the whys and wherefores of the choice of Doris Day for an exercise which perhaps contributed to the renaissance of interest in her career and led to her leaving Carmel for the first time in years to receive her Hollywood Foreign Press Association's Lifetime Achievement Award from Clint Eastwood at the

Golden Globe Awards in Los Angeles, at which she proved as much of a showstopper as in her heyday – a heyday which seems to have clung obdurately to the star who insisted she never retired, just grew a bit tired.

Christopher Frayling explained the story behind the occasion. 'Producer Margaret Sharp and I have made a series of programmes over the years structured around seasons of films on BBC Television and they depend very much on there being enough audience demand for a season of the films of . . . somebody, usually a director or a star. It transpired that the BBC at the time owned most of the greatest hits of Doris Day for transmission – not all, but most of them, and as we went through the lists of films there were two big omissions – *Calamity Jane* and *The Man Who Knew Too Much*, but they had all the rest of the big ones, like *Love Me or Leave Me* and *Pillow Talk*, so we decided there were quite enough to make up a season. One consideration here is that when you make a television documentary you can 'quote' short extracts from the films that are going to appear in the season. We thought, 'Yes . . . Doris!' The moment we talked to anybody about her they said, 'My God, why hasn't this been done before; she has a staggering following among television viewers.' Whenever a Doris film appears on television she's right there in the 'Top Fifty'. There are certain films that if they are shown on television you know the whole world is going to watch – one of them is *Dirty Harry* with Clint Eastwood and another one is *Calamity Jane* – people love it – another favourite is *Psycho*, so there was much support for the idea.

Then I discovered that among my students on the Fashion Course at the Royal College who weren't even born when Doris made her last film in 1967 were those who were designing clothes as neo-Doris Day, basically; Jean Louis-type gowns, only with an Eighties twist –

tentlike constructions with hats and matching access-
ories – and 'The Look', three years ago was, or one of
them was, definitely Doris Day. I went to talk to the
students and said, 'Who's Doris Day? You've never seen
her –' 'Oh, yes, we've seen videos, we've seen television;
we've seen stills; we've got tapes . . .' This was in 1987:
there was an article in the *Sunday Times* fashion section
with the headline, 'This year the style is Doris Day'
which talked about how the London Art Schools were
obsessed this year with the Fifties and Sixties Doris
'Look'. Rather touching, because these were young
people who were not born, as I said before, in 1968.

Putting the two factors together – the enthusiasm of
anyone we spoke to about why hasn't Doris been interviewed before? – and the knowledge that it wasn't just an
age thing, and it wouldn't only be enjoyed by people
over thirty, we thought it would make a really interesting
programme. So Margaret wrote to Doris's agent – I
believe she got the details from the Appreciation Society's Martyn Daye. A couple of months later we had a
reply from the agent, polite but guarded, to the effect
that she hasn't appeared before the public for a long
time, she's no longer concerned with the film business,
though she loves her fans: she thinks they're very loyal,
particularly in Europe. Indeed, she said to me after we
had done the programme, how unbelievably constant
her European fans are, compared with their American
counterparts; here it's a case of once a star, always a star,
whereas in the States you're only as good as your last
film. For instance, in Italy there's always a film being
made with Jack Palance or Farley Granger in it – there
they are still stars. Similarly Rita Hayworth's last film
actually to reach the screen before her tragic illness was
made in Italy.

Margaret wrote back – we were getting quite good at

this, because we'd approached one or two not entirely willing customers before, and survived to tell the tale after interviewing Woody Allen and Francis Ford Coppola, so, undaunted, we wrote again – and, eventually, she said 'Yes,' she'd love to do it. There were various changes of date, because, perhaps astrologically, like other great stars, notably Dietrich, she feels that certain moments are more appropriate than others for doing such things – Doris was born under the sign of Aries, so maybe there's a clue to the way things turned out. I don't know – all very Californian.

Finally it was agreed that we would film in the first week of January 1989, so off we went to stay at Doris's hotel in Carmel – The Cypress Inn, with 'Pets Welcome'. There's a leaflet in every room, explaining how our little friends are very welcome to stay in the hotel: too many family holidays are spoiled when pets have to be put in catteries and kennels and so on. It had been settled that we would do the filming in the hotel – the Cypress Inn is situated in the centre of Carmel and this was at the time Clint Eastwood had just completed his term of office as Mayor so we were in 'Clintville', with all these yellowing posters saying, 'Clintville by the Sea'. The hotel's about a quarter of a mile away from the sea – a lovely beach, a lovely hotel; of which Doris is the co-owner. What a wonderful way to start the New Year. Doris preferred, perhaps for security reasons, not to be interviewed in her own home.

We had put together a crew: the cameraman was Dick Rawlings, and he was the man who shot – not Liberty Valance – but the man who shot Doris's television shows in the late Sixties, so he knew Doris very well and I believe he was the one she approved from a list presented to her. Rawlings also won an award for his lighting camerawork on *Dallas* – in which he 'heightened' the look and colour and everyday life. It was felt that Doris would prefer someone she had worked with before and whom she trusted, and that was fine, making it easier all round for everybody. Dick is American – Margaret and I were the British contingent; she the producer-director, me the presenter-writer and interviewer, and the cameraman, sound crew and all the rest were to be Americans. The production manager who held it all together was a man called Bobbie Anderson: I got to know him quite well, because he co-ordinated the American side of the technical team, so he was the way to get to know the crew. He'd had a most interesting career – he played Jimmy Stewart as a child in *It's a Wonderful Life*, directed by Frank Capra; in the first segment of the film there's this little boy working in Gaver's drugstore, Bedford Falls, and that was Bobbie Anderson, aged nought, the one who puts his hand on the old cigar lighter and says, 'I wish I had a million dollars.' He then had a career as a sidekick to the hero in 'B' Westerns for one of the poverty row studios in the late Forties: he's in all the western encyclopaedias – I know, because I checked it out when I came home. He's a hero among the 'B' Western buffs and goes to their conventions, where they've seen all his films. The sort of films which are now appearing in American cult video shops. Then he drifted into admin, as a lot of people do on the fringes of Hollywood, having obviously not made the transition into adult stardom.

We did not actually see any of the pets at The Cypress Inn, but there was a parrot in a cage just outside the main entrance squawking at everyone: whether he counted as 'Pets Welcome' or was a fixture of the inn or an extra in a private movie I'm not quite sure. I should have asked him. It was arranged that we should go up and see Doris on the evening before the interview, just Margaret and I, to have a drink at her home, with Dick Rawlings, and to talk through the interview. It's always good to do that, because you get the agenda set and plan the set-ups, where the close-ups and medium shots will be and that sort of thing. Margaret and I had done a lot of research – I'd watched wall-to-wall Doris videos for about two months till my wife – sacrilege! – said, 'If I see or hear another Doris Day movie I'll scream.' I'd got to know the complete works of Doris Day very well: the point is that with the more mature stars they do sometimes need their memory jogged, and you have to know immediately when they say, 'Who was the man that directed So-and-So?' – you jump in with David Butler, Jack Donohue, or whoever. It's dreadful, if there's a silence when that happens, but when you provide the clue or the keyword, suddenly we're off. You have to know all the answers: I could have done *Mastermind* on Doris – I couldn't now, but I could then.

Doris turned out to greet us on arrival just as one would have dreamed one's favourite star would do. She looked stunning. There's a kind of wooden stockade around her house which overlooks Carmel golf course, some greens of which she owns. We came through the stockade, which is rather like Fort Apache, to be confronted by this neo-colonial ranch house with neo-colonial additions (which it transpired were dog kennels) and there was Doris, dressed in pink, very excited to see us, with, 'Come in and have a drink'. There were dogs, especially fluffy ones very much in evidence and she was enthusiastic over a photograph of my wife and myself in Ireland with some Golden Retrievers. 'Lovely!' – I was a dog person and had passed the crucial test.

We chatted through 'the story' and she was less interested in the questions about her film career than in talking about the Foundation. I was slightly worried –

it's rather like Marlon Brando: to get an interview with him you have to be committed to talking about the liberation of American Indians, but you don't want the whole interview to be on that subject – we also want to hear about *The Godfather*. One reason Doris had agreed to do the interview was that we said we would talk about her work for the Doris Day Pet Foundation as part of the programme, and I was slightly concerned about how we would make the transition from canines to Hollywood. She really took off when talking about the Foundation: her face lit up, she became very animated and very sharp about all the different aspects of the Foundation's work, like the lobbying office in Washington which lobbied her friend Ronald Reagan over legislation, the local office, which deal with strays – she doesn't call them strays, she calls them orphans – and the various offices of the Foundation in Los Angeles. She talked about all these as though she were inspired, then when I mentioned the films she slightly glazed over and I felt a twinge of apprehension. Anyway, we had a nice gin and tonic and we all got on very well. She has created the interior design of her house, which fits her like a well-decorated glove – in all the Doris colours – beige and peach – and very open-plan, with a huge ranch-style living room: very much in keeping with the lady of the house.

We went back to town, where I met her assistant and butler Syd – Sydney Wood. His story is that, hailing from Dagenham, he was an official in the British branch of one of the Doris Day Fan Clubs, went over to the States on a 'Meet Doris' symposium – and stayed! It was so strange to be sitting in down-town Carmel drinking draught English bitter, discussing Doris with this man from Dagenham who was Doris's butler, a sunnier version of *Sunset Boulevard*. I wanted to talk to him about the areas one should perhaps avoid and he said that one area in particular was the recently published Mamie Van Doren's memoirs – a sore point because of her accusations of Doris being stand-offish on the set. I said I had to mention that because the book was then so topical, and it's the perfect TV story, because you can show the clip from the movie of Doris, seated with Gable, glaring at Mamie as she bumps and grinds her way through 'The Girl who Invented Rock and Roll' in *Teacher's Pet*. There weren't really any other danger zones and Syd obviously knew everything there was to know about Doris in that respect. He lives in the gatehouse on the perimeters of the stockade and works in the main house during the day. He said she hasn't been in direct contact with the film business for a very long while and is in some ways less interested in the gossip of Hollywood than a lot of film buffs are – but good luck all the same.

The next morning we set up the camera in a – peach again, Doris's choice – room on the ground floor of the hotel: Dick Rawlings lit it very cleverly. We had a window open beside Doris, a bunch of flowers in a vase next to her, so we had side-lighting coming in from the window, which I love – *Citizen Kane*-style slats of light – and meanwhile he'd filled the room with light, so the whole room was suffused with a glow, which probably gives the lie to those stories about gauze over the lens. It's more to do with generalized soft lighting than with synthetic tricks – certainly where Rawlings is concerned. He spread the soft lighting around, so there isn't a sharpness, a kind of harsh beam which shows up people at their worst: anyone who has been lit badly on television knows this. Harsh lighting can add half a stone to your weight and make it look as though your eyes are disappearing through the back of your head. He placed the light very subtly, and I think that is the secret. Doris trusted him entirely as she does with anyone who is thoroughly professional at the job in hand, and especially anyone who has worked with her before.

Her son Terry Melcher, who is producer to the Beach Boys and helped to write some of their hits, arrived – 'Christopher, I hear you are the new David Frost' – later to be joined by his wife and son Ryan, and, because American crews tend to be rather larger than British ones, it was getting to be a little bit like the Marx Brothers in *A Night At The Opera*, where they open the door of the cabin and everyone falls out. It was a full room and because Doris hasn't done this for a very long while, it was also tense, not because of anything she said, but she's a lady in her sixties who hasn't made a film for nearly twenty years – would she remember? – would I say the wrong thing? – would all the people in the room keep quiet? So I found it tense to start with – not as tense as our Woody Allen interview – but that's another story.

I made the mistake of starting off with rather general questions, like the classic question about her going down in the history books as, 'American as Apple Pie' and I already knew the answer, because her book starts off by refuting all those tags and saying, 'They really get on my nerves – I'm going to tell people what I'm actually like.' It was too broad and abstract a question to start with – she was a bit thrown by it, I think, and I found the questions which were more precise, like, 'What did you do then?', 'When did you audition?' or, 'What was it like on the set?', she was very good, very sharp – on the questions about her *craft* – but broader questions like 'What do you think about feminists who consider you a great role model?' she wasn't very happy with: it's not her way of thinking. She's a lady with her feet planted firmly on the ground: some of my early questions made it look as though I had mine planted equally firmly in the air! It wasn't possible to plan exactly; we did not have a run-through as such. We chatted and got to know each other while they were setting up the lights, and decided that 'on the air' I would call her Doris and she would call me Christopher. I'm a great believer that in this sort of interview the audience is much more interested in the subject than they are in me, so, basically the camera should be on her for most of the time. Some presenters interpose themselves too much between the subject and the audience; we worked out when the moves would take place, where the camera would be, which films we would cover, which songs and so on. If I'd been from the British Film Institute Seventies-style I'd have started the intellectual ball rolling with some incomprehensible question about an obscure French philosopher, Roland Barthes, and she'd have clammed up immediately. I'd got the feeling that had happened once or twice in newspaper and magazine interviews when radical feminists had charged straight in like that and she had just changed the subject.

The moment I got onto the 'story' – growing up, her father as choir master, her relationship with her mother, who was obviously very ambitious on her behalf, her accident in her teens – with those sort of things, she was away and it was a joy to hear. To be honest, with a lot of these interviews, you enjoy the answers to at least half of the questions – word for word, sometimes – well before you start. You've read the book, you've seen the movies, you've read other interviews – but what's lovely is when the subjects say something unexpected, where the story is slightly different, or where a memory comes into focus that you, or anyone else, come to that, haven't seen in print before. That happened quite a few times during the interview and they were the best moments. She was very emotional throughout, which added to the tension in the room: characteristically as a repressed Englishman I'm not very good at what happens when people are over-demonstrative emotionally, especially in public. I'm sure Californians find this the most normal thing in the world – after all they've had a lot of practice with their analysts – but I do find it difficult. It's a very sad fact that many of Doris's leading men are no longer with us – Cary Grant, James Cagney, Rock Hudson, Gordon MacRae, Jack Carson and Clark Gable among them, and every time I mentioned them she would get very emotional at the memory – she was obviously aware of the passing of time.

I wanted, in as tasteful a way as possible, to ask her about her friend Rock Hudson – the public were natu-rally interested in her memories and feelings – and she handled the questions very well. There were a lot of tears, very few of them in the programme itself – except at the very end, when I thought it would make a nice coda and be rather sweet, that Doris would get very emotional about that public out there whom she really does adore. If you look closely at the continuity of the programme it's the Case of the Disappearing Hand-kerchief: in some shots she has a Kleenex, in others she doesn't. Only a really practised viewer would notice because the handkerchief is in her lap and the camera is usually on Doris's face: but there are moments when 'now you see it, now you don't'. That was the one continuity error we could do nothing about. She would chat to Dick 'Didn't we have good times together?', or her wardrobe lady from Warners, who was there in that Marx Brothers room. And she would cry. We thought, on the whole, that viewers would not be comfortable about this. Except that once. In a way, it showed how relaxed she was – and how well we were getting on together. That old word 'rapport' I suppose. In fact, after the interview was over – I was trying to look terribly

English and wearing a blazer and a club tie, with blue handkerchief in the top pocket – she said, 'You know, Christopher, there are times when you remind me distinctly of David Niven.' I thought it was a terrific line and, needless to say, I told my students, who were singularly unimpressed – they considered David Niven to be, 'a bit of a lounge lizard and a grade "A" chauvinist'.

What we wanted to do was to frame the interview with some shots taken in the garden of her home with her dogs: the last ten minutes or so was her talking about the Pet Foundation, and you can see in the programme that she really does become more animated; although she was remarkably 'focused' about the films, clearly what's on her mind are the animals – it's the thing she lives and breathes: it's her life; she opened up more and you could tell that it's something she cares deeply about. The trouble was that we got on so well and spent so long talking that the light was failing. We started shooting about eleven o'clock in the morning and by now it's about three and the crew have to move the lights and camera and so on – a complicated process which takes time, to set up the shots of us standing outside with the dogs: the only satirical letters I got as a result of the programme were from friends who said, 'Never, but never, appear with fluffy dogs again!' – W. C. Fields was right. The dogs were very endearing, but it looked a bit like a home movie, and I do seem to be ill at ease – I'm looking at this dog as though it's about to pee over my shoe, whereas Doris evidently feels utterly at home: it's all too obvious that I'm not used to being in the company of fluffy dogs and I'm not in the habit of talking to them. You can tell, also, that it's twilight – the light's entirely different from the effect we had in the room; in fact, we only just made it. We got enough footage to have just a little bit of atmosphere for the beginning, with her in the open air, in a tracksuit, relaxing with the dogs; she had changed since The Cypress Inn. We did not have enough light for our original ending.

She then said, 'Who'd like to come out to dinner tonight?' I said, quick as a flash, 'Me!' This was after I'd gone in with my much-thumbed copy of the music of 'Que Sera, Sera', which I wanted her to sign, which she did – 'I love you Christopher. Doris' – now a treasured possession. What tends to happen after the crew had finished shooting is that they prefer to be by themselves – it's a job, it's been done, but presenters like myself who enjoy working on a star, and, indeed, like the producer Margaret Sharp, who has always been a great admirer of Doris's films, said 'Yes, we'd love to have dinner.' So we all went to a restaurant on a mall just outside of town, which is designed in the style of the paintings of Edward Hopper, who painted American urban life of the Thirties – neon, long bars, low-slung lights, Venetian blinds. You may remember the 'look' in a lot of Ken Adams designs for the movie version of *Pennies from Heaven* came from Hopper.

She parked her van with favoured dogs in it, but they were rather a long way away from the restaurant, where we were seated in the corner. She was treated as a conquering heroine by everyone in the restaurant – 'Oh, Miss Day, its so lovely to see you again. You don't come here nearly often enough – you don't get out enough . . .' 'Well, it's the dogs – I don't like leaving them . . .' She gave me a little American flag as a souvenir of the occasion – I felt she wanted *me* to be as American as Apple Pie: a good moment.

Her eyes kept wandering to the left: she was obviously concerned that this estate car was parked the other side of the parking lot and she couldn't keep an eye on the dogs. I got the impression that her life revolves around the dogs, and this was quite an unusual event. I was quite touched by that. Eventually the car outside the window moved, leaving a parking space immediately outside the window: I said, 'Doris, I'll rush out and stand in that space – you go and get the estate wagon while I reserve the space.' She said, 'Oh, would you – you're so chiv-alric, you English people!' All of a flutter, out I went and stood on the space and, lo and behold, the moment she got to the other side of the car park another car pulls in and tries to run me over. They said, 'Get out of the way! I want to park there' and they started hooting. It was all getting a bit acrimonious. A John Cleese-style situation – I said, 'No, I'm keeping it for somebody', but eventually Doris appeared on the horizon and I said, 'Look, it's extremely important to me the person driving that car parks outside this window, OK? Would you *please* move on?' There was much swearing, but off they went. Doris moved in and parked outside the window: from then she visibly relaxed, because she could look out of the window, and see all those doggies, paws against the glass and she felt all was well with the world. I wish I could have said that the owner of that displaced car had exclaimed, 'My, it's Doris Day – I'd be charmed to give up the space to her', but it didn't seem to work that way on a shopping plaza in California.

After that high spot we came home. The film looked lovely – Dick Rawlings really earned his money – it was beautifully lit, and we had tons of material. While we were working in the cutting rooms at Lime Grove, the old BBC TV Studios where our nearest approach to Doris Day, the cockney song and dance star, Jessie Matthews, made her biggest hits for Gaumont British. The sound of the movieola was turned up full and there we were deciding what goes in and which clips go where

– it's quite an art, choosing the film clips and integrating them – so there was 'Que Sera Sera' and 'Secret Love' and all the other classic songs, and people would look in on the editing room and say, 'What's going on? Isn't that Doris Day?' Again young junior employees of 'the Beeb', aged twenty, twenty-five would say, 'My God, isn't she terrific?' I can't think of anyone else who can still have that effect except perhaps, Marilyn, and that's different; because she died she's frozen in time, and rather like James Dean and Montgomery Clift she will never be able to grow old. People worship a kind of icon that's ageless; that gives them a special place in people's affections because they died so young. Forever young. Doris is unique because they still like her, though she is a mature woman, who graduated from pigtails and base-ball bats via young 'Secret Love' to playing a mum with several children in *Please Don't Eat the Daisies* to becom-ing in her TV series a mature career woman who could also hold together a family.

What would Marilyn have been like in her fifties and sixties? Would she have proved as adaptable? Would she have provided such a developing role model as some of her contemporaries? I doubt it. I think her vulnerability, which was so much part of her appeal, would have militated against it: Marilyn in character parts is almost unthinkable. As is Marilyn as a career woman with responsibilities. Doris effected the transition with charm and subtlety: I think personally, the only film in which she tries to play herself too young – to hold back the hands of the clock – is *That Touch of Mink*: there is something slightly distasteful about an attractive woman in her late thirties so frantically protecting her virginity against a Cary Grant oozing charm and we can't help thinking sacrilegious thoughts like, 'Why doesn't she stop being so smug and just pop into the sack with him?' It's really the only film that deserves Oscar Levant's famous quip, 'I knew Doris Day *before* she was a virgin.'

The programme was a great success – I've never had so many letters in my life. I did a programme on Deborah Kerr, *Not Just an English Rose*, with much of the research from your esteemed book; that was a success and I got some letters, especially from the Deborah Kerr Appreciation Society, but on the Doris occasion I was swamped with letters – not all of them saying, of course, what a wonderful person I was; a lot of them asked can you please get in touch with Doris for me, I've wanted to see her for years, and here's a photo of my dog/old horse/elderly cat etc. – all of which I sent on dutifully. When I did the Woody Allen programme with the same team of Margaret Sharp and myself, in New York, the tradition started of doing a phone-in with people calling in live the following day to say 'What's it like to meet Woody Allen?' One of my students phoned me up on that occasion and tried to put me on the spot, which was a bit naughty: I had to say, 'You're supposed to be at a seminar, not sitting at home phoning me up!' They thought it would be fun to do a phone-in about Doris, so I went into the studio at the unearthly hour of seven o'clock in the morning for the television broadcast and answered all these questions about, 'Was Doris Day nice?' – 'Yes very nice'. I was sitting there with the earphone to my ear and suddenly this voice comes down, 'Christopher, how *wonderful* to speak to you again. How are you?' It was one of those moments. Panic. Live. You say to yourself, 'Is this a Doris Day impersonator or is this Doris Day speaking?' I've seen impersonators but . . . she it was. I said, 'Doris, is that really you?' – Doris Day, phoning me, live, from Carmel, where it was about two in the morning on this

BBC programme – 'the Beeb' had set it up. Apparently, my face was like a cartoon double-take! She said, 'How wonderful it is' and how marvellous it was to reminisce and how much she'd enjoyed making the programme, and a great big hello to all her loyal English fans, have some fish and chips on me and think of me when you do all these British things. It's her second favourite country. The following morning another deluge of fan mail.

The second showing of the original programme was an odd one. It's rare to repeat film profiles, because the clips cost so much second time round. Our repeat was during the BBC strike. *Wogan* was off the air because it's presented live, and so they put on '*I Don't Even* Like *Apple Pie*' as a substitute. That was Tuesday, 9 May, 1989.

For fifty minutes of my life I had become the Wogan of the Upper Fourth! It got a huge number of viewers because it was screened at 7 p.m., whereas it was put on slightly later first time around. Just before *Love Me Or Leave Me*, with which we decided to couple it, because I think that's her best film, by a long way – for once a vehicle that was really worthy of her, and great for Cagney.

Her attitude to directors was interesting: of David Butler, with whom she made so many musicals, including the charming *By the Light of the Silvery Moon* and the smashing *Calamity Jane*, she said she felt very comfortable working with him, but I don't think she thought of him as a high-flier like Hitchcock. As a director she considers Hitchcock in the first eleven, David Butler not. She was, nevertheless, unnerved by the fact that Hitchcock was very strange to work for in that he never seemed to direct her or told her what she was doing right or wrong. This concept of the director as the artist – *auteur*, as they say in the movie journals – is quite recent:

in her day it was the star who counted. She didn't think like that – it wasn't so much a question of the quality of the director, it was whether they saw eye to eye, was it a good working relationship?

The thing about Doris is that, not only is she a professional to her fingertips, but she's a pleasant person, without a discernible trace of malice. Even about Sinatra, who, after all, had her husband barred from the set, fired the cameraman and had the script of *Young At Heart* altered to suit himself, she could only express deep admiration and affection. The BFI's interesting dossier 'Move Over Misconceptions' preceding the 1980 season of Day movies – eighty pages of it, which in turn spawned a *Time Out* enquiry 'Reclaim the Day', about why she 'deserved' a major season at the National Film Theatre and why an actress with a 'virgin next door image' should be 'reclaimed' by feminists – is just the kind of writing and criticism to which she cannot readily relate. All that thinking has happened since she made her last film in 1968. For all her professionalism and dedication to the work in hand – you had to be punctual, and turn up in time for your make-up call, even if it was five in the morning – something she did for twenty-five years, there's a paradox about her, which is also interesting. Although she inspires such enormous affection, such wonderful memories of her films, I think she was always quite detached from the work she was doing – very professional, arrived on time, you did your work, learnt your part for the following day and went to bed at eight at night. She did this all during her film and TV careers assiduously, but not in a sort of 'It's my whole life' way: there was a corner of her which Hollywood never got to, like the Christian Science thing with Melcher – her interest in spiritual things as well as the material. Unlike a lot of Hollywood stars, where they couldn't spot the join between their careers and their own lives, she didn't go to the parties, or get involved with movie people, she didn't concern herself with the gossip columnists: I think when she went home she went home and shut off, and that was the end of the day's work. The paradox is that, thanks partly to articles like the BFI one I've just mentioned, which have, in their way, enhanced and prolonged her hold on the public, she's so confused with the parts she played that you'd think that her identification with films is total: I think she pragmatically saw it as a way of making a living, and that's what protected her. Those who saw it as more than that were destroyed by it: Bela Lugosi was the prime example. Have you seen that last interview of his, in which he's sitting in a coffin? By then he thought he really *was* Dracula, and he's sitting in this coffin, talking to the journalists. He had also become a heroin addict: it's just appalling – he's living the Hollywood fantasy, and he can't tell the difference. He died in the middle of the film he was making at the time – the terrible *Plan 9 from Outer Space* which was directed by Edward D. Wood. The director's chiropractor, who was roughly the same shape as Bela Lugosi, appears in the second half of the film with his back to the camera. It's a dreadful tacky story. Doris wasn't like that: she disengaged herself and off she went to live the life she wanted, and I do admire her for that.

I phoned Doris up afterwards, through the Beeb, to give her a progress report on the programme: she retained an active interest in it, but I sensed she felt she'd done it, and 'let sleeping dogs lie'! She said, 'Oh, I'd *love* to make a come-back: you make it sound so appealing. But I don't know . . .'

Just to end with a little story about Carmel while we were there: the residue of the Clint Eastwood mayoral campaign was everywhere – Clint Eastwood campaign buttons and posters saying, 'Make My Day', and one put out by the opposition, which I actually purchased – someone had steamed it off a lamppost and was selling it in the shop: part of his campaign was how outrageous it was you weren't allowed to sell ice-cream on the streets of Carmel, a big issue in a town which seems to exist in a cocoon – this poster has Josey Wales with his arms folded, and instead of clutching Colt .45s he has an ice-cream cornet, and across the top the words, 'Law, Order and Ice-cream'! I couldn't resist that; I think it's wonderful. Like I say, California is one hell of a different place.

When Doris worked before the cameras again for Christopher Frayling's documentary it certainly seemed to have reactivated her awareness that there was a great big world outside Carmel – a world that had not only not forgotten her but to whom she was still a vital entity. If she ever had any doubt about this, the reception she received when she undertook her first long journey in a very long time away from Carmel to Los Angeles for the Golden Globe Awards at the Beverly Hilton Hotel on 28 January 1989, should have reassured her in a very positive way. Leaving her beloved charges, in itself, for the first time in five years, was significant, and this kind of spectacular public appearance was something she had not undertaken for some twenty-one years. Her peers, many of whom had been working in films during her reign as 'Number One Box Office Star', were there to applaud: they included the Golden Girls and Dustin Hoffman, who would have been her co-star in *The Graduate* in 1967, had she not considered the film too explicit in its treatment of the affair between a college boy and an older woman, leaving the field clear for a triumph by Anne Bancroft. Other luminaries included

Robert Mitchum, Shirley MacLaine, Gene Hackman and Joan Collins, the great survivor, who was making her film début in Britain in *I Believe In You* in 1952, four years after Doris's meteoric rise to stardom, when she was filming one of her least auspicious movies, *The Winning Team*: her co-star was Ronald Reagan, and neither of them won that round. They made a fascinating contrast – Collins orchidaceous as always, Day in a vanilla trouser suit, blonde hair gleaming, looking as fit and trim as the day, some years ago, when she cycled out of frame in her famous Blue Band margarine advert, directed by our own Nicholas Roeg. Joan, ever the pragmatist, conceded the round in the glamour stakes, with a cheerful smile, *faute de mieux*.

Representing the 'new kids', Steven Spielberg seemed impressed with his 'Close Encounter' with a legend and Meryl Streep presented her mother, a firm fan of Doris's. Clint Eastwood, whose close proximity to the winner of the Lifetime Achievement seemed to cause him to lose some fifteen years as he stepped into the spotlight to present Doris with her Golden Globe, glowed as much as she when she told him, 'By the way, I'd love to work with you.' The King and Queen of Carmel could be quite a team. 'I never said I'd retired,' she insisted, and, improbably, 'I'm a wreck. I don't do this any more. I've got to come to town more often.' She was obviously deeply touched by the standing ovation she received, and said, with genuine modesty, gazing at her Award, 'I don't understand why I've got this, but I love it. This business has given me great happiness. I've worked with the cream of the crop' – which was when she made her aside to Eastwood – 'and every minute of every day was a joy. I mean that. I really do.'

In November of that year the press announced that she had agreed to star in three two-hour TV specials for

MGM, playing an insurance investigator. The report stated that she would receive half a million pounds per film, plus an air-conditioned motor home exclusively for her dogs. 1990 came and went, with a conflicting report in October that Doris had signed with ABC TV to star in three telefilms per year as a 'recurring character' with production expected to begin on the first before the end of the year, with her son Terry Melcher as executive producer: the terms this time were vaguely named as 'a one million pound deal' – confusion between pounds and dollars is the norm in such stories, some of which reported that her work would begin early in the new year and that the 'recurring character' would be 'young at heart'. Well, she would be, wouldn't she? Her admirers have written in anxiously hoping it is not a case of, 'this year, next year, sometime – never'.

2

Childhood, Into Salad Days . . .

Doris Day was born, according to the most reliable reference books, Doris Mary Anne Kappelhoff to German Catholic parents Alma Sophia and Frederick William von Kappelhoff, in Cincinnati, Ohio, on 3 April 1924 – the von was dropped at her birth. She was christened Doris because her mother, an ardent film and theatregoer was a devoted fan of Doris Kenyon, who was at her peak at the time of her namesake's birth, and that very year was leading lady to the most famous heart-throb in motion pictures, Rudolph Valentino himself in *Monsieur Beaucaire*. She went on working on stage and screen until 1939, when she played Queen Anne to Louis Hayward's *The Man in the Iron Mask*, with Joan Bennett as Maria Theresa. Doris Day, in *Her Own Story*, written with the help of A. E. Hotchner in 1975, when she lived on North Crescent Drive in Beverly Hills, wrote that only a few houses away from her, on the same street, lived that same Doris Kenyon, 'a beautiful, vibrant chic lady', whom she occasionally saw.

Mr and Mrs von Kappelhoff, at the time of their daughter's birth, lived in a red-brick, two-family house in Evanston, a suburb of Cincinnati, the town where they were born of German immigrant parents: her maternal grandfather left his hometown of Berlin to avoid the conscription of which he heartily disapproved. He had heard there was a large German community in Cincinnati, which is where he settled and with Doris's grandmother opened a pretzel factory, where the whole family worked and lived in the apartments above the bakery. Grandfather, described by Alma Sophia as, 'the kind of man, not too many tears were shed when he passed away' died at the age of forty from pneumonia, but Grandmother, Mama Welz, was adored by all who knew her and moved into the house in Evanston to live with her daughter and son-in-law, when she bequeathed the bakery to her sons on her retirement from the family business in her late fifties, leaving a void in Alma and Doris's lives when she died in 1934. Mother and daughter seem always to have been very close – far closer than Alma and William, to whom two sons were born some years before: Richard, who died at the age of two, before Doris's birth and Paul, her senior by a few years. The marriage seems to have been a very unhappy one from the beginning: the wonder is, how it came about in the first place. But, as Beryl Reid is apt to say, 'God's a funny fellow' and He obviously ordained that, to make up for this mismatching of opposite souls, the world would be the richer when their progeny first raised her voice to sing His praises.

Alma was gregarious in the extreme, loved parties and Country and Western music: it was her great pipedream that Doris would one day make a Country and Western movie – maybe *Calamity Jane* came near the mark for her – or did she dream of a *Louisiana Hayride*-type hillbilly scene like Judy Canova did when Ross Hunter was her handsome leading man, many years before he was to take a different kind of leading role in the life of Alma's young daughter? William was the exact opposite to his wife: quiet, introverted, an opera buff who adored the classics, which she disliked passionately. It is clear that Doris admired her father and his handsome good looks, but he was too busy with his classical career as a choral master and teacher of violin and piano to have much time for his family, who attended Mass regularly at St Mark's Church, which served the Catholic parishioners of Evanston. William tried to interest Doris and Paul in taking piano lessons, with some success where his son was concerned, but a family crisis soon put paid to his potential as a budding Paderewski.

Doris was about eight when she discovered that her father was having an affair with her mother's best friend: after a rare party at the house Doris, after peeking from upstairs at the grown-ups enjoying themselves downstairs, retired to her room and pretended to be asleep when her father came through her room to reach a small guest bedroom beyond, which was the only way of access. He was not alone, and the unsuspecting child was unable to avoid hearing what was going on, as the head of her bed was against the wall of the spare room. Though her world fell apart that night, she went on loving her father and wanting him to go on living at home with them all: she said, revealingly, about that episode that she did not condemn her father – 'it is my nature to forgive, to try to accentuate what is good, and not to pass judgment. Hate is simply not in me. I am often made sorrowful by the disappointments and disillusionments I have suffered in people, but hate or condemnation is not a part of it.'

It is not surprising, as that was always her outlook, that she took so readily to Christian Science in later life: Mary Baker Eddy's philosophy is one that seems to have given a special strength and resilience to many people in show business, among them one of the world's great actresses, the late Dame Edith Evans, Ginger Rogers, Dorothy

Dickson and Deborah Kerr, who explained her calm attitude on the film set in the face of crises that caused others to tear their hair and rant and rave by saying that if you do that you simply upset yourself more than anyone else, and achieve absolutely no good in the long run.

Alma did, of course, find out about the affair and Doris's parents were divorced: as that is anathema to the Catholic tenets, William had to abrogate his standing in the Church: despite her Catholic upbringing and attendance at convent schools, Doris found the dogma unyielding and unattractive, as have so many free spirits before her. *Once a Catholic* was not only the title of an outrageously irreverent look at the Church, but it contained more than a grain of truth: so many lapsed Catholics return to the faith after sowing their wild oats: there is something comforting about a Mother Church prepared to absolve all one's peccadilloes, great and small, as long as one is prepared to admit all to the priest, as God's representative in the confessional. The condition of 'a firm purpose of amendment' is, in the nature of things and people, unlikely to hold good when the next attractive forbidden fruit is flashed before one's eyes. As Mae West's Eve said to Don Ameche's Adam in a broadcast which rocked pious souls everywhere and affronted not only William Randolph Hurst but the Catholic Legion of Decency to its very roots, 'Will you, Adam, take a bite out of this here apple?' Well, the rest is history, and if he hadn't maybe we would not be here to write about it. The unrepentant Mae was still rockin' 'n' rollin' about it in her eighties; 'You Gotta Taste All The Fruits'.

To Doris, with her essential honesty, that was something of a cop-out; the dogma of, 'absolved today, sin tomorrow,' was not one that appealed, and the example of her much-loved but elusive father was unlikely to have strengthened her already none-too-secure faith. The divorce took place in 1936 when Doris was twelve and Paul fifteen: the boy helped his father carry his bags to the door when he moved out of their home – he did not say goodbye and Doris was amazed that Paul was not crying when he came back into the living room, where she was hiding tearfully in the draperies. The event did not, surprisingly, affect her dream of a happy marriage in the future for herself: she insists that was her only real ambition, although she had come to terms with the fact that the ideal marriage she wanted for her parents was not to be. Her loneliness was assuaged a little when her mother allowed her to sleep beside her in the twin bed that had been her father's: from then on her brother and she took turns to sleep next to their mother, which somehow made them feel less bereft.

She visited her father once a week on Wednesdays at her aunt's house, to which he had moved. So had the lady in the case, which was a source of great distress to her mother, and their marriage did not take place for some years, by which time Doris was singing in a band. The union was a happy one, but William's second wife died from cancer not long after, an event which turned him, years later, away from the dour and rigid man with his racialist and religious prejudices into a complete volte-face – a metamorphosis that occurred after Doris had become a film star.

Alma took a job in the Evanston Bakery to support her children: with the example of shining Doris Kenyon before her eyes she was keen that her daughter should somehow end up in a theatrical career, and enrolled her – Doris says as a result of her own nagging, because she was crazy to dance – in Pep Golden's School for tap and 'personality dancing'. Mother soon moved her to

Shuster Martin's Ballet School, and then to Hessler's, where they also taught elocution and singing, besides acrobatic dancing, which she loved. She easily won first prize of twenty-five free lessons for the pupil who could stand on his or her hands the longest.

Doris advances an intriguing theory to account for the fact that, despite all her years as a band singer, she has a rooted dislike to performing before live audiences. She was still in the kindergarten when she made her first public performance in the warm-up to a Minstrel Show. Alma had made her a red costume in satin for her to recite a piece of doggerel which has stayed in her mind, unsurprisingly, ever since:

> 'I'se goin' down to the Cushville hop,
> And there ain't no niggie goin' to make me stop!'

Alma had, unfortunately, pinned Doris into her costume, and during the seemingly endless wait backstage for her to go on and strut her stuff, nature took its course. When she went out, did her bow and began her recitation, audible giggles were to be heard. Her mother, looking round indignantly from the front row did nothing to quell the laughter: Doris burst into tears and blubbed, 'I'm sorry, Mommy, I couldn't help it!' The embryo star had wet her pants and the red satin had turned black. She was already enough of a professional to remember her curtsy before she ran off. 'Wet pants Kappelhoff' is how she dubbed herself!

By the age of twelve she had evolved a dance act with a boy of the same age called Jerry Doherty: they had met at dancing school and had a routine entitled 'Clouds', which they sang with Doris stepping out in front, while Jerry walked behind her with his hands on her hips, back and forth, until they stood together and went into a fast buck-and-wing, in clothes which Alma designed for them: the motif was blue. They were in great demand all over Cincinnati to perform at various church and charity functions, with the few dollars they were paid helping to cover their expenses. The Kappelhoffs had moved to a smaller house in another suburb of Cincinnati, College Hill, where she attended Our Lady of Angels School, less prestigious than Regina High, to which all of her friends went.

The high spot of the Doris and Jerry dance team was winning first prize of five hundred dollars in a big city-wide contest for amateur talent run by a local department store: with their comedy song and dance routine *The Funny Little Bird on Nellie's Hat* they swept the board against hundreds of entrants. The interesting thing is that, even in those early salad days, Doris never had any doubt they would win. The money seemed irrelevant to her, just as it was to be after she achieved fame and fortune: apart from the practicalities of supporting anyone dependent on her, she has always been content to let others manage her financial affairs, an attitude she later had cause to regret, or would have, were it not that 'regrets are vain' is a belief which must have sustained her through many a major crisis in her life. The song which won them the contest was an old music hall ditty which Roy Hudd, our leading exponent of the genre, readily associated with Maidie Scott.

The contest had gone on for months, having been held every weekend in a local radio studio, amassing enviable publicity for the Alms and Doepke department store, the enterprising sponsors. A meeting was held the same evening in the Kappelhoff kitchen – Doris had met her partner at a service club, when she mentioned casually to a lady nearby that the boy going through his tap routine on stage was 'awfully cute': the lady said,

'Why, that's my son', introduced Jerry and the potential Astaire and Rogers got together without further ado. Mrs Doherty and Mrs Kappelhoff asked their progeny if they would like to spend the money on a trip to Hollywood to study at the famous dance school, Fanchon and Marco, under the leading teacher of tap, Louis Da Pron.

Though a confirmed movie fan, Doris had no thought of anything like that where she herself was concerned. Her big thrill had been her Friday night visits to the major cinemas in the locality, the Shubert or the Albee with her mother after their favourite eating-out dinner of spaghetti at Caruso's, the home of haute cuisine for the Cincinnati of those days. Once at the Albee she had seen Betty Grable dance, which started her early devotion to the then Mrs Jackie Coogan, later to be Mrs Harry James and already on the way to becoming box office star 'number one' in the Hollywood firmament. This strikes a nostalgic chord in the present writer: when Coogan became world child star 'number one' after playing with Charlie Chaplin in *The Kid*, Coogan dolls in the little boy's Huckleberry Finn outfit, with a peak cap pulled sideways on his head, were marketed worldwide, and that's how I got my first doll, equal in rank to Teddy Bear, but, unlike him, the innocent recipient of all my childish tantrums and nastinesses. Jackie was regularly beaten against the wall like a gong, and rescued from the railway line by my Nanny, who was understandably more devoted to Jackie than to me. Not too surprisingly, he became a very battered and sad figure, whom I used to take everywhere, on holidays and even to church, because underneath all that I really did love him, and probably making up our quarrels was what made it all worthwhile.

So, Mrs Jackie Coogan played a key role in my life, as well as Doris's, although she admits, 'Much as I adored

Betty Grable, when we played movie stars I was always Ginger Rogers . . . and I had only one movie boyfriend – Lew Ayres, because at that time he was married to Ginger Rogers.' Many years later, Mr Ayres was a guest in *The Doris Day Show* television series – a beautiful person, she says, who shared her passion for chunky peanut butter!

Mrs Kappelhoff rented a small apartment for four weeks, which she and Doris shared with Jerry and Mrs Doherty: there was one bedroom and a living room with a folding bed attached to the door – they had a roster for who should sleep on this contraption and who should occupy the bed. Louis De Pron, their dance teacher, who had featured in film musicals, was impressed with the young couple's terpsichorean abilities, and they were soon signed to tour with the Fanchon and Marco stage show at venues in and around Hollywood, becoming starstruck enough to buy one of the maps on sale detailing the locality of the stars' homes. They never saw one, not even Ginger Rogers', despite driving at a crawl by her house. Their four weeks' taste of touring with the stage show was such a success, with much encouragement from Fanchon and Marco, that their mothers decided to move to Hollywood for good.

Back in Cincinnati they made their plans to leave at the end of October 1937. That Friday the thirteenth, defying the auguries, friends of theirs called Holden gave a farewell party at their home in Hamilton, some twenty-five miles away from Cincinnati. By then Doris, in her fourteenth year, had a regular boyfriend, Larry, the brother of her dancing partner Jerry Doherty; Larry telephoned for her to join him and two other friends, Marion Bonekamp and Albert Schroeder, to pick up hamburgers at a joint on the other side of town. After a short stay for milkshakes they set out to return Doris to her party in Hamilton; she was in the back seat behind Albert, who was driving, with Marion beside him in the front. Doris describes the most traumatic experience of her young life:

It was a cold, rainy night. The steamy car windows were all closed, the radio going full blast. We were driving rather slowly, talking, Marion with her head turned towards us in the back. There was a flash of the locomotive's light, a moment when I became aware of its black, looming hulk, but no sound, no warning, a crossing with no lights or signs, just the giant presence hurtling at us, a split moment of our screams, then crashing into us, not once, but twice as we were struck again by a freight car in back of the locomotive. Albert and Marion were both driven through the windshield, embedded in the shattered glass. Albert's seat had first pitched forward, driving him into the windshield, but the second impact knocked him free of it and his seat came crashing back. Marion's head was trapped in the windshield, and she was severely cut and bleeding profusely.

The initial crash knocked me down in the seat with my legs forward, but as the train screeched to a halt I was able to react to what had happened. I felt all right, that I hadn't been hurt, Larry was all right too.

People were running to our assistance. Albert, bleeding heavily, was helped from the front seat. I pushed his seat forward and started to get out to see if I could help Marion, who was still pinioned in the shattered windshield. I collapsed. My right leg wouldn't support me. I pulled myself along the ground over to the kerb. I felt no pain. I probed my leg and discovered I was bleeding. Then my fingers came to the sharp ends of the shattered bones protruding from my leg. I began talking to myself about my leg. 'How will I dance? How can I dance?' I kept repeating it. Then I fainted in the gutter.

Doris was taken to the Mercy Hospital at Hamilton, Ohio, and they diagnosed a double compound fracture of her right leg. Her mother was with her when she regained consciousness. This shattering account of Doris's accident – the more graphic for its laconic style, almost in semaphore – must surely be the herald of the most unlikely total recovery ever to have gone on to such unimaginable triumph in later years: after fourteen months in hospital she was fortunately able to return to the apartment her mother had rented out prior to their planned move to Hollywood. Mrs Kappelhoff was able to persuade the new tenants to let them have it back. Jerry Doherty and his mother had visited her in hospital the day after the accident: his injuries were relatively minor, quite miraculously, in those days before seat belts were compulsory – the real blow came when he realized that a future dancing partnership was out of the question. The discovery must have destroyed something in his will to succeed in showbusiness: after high school he became a milkman.

Four months in a wheelchair, followed by slow progress on crutches, put paid to Doris's academic career: return to high school was a nightmare, unable as she was to get around without extreme effort and in constant fear of having the crutches knocked from under her, and wisely Mrs Kappelhoff assented to her staying out of school until her recuperation was complete. The family moved to a house she loved in Price Hill, Sailor Park, on the proceeds of the family bakery's sale by her Uncle Charley, but the inactivity, after years of hard graft as a master baker, soon impelled him to buy a tavern, where mother did the cooking and they shared an apartment upstairs. Doris's pragmatic nature asserted itself immediately; she enjoyed the sound of the tavern's jukebox and the glorious freedom of bumping down the stairs on her seat to help herself in the kitchen, where chilli and roast beef were the order of the day.

With time on her hands, *faute de mieux*, Doris became an ardent radio aficionado: these were the great days of the wireless – in fact, in a way it was an invention more totally universal than any other, and one that, despite all vicissitudes, is unlikely ever to be totally supplanted – and the great bands came into everyone's home; Glenn Miller, Benny Goodman, Duke Ellington were all there on tap, to sing along to. Doris Day became a Big Band Singer in the parlour above her Uncle Charley's tavern, long before any thought of turning professional entered her head. Then there was Ella Fitzgerald – the great Ella, still the living proof that the infinite variety of the human voice can rise above all considerations of class, race, creed and nationality: significantly, Doris found a fascinating quality in her voice perhaps above all others, and she would join her in song, trying, as she has said, 'to catch the subtle ways she shaded her voice, the casual yet clean way she sang the words'. The influence is still discernible: though Ella is still unmistakably Ella and Doris inescapably Doris, as subtly different as a lute from a lyre; they share a purity of tone that the passage of time has clarified rather than muted.

One man's joy is another man's anathema, in music as in any other field: this difference was highlighted in the Kappelhoff household when Alma was persuaded by a musician friend who heard Doris's impromptu duetting that she should take singing lessons. Jeanette MacDonald was riding the soprano range, never higher than in those days, and Doris found herself set to carolling 'The

Indian Love Call'. The thought is a fascinating one: Doris Day and Nelson Eddy in *Rose Marie* might have enchanted her mother, but was a definite no-no for Miss Kappelhoff. MacDonald, a sturdy opera-trained musical comedy lady *assoluta*, had an enormous following in her MGM operettas, especially those with Nelson Eddy, and a sharply satirical sense of humour, evident in her early singles like the Ernst Lubitsch–Maurice Chevalier movies, which was well doused by order of Louis B. Mayer, to whom *New Moon* and *The Firefly*, with Jeanette for once silently swooning over Allan Jones's hearty tenor 'Donkey Serenade' spelt more ringing box office gold than the sophistication of *One Hour With You*.

So, no Friml or Sigmund Romberg for Doris: instead a song-plugger friend of Alma's introduced a voice teacher called Grace Raine who, Doris told Christopher Frayling in their interview, had the biggest influence of anyone on her singing career. They discovered instant rapport: Miss Raine told her new pupil's mother she believed Doris had tremendous potential and that she would like to see her three times a week. Told that Alma could only afford one lesson at five dollars weekly, Grace Raine volunteered that the other two lessons were on her. That deserves a special Oscar for her perceptive kindness, and Alma a big bouquet by becoming perhaps the nicest kind of stage mother, obviously living out her own undefined ambitions through her daughter, but in allowing Doris to make her own decisions, and supporting her whenever she could. She helped pay for the lessons by taking in sewing. Doris explained to Christopher Frayling that Grace taught her the importance of imagining that you're singing to a special person – 'It's really like playing a scene.' Those early lessons with Grace Raine were more effective than any formalized dramatic coaching could have been and she took that training with her, first into her singing with bands and then into acting.

Grace was not only the ideal voice teacher for Doris, she also had contacts, through being coach at radio station WLW: she knew a man called André Carlin, who had a two-hour Saturday morning local radio show in a department store called 'Carlin's Carnival' – in which he introduced students with ambitions to appear on radio: after a little biographical build-up the potential radio personality would sing a song of his or her choice, accompanied by a pianist, who did sight-reading from sheet music. Doris chose 'Day After Day' for her introduction to the airwaves: she claims not to have felt nervous, but to have experienced considerable curiosity over how she would feel singing into a microphone. Her teacher, listening at home, said Doris's voice came over charmingly, but that she needed practice to polish her delivery. She taught her all the tricks of the trade and Grace's husband, a song plugger by profession, told her about a Chinese restaurant in downtown Cincinnati, called the Shanghai Inn, run by one Charlie Yee, who was looking for a girl singer for Saturday evenings. This engagement netted five dollars a session, a handy increment to the radio show, which paid zilch, but was a beginning.

To reach the restaurant on the second floor the new cabaret star had to inch up the stairs on her backside before making her entrance on crutches to front a three-piece combo; an even more original way into a floor show than Beatrice Lillie's celebrated roller skates routine in the Twenties. Doris looks back on this introduction to live audiences, talking away and masticating their oriental delicacies as a nice way to have made her debut: at fifteen she claimed to be eighteen and the amiable Charlie never questioned it. At this early stage in her career the Betty Hutton influence was already present: despite the crutches Doris managed to belt out 'Murder, He Says', which was one of Betty's frenetic *pièces de resistance* in her Paramount movies, into which she erupted in 1942, some three years after Doris's humble beginnings at Charlie Yee's. Betty, undisciplined and explosive, was one of Hollywood's all too frequent casualties. Her blonde ebullience in *The Fleet's In* and *Star-Spangled Rhythm* was never better displayed than as nightclub queen Texas Guinan, a soul-sister to Ruth Etting, who was living out her traumatic and meteoric career when Doris Kappelhoff was singing at the Shanghai Inn: like Doris's portrayal of Etting, Hutton's *Incendiary Blonde* was a great compliment to the original – both nightclub queens were bordering on the plain.

Betty was too busy with *Dream Girl* when *Romance On the High Seas* was mooted for her: two years later, in 1950, she had her last big opportunity taking over from the ailing Judy Garland as Annie Oakley in *Annie Get Your Gun*. From then on, after impersonating another nightclub diva, Blossom Seeley in *Somebody Loves Me*, it was downhill all the way for the mercurial Hutton: she seemed bent on emulating Judy's misfortunes in walkouts, on-set explosions and nightclub engagements ending in fiasco. Her singing voice, sweet and mellow in its softer moments, was burned out through perpetual belting: at her London Palladium engagements, despite some fairly sensational trapeze work she had learned for Cecil B. de Mille's *The Greatest Show on Earth* in 1952, a distressing story was printed in a Sunday newspaper that her singing was 'ghosted' by one of the group accompanying her on stage. Even more sensationally, in 1974, after a minor film comeback seventeen years previously in *Spring Reunion*, her voice a whisper of its former self, she was discovered broke in a Catholic Rectory on

Rhode Island and subsequently taken into psychiatric care until she returned to the Rectory where she had worked as cook and housekeeper.

A sadder contrast to the always disciplined Doris Day, even at her most testing times, can hardly be imagined: when she performed the songs that Betty did she could be as peppy but it was a performance filtered through the control she had learned from the start through her training with Grace Raine, and, even more to the point, her innate balance as a human being. Protest though she may – 'I'm *not* Miss Goody Twoshoes' – there *is* a special quality that pervades everything she does and which must have contributed to her abiding popularity, some seventeen years after her last major television show.

It was eighteen months before Doris finally was able to swap her crutches for a cane. The first time it seemed that the doctor would be able to remove the heavy plaster cast on her leg she all too impetuously decided to try a little modified tap to the rhythm of 'Tea for Two' on her mother's Victrola. Doris supported herself on her crutches to move her good foot to the music; one of her crutches slipped on the edge of a rug and she fell heavily on her injured leg, which put it back at least another year. Her already formulated acceptance of what fate had in store without bewailing her misfortune eased her passage through those eighteen months of slow convalescence, with the radio and cabaret work she was able to do, despite the crutches. There was also another factor to keep her looking on the bright side: Tiny, a little Black and Tan, who never left her side, understood her moods and gave her the kind of companionship that only a dog can bestow: it was, Doris says the start of what was to be for her a lifelong love affair with the dog, a sentiment known only to dog lovers and, many would claim, cat lovers as well. They can be affectionate and caring, a relief from tensions and anxiety, a theme Beryl Reid, the brilliant star of the stage and screen versions of *The Killing of Sister George*, developed in her best-seller *The Cat's Whiskers*. However, a cat's devotion is on its own terms, while a dog's is all-embracing. Writing this book, for me illustrates the difference between feline and canine devotion.

My dog, Swanee, will lie quietly, all day if necessary, beside me until the great moment comes for 'walkies', or, in our case, 'runnies', as he gallops beside my bicycle along the towpaths and meadows near our home. Fluffy, the cat, *has* to be on my lap during her visits, which means re-arranging mounds of reference books and the typewriter itself, as my lap is my favoured position for writing. She will prowl meaningfully round and round until the necessary adjustments are effected, then settle down contentedly. If this diagnosis upsets cat lovers, I'm sorry, but it has always been my experience; on final analysis, as Doris wrote to me, 'Aren't they *all* wonderful?'

Tragedy struck where Tiny was concerned: he used to walk beside her on the pavement as she eased herself along on her crutches, and one day, for no reason she was ever able to find out, he scampered away from her and into the street. Tiny was hit by a car and killed instantly. From that day forward she has felt deeply and passionately about dogs not on leads in the street: if she finds a dog running loose, she will catch it if possible, and if there's a name on the tag that should be round its neck she contacts the owners and that is one time the sweetness and light associated with the Day persona will be found to be conspicuous by its absence.

Doris was free of her crutches by the time Grace Raine was approached by a bandleader friend, Barney

Rapp, who had heard her protegée singing on 'Carlin's Carnival' and enquired whether she would be interested in singing with his band in a club that he was planning to open in Cincinnati, called the Sign of the Drum. Rapp and his New Englanders specialized in playing smaller hotels around the country; Doris was familiar with his music from broadcasts and agreed to audition at the Hotel Sinton in downtown Cincinnati, where they were playing. Although she had never had doubts about her ability to put over a good show, for the first time she experienced a nervousness she can recall to this day over singing to professionals in public. This was a big band and she would have to measure up to top standards. The song Rapp asked her to sing was one she loathed – 'Jeepers Creepers', surely the nadir of all crass jingles of the Thirties, but vastly popular at the time.

She was still limping as she walked to the microphone but her voice warmed as she continued with the song, the audition was a success and Barney Rapp hired her in preference to 200 other vocalists he had tried out at the Sinton Hotel. The band manager told her her salary was to be twenty-five dollars a week: much later she found out that her actual salary should have been fifty dollars – half he was keeping for himself – a situation familiar to all too many young hopefuls starting out on a musical career. This was Doris's first experience of her trust being abused, but, far from it souring her trust in human nature she continued to let others manage her affairs: despite later, far more costly, examples of being conned, she can still say it is in her nature to be trusting and she wouldn't have it any other way.

At the opening of the Sign of the Drum, Doris discovered that she was expected to dress in the Ladies: while she put on the new frock her mother had made for the occasion she suffered the considerable embarrassment of changing while females whom Alma had not been able to waylay at the entrance kept coming through, gazing at the new vocalist with unconcealed curiosity. Her opening number was Gershwin's 'A Foggy Day In London Town': she later found out that no one had been able to hear a word, due to the tightness of her vocal cords – no wonder, in the circumstances, in her book she called the song 'A Foggy *Night* in London Town': Barney Rapp, with great understanding, did not embarrass her further by commenting on her almost silent performance, and as the evening went on she gained in confidence and began to feel that she was really enjoying herself – an ability which has communicated itself to her audiences ever since. She says, 'I really like to sing; it gives me a sense of release, another dimension – it makes me happy, and I think that the people who listen to me instinctively know that and feel it.'

One of Doris's numbers on her opening night was one she had been making her own on the air, 'Day after Day'. As always, it went down particularly well, so when the time came for Barney Rapp to put her name on the marquee outside the club, after some discussion he suggested Day as a surname, having rejected Kappelhoff out of hand and her mother's maiden name Welz, and pointed out that if she called herself Doris Kenyon, as she suggested, people would come in expecting to see Valentino's ex-leading lady burgeoning as a nightclub queen. Doris herself was not too excited over the proposed new name, but Barney stuck to his guns. He asked her to think about it and said, 'I think it's just right – has a nice fresh sound to it, like the dawn of a new day.' How right he was – it was such a convenient handle for launching publicity campaigns at the start of her film career. Her relatives liked it, but she never has – thinks it sounds phony, and several of her friends were in accord. The late Billy De Wolfe used to call her Clara Bixby – just the sort of name one would expect from that dear, funny man with whom I had the great pleasure of working on the publicity for the London presentation of '*How to Succeed in Business without Really Trying.*' He used to talk a lot about his film career and in particular the fun he had working with that same Clara Bixby – a name that has stuck where many of her friends are concerned.

Rock Hudson used to call her Eunice, Gordon MacRae, also, alas, no longer with us, designated her Do-Do, and, when Martin Daye rang me from the Lake District after the news that I was 'Desperately Seeking Doris' had appeared in the press, he said, 'We've just been staying with Do-Do.'

Nevertheless, Doris Day's billing appeared over the Sign of the Drum, where she worked a six-day week from early evening till two in the morning. By association it's a name with a kind of a glow, and, like the man said, a freshness, as abiding now as it was in 1940. At first Alma used to drive her there and back, but, with her other commitments, it became too much of a good thing, and they were both relieved to discover that one of the trombonists, Al Jorden, lived near them in Price Hill. He did not exactly leap at the idea when Doris suggested he might pick her up as he had to drive right by her door. He raised every objection he could think of, starting with girl vocalists never being on time, and when she finally persuaded him, agreeing to help pay for the petrol, he turned out to be a most unsociable companion, taciturn and silent, for all his slim good looks, and often behaved like a bear with a sore head on the return journey, especially when he had to drive out of his way to Price Hill when he had a date with a girl singer in another band. Doris used to enjoy eating with the musicians after work and delighted in hamburgers loaded with onions and smothered with relish, until Al, waiting outside would toot his horn impatiently, causing her to run out, half-consumed hamburger in hand. Often he complained bitterly about the smell permeating his upholstery and once grumbled that his date was upset by the hem of her dress being smeared with the ketchup which had oozed out of the bottom of Doris's sandwich onto the car floor.

Despite this unpromising beginning, Al Jorden was on the way to becoming her fate – a fate that would threaten to turn to nemesis in the long run. Unexpectedly he rang Alma during a two-week break when the band was taking a holiday without pay while Barney Rapp brought in an out-of-town replacement, and asked if she thought Doris would be interested in going out to dinner with him and on to a movie after. At first she protested that he was a creep and she wouldn't go out with him if they were giving away gold nuggets at the film show. Her mother eventually talked her round, pointing out his good looks and that at twenty-three he was the ideal age for a girl of sixteen – going on eighteen, the age at which she was listed on the records as being able to work at the club.

Al turned up when Doris finally agreed and was the antithesis of the grumpy chauffeur she had learned to dread – charming and a good companion – the definitive Dr Jekyll to his alter ego Mr Hyde. In her innocence she agreed to go boating the next day in his sixteen-foot speedboat on the Ohio River with Barney Rapp's drummer Wilbur Shook and his wife Virginia. The trip ended in disaster after Al took it into his head to ride in the wake of the steamboat, *Island Queen*, that used to take excursions up the river to Coney Island. A huge wave struck their speedboat amidships, they were all flung into the muddy water as their boat plunged to the bottom of the river, and they clung for dear life to the inflatable cushions that surfaced from the craft until rescued by a reporter from the *Cincinnati Times Star*. The next day's headlines did not entirely make their journey worthwhile.

Despite this ominous portent, Doris decided she was in love with Al: as a sixteen-year-old the incident probably struck her as a sign of youthful unconventionality – she explained his jealous rages to herself whenever she talked to another man, which was fairly unavoidable when working in a band, as rather flattering devotion, and even a meeting with his mother after he had been injured in a motorcycle accident failed to signal the warning signs that would have been plain as a pikestaff to anyone less naïvely starry-eyed. Mrs Jorden warned Doris against any thought of marriage to her son in a doom-laden voice that would have done credit to Judith Anderson's Mrs Danvers warning Joan Fontaine's Rebecca that she was not, repeat *not* welcome at Manderley. 'Albert is never going to get married. He has promised never to leave me and his father, and I think it's only fair that you know that.'

But she did marry the guy eventually, by which time several changes had taken place in both their careers. Al had left Barney to accept a job with Gene Krupa's new band, which the ace drummer had quit Benny Goodman to form, and Doris, after starting on as a singer at the Sign of the Drum, agreed to go out with Barney Rapp on a tour of band dates after the club folded. She was disconsolate without Al: his letters helped fill the void, but there was little time to brood, playing at least four one-night stands a week, sometimes after a hundred-mile journey in a travel-stained band bus. When Ferde Raine, Grace's husband, suggested she try out for the vacancy Bob Crosby and his Bobcats had for a vocalist, she accepted the idea with her usual equanimity, reflecting that she had never really thought about trying the big band world outside Cincinnati. She let the Raines drive her to Chicago, auditioned without rehearsal for Bob Crosby at the Blackhawk where the Bobcats were playing – a live audition, from which only the persuasive insistence of Grace Raine stopped her from fleeing – and after three songs found herself signed by Crosby's manager, Gil Rodin, for seventy-five dollars a week. Though in shock, and reluctant to go on with the audition until Crosby's laconic announcement, 'We have a little lady who's come all the way up from Cincinnati to audition and let's all be very nice to her' Doris was, again, in no doubt that she would get the job. This dichotomy between possessing no overt ambition and total self-confidence poses a fascinating paradox and is surely the clue to what Christopher Frayling defined as her completely pragmatic approach to her work. Having got the job she was, by her own admission 'excited and pleased', not least with the new salary, from which she was able to send money home to her mother to pay for her beloved brother Paul's medical care after he received a fractured skull from a baseball pitch square on the head while playing for the famous Cincinnati Reds. Paul suffered brain damage which in turn led to epilepsy.

With the Crosby Band Doris eventually made her Broadway début, at the Strand Theatre. For all the experience and excitement of travelling with the Bobcats, who treated her with respect, like a sister figure, giving the lie to Alma's fears when she was not able to act as Doris's chaperone on the tours, she does not seem to have established any particular rapport with Crosby himself, who, she says, contributed little or nothing to her singing education, as he was not really a musician, just a frontman for the band. When his manager told Doris they were having to let her go, in favour of the other girl singer, who was the girlfriend of the man who handled the account for Crosby's weekly commercial radio programme, she was not too distressed, particularly as he had brought the new band sensation Les Brown to hear her and he was keen to sign her to tour with him. Gil Rodin admitted that Brown's band was the one that everyone was talking about; they had the new sound and were really going places.

Doris seems to have taken to Les Brown immediately, at their first meeting. He says he went backstage and signed her after listening to her for five minutes at the Edison Hotel in New York. 'She was every bandleader's dream, a vocalist who had natural talent, a keen regard for the lyrics and an attractive appearance.' He places her firmly in the company of Frank Sinatra and Bing Crosby, rating Doris next to Sinatra in the business of selling a song. Actually, at the start of her meeting with Les Brown, Doris had told him she was ready to quit and go home. Brown persuaded her to stay, being aware that his musicians were such a straight bunch she had nothing to fear from them. Her pay then was seventy-five dollars a week; when she left in 1946 it was 500 dollars a week. She had constant offers of film tests but she remained loyal to him, probably, he thought because of his insistence of no drugs, alcohol or strong language. The reason she was so much in demand by Hollywood was that she had one hit after another with the band and so almost every other band tried to hire her away which made her earnings rise so astronomically. She preferred to stay with Les because his musicians were always so disciplined.

Their first appearance together was at Mike Todd's Theatre Café in Chicago, where Gypsy Rose Lee was starring. The band did two twenty-minute dance sets during which Doris sang four songs. She rated Les Brown highly as a 'strong father figure, despite his youth', and admired him as a musician – a marked contrast to her experience with Bob Crosby. Brown's new band sound, different from all the others, was typified by his theme song 'Leap Frog' – staccato, like the unexpected jumps and bounds of that lively amphibian: he did most of his own arrangements, helped by a member of the band, Frank Comstock, who had considerable experience as an arranger. Another talent of Les Brown's was his ear for phrasing and it was he who helped Doris eradicate a slight southern drawl, which he pointed out to her at their first recording session together.

Doris's career was proceeding very happily, yet she was still pining for Al Jorden though sustained by his letters, which he contrived always to have waiting for her at the band's next stop. He had left Gene Krupa for Jimmy Dorsey, and when Les Brown's 'Band of Renown' hit New York and the Dorsey Band happened to be there at the same time, Doris and Al were reunited ecstatically, albeit briefly between shows, for which they made up by being able to stay together every night. It was at this time that he made their engagement official by presenting her with a ring, they exchanged vows to get married as soon as circumstances allowed, and in the meantime separated again when Doris accompanied Les Brown on a long tour of one-nighters, ending in a month's engagement back at the Theatre Café in Chicago.

Les Brown's remark about the film studios constantly being at Doris to make tests highlights the essential difference between American and British attitudes towards success. In the States when a star is born in one medium, particularly someone young and attractive, immediate feelers are put out by the motion picture people to cash in on that success. In Britain, it took a war to propel our nearest equivalent to Doris Day, Vera Lynn, into movies, though she is now a Dame of the British Empire and a National Institution of the kind they don't appear to have in the States – perhaps the nearest approximation was the late Ethel Merman, or her male counterpart, Jimmy Durante, with whom Doris was to appear in one of the happiest musicals of her career, *Billy Rose's Jumbo*. In the late Thirties a young vocalist, Britain's Vera Lynn was becoming famous though singing with our own Big Bands, finally being associated most definitely with that of Bert Ambrose, and the seal was set upon her international status when she was given her own programme by the BBC to sing to the Armed Forces in 1941. She achieved immortality as 'The Sweetheart of the Forces' with her straightforward, sincere way of addressing the public through the lyrics of the popular songs of the moment.

For once, the British film industry was not slow to jump on the bandwagon, and Vera was signed to do three films, the first of them entitled *We'll Meet Again*, after one of her hit songs, with Geraldo supplying the music. They were cheaply and quickly made, proved just the ticket for wartime audiences as well aware of Vera Lynn as Americans were of Doris Day, and that was that. *Rhythm Serenade* and *One Exciting Night* were the others – the latter title somewhat overstating the case, perhaps – but no follow-up, as far as films were concerned, although Dame Vera's career has gone on from strength to strength, thanks to the careful nurturing of her manager-husband Harry Lewis. Like Doris, *au fond* Vera has notably lacked ambition for herself, accepting the assignments as they came along and doing her considerable best, but content otherwise to remain with hearth and home, a condition which has consistently eluded Doris, though she proved that was where her real ambitions lay when she turned her back on the glittering prospects before her with the Les Brown Band to accept Al Jorden's proposal of marriage shortly after her seventeenth birthday, about the time of Vera Lynn's sensationally successful broadcasts to the troops.

Once the Day film career had taken off there was no looking back, which was the exact opposite of Vera Lynn's experience. In her book *Vocal Refrain* she commented, more in sorrow than in anger, 'One of the problems was that I was just Vera Lynn: it was difficult for them to take me out of that established character and get the public to accept me as a different person. I was so *me*, it was hard for anyone to write a different kind of part . . . I'm forced to admit that the British have never been good at musicals. It's a great pity, for I enjoyed making the films, and I would have loved to have found a whole new career for myself in pictures.' Whether that could have been her *métier* we shall never know.

Lucky Doris, that she was not born in Britain, although she just might by now have been a Dame of the British Empire. It's an intriguing thought.

3

Motherhood and a Million Seller

When Doris told Les Brown she wanted to leave the band to marry Al Jorden, Les was aghast. He pointed out that she was liable to throw away what was starting to be a glorious career for the bleak prospect of being a band wife – a miserable life either being lonely at home or hanging around dreary hotel rooms when the band were booked in somewhere for a stand. He did not mince words about his attitude towards Jorden: he said he did not think he was much of a prize as a husband – which turned out to be the understatement of the year – and, as someone who cared for Doris and her welfare, he begged her to reconsider her decision.

She was adamant: when she said that home and marriage were the only career she wanted – the kind of relationship that had eluded her parents – she really meant it. Alma, desperately unhappy at the chances her daughter was throwing away, pleaded as strongly as Les, pointing out that nobody liked Al Jorden, and, in any case, what was the hurry?

When Alma saw that there was no alternative but to concede defeat she set to, readied a wedding gown and drove Doris to New York's City Hall. The Les Brown Band of Renown were appearing at a venue called the Strand, the Jimmy Dorsey Band at the Martin Beck

Theatre, so they were married between shows, with one of the members of the band and his wife as witnesses, while the rest of the guests were the other musicians and their wives. There was a hurried reception at a small hotel opposite the Strand – a gulped mouthful of champagne, a couple of hors d'oeuvres – and everyone dashed off to their respective engagements. Alma returned home to Cincinnati the afternoon of the wedding, trying desperately to put a brave face upon things.

The 'honeymoon' was at the two-room apartment Al had rented at the Whitby in Times Square, where visiting band wives would stay because it was cheap, if not cheerful. There and then Doris, with no experience as a housewife or cook, learned the hard way what it was to be one of the *Orchestra Wives* – not the glamorous type in the film featuring Glenn Miller – but an aimless, barren existence passing time until her husband arrived home in the early hours of the morning, when the blushing bride would set to and prepare a meal. Blushes were in order when she tried spaghetti for the first time and found there was enough to fill the kitchen sink.

None of this would have mattered had she not been forced to come to terms with the darker side of Al's nature almost immediately. She had had experiences of his unreasoning jealousy in the past, always rationalizing it as the extreme evidence of the way he cared for her. Even at this remove she is convinced he did love her, but in his own way, and that turned out to be the way of madness. She went to meet Al at the dinner break at the Strand, on the second day after the wedding, and waited for him in the ante-room as the show was about to end. On the first floor the manager of the Dorsey Band and Jimmy himself shared an office-cum-dressing room, from which Billy Burton, the manager in question, called down to Doris to ask her to come up for a moment, as he had a wedding present for the happy couple. It was a leather make-up case, which she had just opened, when Al burst into the room, with a manic expression on his face. He grabbed her arm and propelled her down the stairs; she just managed to hold onto their wedding present with her disengaged hand as he marched her through the streets to their apartment.

When they got indoors he struck her in the face, calling her a whore and a tramp, and beat her up, slamming her around the apartment, accusing her of running up the stairs so the bandsmen would be able to look up her skirts. He ended by saying he would kill her if she ever did it again. He stood over her as she collapsed onto the floor, and, minutes later, in a complete volte face flung himself on the floor beside her and begged her forgiveness. Of course, being Doris, she forgave him and remembered all the loving, funny moments they had enjoyed together and how good he was in bed. She admired him as a musician, and, more importantly, she was in love with him. Photographs of Al Jorden show him to have been a glamorously handsome man, although, in hindsight, it is easy to detect a touch of the sinister.

The situation was repeated over and over again: the beatings, the tearful reconciliations, and in his rational moods, when he was the loving husband in bed he would admit the groundlessness of his paranoid jealousies. Doris discovered in the second month of their marriage that she was pregnant: Al received the news with tears; she could not decide whether they signified joy or unhappiness. She did not have long to wait: the same evening he returned after work and told her about an abortionist with first-class credentials, according to one of the boys in the band. Doris was sickened by the proposal and refused categorically to have anything to do with it. She wanted her baby and deep down hoped that this would bring about a change in her relationship with her husband. However, having agreed that Doris should not have to undergo the painful humiliation of visiting a back-street abortionist, he came up with another scheme, involving putting her feet in a basin of near-boiling water and taking some nauseating pills which made her sick. Her resistance worn down by his callous and totally uncaring behaviour, she allowed him to put her through the obscene charade, whose only effect, in the long run, was to renew her original determination to see her pregnancy through to its logical and, by her, longed for, conclusion. She also made a silent resolution to leave Al after the baby's birth.

On the way to an engagement with the Dorsey band in Chicago he drove them to Cincinnati to stay with his parents and to visit her mother, who at once diagnosed Doris's pregnancy, although she was only in her third month. There were celebrations that evening at the Welz tavern, with the family present in force, singing, dancing, a beef barbecue, beer and conviviality all round, even from Al, who was at his most charming, giving Alma pause for thought over her originally uncompromising attitude towards her son-in-law. Doris was happy and relieved by the time the party ended at midnight. There had been toasts to the impending arrival and Al had lifted his glass with the rest of the family.

Her joy was shortlived: he turned on her in the car and ranted on about how he was sure Doris had disobeyed his orders to tell no one about her pregnancy and he had watched everyone lusting over her enlarged breasts – surely very slightly, at that stage. When they arrived at his parents' home he employed his usual strong-arm grip to propel her into the house and when she managed to free herself to run up the stairs to their bedroom he followed and subjected her to another violent attack, knocking her around the room, punching and hitting, sending furniture and ornaments flying, with the un-surprising result of waking his parents. Only his father's prolonged thudding on the door eventually brought the attack to an end when Al stopped to admit Jorden Senior, who took his son away downstairs. Doris locked the door and sat weeping on the bed, until a knock heralded the arrival of her mother-in-law.

Mrs Jorden's 'Judith Anderson' persona had in no way softened: in fact, her attitude was so hurtfully insulting – 'From the looks of you he didn't hit you very hard' was the only consolation she offered – that Doris stepped far enough out of character to push her out of the room, telling her she never wanted to see her again, and locked the door behind her. She resolutely refused entry to Al when he returned to beg admittance with his usual after-violence conciliatory tones: she sat up all night and crept out of what had become to her a house of evil as soon as it was light. She told Alma just enough to enlist her assistance with secret plans for the baby's birth: when Al came to collect Doris for the return journey he played his little-boy – contrite – scene so effectively that her mother, to whom the performance was entirely new, seemed to have some sympathy for him.

The situation worsened during the succeeding six months: twice in the car he threatened to kill her, the first time by plunging at full speed over the side of a mountain road, the second by pressing the gun he always carried in the car into her stomach and saying he was going to kill her and her baby. She was eight months pregnant when he came home drunk one night and gave her the worst beating of all, pulling her out of bed and dragging her round the room until he got her up against the wall and began pummelling her before slamming out of the house. Terrified as she was by his violence, her dread of being alone was even stronger, and she ran through the freezing streets of Chicago looking for him, with only a raincoat over her nightdress. She never found him and returned to the lodgings, physically sick and frozen, certain that she would lose the baby. That she did not do so was surely a miracle, as indeed was the fact that she survived those nightmare months of pregnancy at all.

When her husband appeared at dawn he was his Dr Jekyll self again, and explained that he had jumped to conclusions that she had been unfaithful to him with the friendly barman at Michael Todd's hostelry, simply because he had enthused over how lovely Doris was and how she used to talk to him about Al and showed their engagement ring. Again Al wept and crept into bed beside her, seeking comfort: although she knew by then that her husband was a sad schizophrenic and no more capable of controlling his moods than the sun could prevent itself from rising. She was dreadfully in fear of what he was apt to do if she tried to get away from him, so all she could do was to cradle him in her arms while his sobs shook them both. Of that experience Doris wrote, 'No matter how many lows I would have in my life, none would ever be lower than that night in Chicago.'

Years later the situation would be re-played for her in the film *Julie*, when she has to hold the husband she has discovered is planning to kill her. Louis Jourdan, like Al Jorden, playing the psychotic wife-killer, is dark and handsome, as was Al – even the name similarity is striking – and their scene in bed together as he begs her forgiveness for his unreasoning jealousy was one of the most traumatic of her acting career. No Method actress she – Doris could not switch moods on and off like a light, which surely accounts for the veracity of her portrayal.

Al had gone to Buffalo with Jimmy Dorsey when the baby was born, and Alma had come to stay with her daughter at the Whitby: they took a taxi to the hospital and after twelve hours of tortuous labour, on 8 February 1942, her son was born and christened Terry, after Doris's favourite childhood tale, *Terry and the Pirates*. Al arrived at the hospital two days later: Alma had tried to reach him by phone without success and later revealed that she had discovered, via a letter he had left in the pocket of a suit he had asked her to send to the cleaner's, that he had spent three days with an unknown girl at the time of Doris's accouchement.

Her plans for escape after the birth received a bad jolt when her husband suddenly declared that he was going to return to Cincinnati with them to the little house that Alma had found not far from the Welz tavern. Al said that he had left the Dorsey band and would find local work, which he was well able to do with his talents as a musician. He insisted Doris drive back with him in the car and arranged for baby Terry to travel by train with his grandmother: comforted by the thought that at least back in Cincinnati she would have the protection of her family and to avoid a violent scene in the baby's presence Doris agreed and they moved into the new home that she had planned to share just with Alma and the baby. Nearby were Uncle Charley, Doris's brother Paul and, right next door, her favourite Aunt Marie – large, capable, full of good humour and nicknamed Rocky: she was indeed a bastion of strength.

At first Al conducted himself as Dr Jekyll, attentive

and on his best behaviour where Doris and the family were concerned, with plenty of work on radio and with local musicians, but betraying a more subtle type of sadism in his attitude to the baby. Firstly he would not allow Terry to sleep in the bedroom with them – he shared with Alma, whose devotion was total, but who found Al's attitude unnatural and cruel. Then he bought a little dog, on whom, in front of Doris, he bestowed all his affection, while ignoring Terry. He certainly succeeded in upsetting her completely by this ploy: to set the two species she loved most, babies and animals, in rivalry, as it were, was unkind in the extreme, and her affection for dogs showed itself to be so deep rooted that she emerged unscathed from this war of nerves. After a few weeks Al returned to his more familiar battlefront tactics, one night coming home abusive and belligerent, his roars awakening the baby next door.

That finally did it: the straw that broke the camel's back – the camel in this case being Al, who at last got his come-uppance from his long-suffering wife. The following day when he came home from work he was unable to effect an entry: Doris had changed the locks and packed his bags, leaving them outside the front door – she herself had taken refuge at Aunt Rocky's. To their surprise, after some banging and shouting he picked up his bags and walked away from the house. Doris claims that the ten dollars she had to borrow from her aunt for groceries was the one and only time in her life she ever asked for a loan. Subsequently she instructed her lawyer to initiate divorce proceedings.

With her usual self-confidence she applied for a job forthwith and got it, from a Mr Weiner, who ran radio station WLW, explaining to him that she needed to work locally because of the baby. Just one song and she was in, shortly to be featured on various sponsored shows, including *The Lion's Roar*, promoting MGM productions. She graduated soon to WLW's most important radio show *Moon River* for which she was the vocalist four times a week.

In the meantime Al had begun a new war of nerves, having only returned to the house once to collect his little dog from the back yard. He used to tail her whenever she dined out at a restaurant and just sit staring: it is amazing that she managed to eat anything in those circumstances. He made no attempt to talk to her until one night when she returned with some friends from the studio after a double date: a girl called Vivie had agreed to stay the night with Doris and her mother, and it was Vivie who alerted her to the fact that Al's car was parked behind them. In fear and trembling they resisted his demand that Doris get into the car to talk and when they ran up the steps of the house he made no attempt to follow them, but the next time she steeled herself to agree to a discussion and sent Vivie on into the house.

Al was conciliatory and reasonable and made a final attempt to win her back, stressing his need for her and love for his baby, but at last she was purged of her pity for him and the only concession she would make was that he could come and see Terry occasionally, and even take him home for the odd afternoon to his paternal grandparents. These would be part of the normal arrangements after the divorce which was to be handled by a cousin of Doris's who was a lawyer. In the event Al only availed himself of the opportunity to see his son a few times before leaving his home in Cincinnati to join the forces: he found his true vocation as a member of the Great Lakes Naval Station and the saddest phase of Doris's life came to an end. The tragic final curtain came years later when Al shot himself in the head with the gun he always carried in the glove compartment of his car.

Doris finally made her own discovery that the 'Once a Catholic . . .' tenet as far as she was concerned was null and void. Having declined, understandably, into a deep depression after the saga of her life with Al, she accepted Alma's suggestion that she might find consolation in talk with the parish priest. After all, that's what priests were for, wasn't it?

The meeting was a disaster. This particular priest, like Graham Greene's hero-priest in the play *The Living Room*, when his niece goes to him for consolation and sympathy after having transgressed, found his tongue 'heavy with the phrases of the Penny Catechism'. He was unable to reassure Doris when she asked him point blank whether the fact of her marriage not having been solemnized in a Catholic church making it 'no marriage' implied that her son Terry was illegitimate. All the good priest could proffer was 'Let us hope that you will find solace in marrying properly, and enjoying the fruits of such a marriage.' It is not recorded whether the sarcasm in her thanking him for having been a great comfort was detected by the good father or whether he foresaw that to be the final scene of her attempted reconciliation with the Church.

Her work for the radio station had been adequate to keep herself, Alma and Terry until Doris reclaimed their house from Al; then the mortgage payments placed a considerable additional burden on her resources. A call from Les Brown, who had heard her on *Moon River* urged her warmly to go back to his band but she refused because she could not bear the thought of leaving her son. She has always held that the automatic payment of alimony from the husband to his ex-wife after a divorce is farcical, and there was no question of her asking anything from Al. So life became quite a struggle, which she thought worthwhile as she enjoyed her work on the radio and did not envisage leaving Cincinnati. She had made friends with a group called the Williams Brothers, and she was persuaded somewhat against her better judgement to join them, which she did with great pleasure, but only at their home for Monday-night sessions with the whole Williams family. It was this kind of impromptu singing for fun that she enjoyed best and would miss if she left her home town. They never sang together professionally – Doris felt, perhaps, that she was too set in her ways as a solo song stylist for a permanent blending of talents to work out – but she was desolate when they announced they were going to New York to see fame and fortune. She felt she was going to miss the brother who had been instrumental in getting her to join the group on a friendly basis. His name was Andy, and so it was that Andy Williams played a key role in being the catalyst to propel Doris Day into her pre-eminent position as one of the greatest luminaries ever to grace the world of recording – not to mention the silvery-cum-Technicolored screen. The departure of her good friend decided the issue.

The third time Les Brown called, Doris agreed to rejoin him and the band. The casualness of her assent is astonishing. She herself says, 'My mother and my aunt had been working on me, and I was on the point where I felt I should give it a try.' Just like that. She had a tearful reunion with Les in Columbus, Ohio: the parting with Terry and the family had been predictably upsetting, although she knew that Alma would give him her single-minded love and attention and that Aunt Marie next door would back her up with her usual rock-like devotion. Les comments that he saw a change in Doris, 'She falls in love very easily and whole-heartedly, and when it breaks up she suffers whole-heartedly, too. Whereas she used to be scared but fascinated with life with the band, now she was moody and depressed. She cried a lot.'

Nevertheless, she was delighted with the way Les and the Band of Renown set her 'comeback' after more than two years away which had seemed like a lifetime of hard-earned experience. She sang 'Too-ra-loo-ra-loo-ral' on a darkened stage with a pin spot on her and a backing of four trombones immediately behind her. New songs were constantly added to their repertoire, which she was able to sight-read in her own way, although, like Bing Crosby and Frank Sinatra she is unable technically to read notes of music. She had recorded several songs as vocalist with Les Brown, but one night at the Pennsylvania Hotel in Newark, New Jersey, he handed her the sheet music for a song of which he was part-composer, which was to give her her first big hit and ultimately change the direction of her career forever. The song was 'Sentimental Journey' and the dancers went wild. They stopped dancing and just listened: Doris did encore after encore and Les was so excited by the response that they recorded on the Okey label. Doris had her first hit record: Bud Green's lyrics had the quality of folk poetry, and were just the stuff to give the troops, strangely enough, as his most famous hit up till then had been 'Flat Foot Floogie'!

The song, predictably, became a kind of theme song for the Armed Forces worldwide, and Doris joined Betty Grable, Rita Hayworth and Vera Lynn as pin-ups for the services. She received thousands of letters from all over the world, which never failed to touch and delight her, but ultimately she wearied utterly of having to keep reprising 'Sentimental Journey', which spent a staggering 28 weeks on the American Billboard chart.

Thirty years later, in 1975, the song was nominated for honours by the National Academy of Recording Arts and Sciences' Hall of Fame. Then, in 1998, the vintage recording was resurrected to take its prestigious resting place in the Grammy Hall of Fame.

Another big record for Doris was 'My Dreams Are Getting Better All The Time', which was a number-one smash and the second of a total of twelve Top 20 American hits with Les Brown (others included: 'T'aint Me', 'Till The End Of Time' based on Chopin's 'Polonaise', 'Aren't You Glad You're You?', 'You Won't Be Satisfied (Until You Break My Heart)', 'Come To Baby Do!', 'Day By Day', 'I Got The Sun In The Morning' from *Annie Get Your Gun*, 'The Whole World Is Singing My Song', 'The Christmas Song (Merry Christmas To You)' and 'Sooner Or Later').

Three years of touring with Les Brown enhanced her popularity all the time, and led to a final encounter with Al Jorden, a bitter-sweet coda to their unhappy marriage finale in Cincinnati. They were playing the College Inn, Chicago, when he rang her at the Sherman Hotel. He turned up to see the show, and, being Doris, when she saw him, looking distractingly handsome in his naval uniform, standing in the wings behind her, all her resolutions about not accepting his invitation to dinner were gone with the wind. He came back to the hotel with her and again pleaded his case, often very touchingly: all through the night they talked and when he was finally convinced she had no feelings left for him, he wept, and his distress moved her also to tears. She slept with him for one final time. Afterwards he wrote to her, still unable to accept the inevitable, until she wrote back and asked him not to continue with his letters. It seems he capitulated after that and never wrote again. Their divorce followed amicably. He married a second time and Doris saw him just once in a Cincinnati store. He was with a woman, whom Doris took to be the new Mrs Jorden. They did not speak.

Happier encounters during the long tour were with Terry and Alma, who brought him to stay whenever the band were in a town for at least a week. He was growing fast and highly mischievous. One day when he shot away from Alma in order to chase after a policeman's horse the cord of the harness the child was wearing got entwined round his grandmother's ankles and she crashed to the ground, breaking her leg in no less than fourteen places, which necessitated hospitalization and a heavy plaster cast which totally enveloped her leg. Doris's heart bled for her as her mind went back to her own nightmare days on crutches: Terry, with no such memories, thought it great fun to throw Alma's out of the window when she got back from hospital. He was, fortunately, usually most appealing and a great favourite with the bandsmen and their wives, who were always happy to take him on little outings and buy him ice cream cones, which he had to be restrained from trying to feed to the inhabitants of the zoo.

Les has said Doris fell in love very easily – maybe, like the song, it should be too easily; it was only a matter of months after she went back to the band that her eye fell on the lead alto sax player and his on her. His name was George Weidler, brother of Virginia, who was to Hollywood movies of the Thirties the personification of malevolent bratdom, the antidote to Shirley Temple's sweetness and light: by the time Doris and Virginia's brother fell in love, her career as a child menace was virtually over, though she made a good showing in *The Philadelphia Story* and the Lucille Ball musical *Best Foot Forward* in 1943.

Once again Doris thought that her affair with George

Weidler was for all time: not content with sleeping with him every night she romanticized their relationship to such a degree that after he left the band – the original alto sax player Steve Madrick, whom he had replaced when Steve was called up to the forces, returned and George decided to return to his native California – she once more experienced the deprivations of a love affair courtesy of the US mail, and married him at Mount Vernon when he came to see her in New York where the Les Brown band were performing at the Pennsylvania Hotel. Les commented ruefully 'If I had known that was going to happen I would have left well enough alone'. He tried to talk her out of this second marriage, predictably unavailingly and she again handed in her notice, but agreed to stay on until he found a replacement. This was in 1946.

After the fantastic success of 'Sentimental Journey' Bob Hope became interested in using Les Brown on his peak radio show, on which the featured vocalist was Frances Langford, who was having personal problems. This was about the time she was signed to star for Monogram in *The Bamboo Blonde* and shared with opera star Grace Moore and the queen of Broadway, Ethel Barrymore, the dubious distinction of being introduced in the credit titles as 'Miss' Frances Langford: considering the status of the studio in question the idea was slightly risible. However, she made up for her lack of acting ability and pugdog looks by having a warm and mellow voice on her own radio shows and was a popular adjunct to the World War Two Bob Hope broadcasts. She evidently beat her battle with the bottle by continuing her successful career as a singer through the decades, and appeared as herself in the 1954 *Glenn Miller Story*.

Bob Hope, who Les Brown describes as, 'One of the

few genuinely compassionate people in our business', was unwilling to add to Langford's troubles by taking on Doris Day, with her own highly individual and sympathetic style as his replacement vocalist, so there the matter rested for the time being: later Bob had cause financially to regret his altruism, as Les Brown repeatedly warned him.

From the outset Doris had misgivings about embarking on her second marriage: she wrote in her book, 'I should have worn black.' But at that time she echoed the old *Maid of the Mountains* ditty 'Love Will Find A Way' and mentally reassured herself that all would be well once she, George and little Terry found a home together. At the Pennsylvania Hotel an agent named Al Levy had introduced himself and tried to interest Doris in branching out on a solo career as a singer. Her reaction was that if this gave her the opportunity of going to California to join her new husband, well and good, so long as she could earn enough money to support herself and Terry: George's financial resources as a musician were limited.

So was accommodation in Los Angeles: eventually the newlyweds ended up in a trailer in something called the Midway Trailer Camp in an industrial area of Sepulveda Boulevard, to which it was not possible to bring her son, but she determined to put as cheerful a face on things as possible and asked Al Levy to find her some local radio work. In fact she had developed an aversion to singing on live radio, without a backing band, and with no opportunity for reprising a song if it didn't go the way she would have liked. *The Sweeny and March Radio Show* featured Doris as vocalist and provided enough pennies to support Alma and Terry, and though she was grateful for small mercies, she opposed Al Levy when he wanted to discuss her potential as a big star. She protested she was not interested and that all she aimed to do was to look after her family, which was as well, because at that time all that Al was able to come up with was the local radio. The gates to Hollywood did not seem to be beckoning, which did not worry Doris at all, but one event of significance for the future was that Al Levy introduced her to his partners at the firm with which he worked, Century Artists, Dick Dorso and Marty Melcher. They predicted big things on the horizon for Doris: the accuracy of their forecast was not to be tested for some time to come, and in the meantime her next engagement took her away from Hollywood and back to New York.

Al Levy booked her into Billy Reed's Little Club there and she went with George's blessing, after a long discussion: he agreed that it seemed an opportunity not to be missed, particularly as the money was four times what she had been able to earn in Hollywood. She enjoyed working for Billy Reed, an old-timer from vaudeville, and the Club itself, elegant and, she realized at once, eminently suited to her kind of singing. The man whom Al Levy brought in to help select her songs was Marty Melcher; they included two of her hits, the inevitable 'Sentimental Journey' and 'My Dreams Are Getting Better All the Time', besides 'How are things in Glocca Morra?' and 'How About You?' She had bad first-night nerves which eased as she began to sing and found herself going well: Billy Reed took up her option for a second month and *Variety*'s notice was cautiously enthusiastic; 'Miss Day is a charming young songstress, better than average looker . . . who does justice by her pop chores although she'll need a little more zing and change of pace to give her special distinction that really counts for above-par values. Right now she's a shade too "sweet" . . . on the other hand a fetching personality who will more than hold her own in class or mass nighteries'.

Her success was counterbalanced by a letter from George, who at that time was playing with Stan Kenton's band, saying that he wanted to end their marriage of only eight months. She had received no inkling of his feelings when he urged her to take the New York offer. It was a sad letter, the nitty-gritty of which was that he believed Al Levy's contention that she was going to be a big success, did not want to stand in her way, and had no intention of becoming Mr Doris Day. The irony of it was that those were not her intentions at all – at least it seemed to her at that time that her only interest was in saving their marriage. She even believed that she could continue to enjoy her life as a trailer wife, but, with hindsight it looks as though he knew her better than she knew herself.

She struggled through her first month at the Little Club, in tears through most of her songs and only just able to get through her final number 'Glad to Be Unhappy' before the floodgates opened. The understanding Billy Reed reluctantly let her out of her second month at the Club and, like others before him, tried to talk her out of throwing up an engagement to follow her heart. That was one thing at which Doris was especially adept, and she hurried back to Hollywood to try and talk her husband out of his resolve. He had quit their trailer home, but eventually she left a message with his mother; although he had agreed to meet her at Pasadena, he did not show up at the station. Again she left word with his mother and eventually George came to collect her at the hotel into which she had registered: the same evening they returned to the trailer and talked until well into the night. George showed himself more prescient than she, reiterating his conviction that she was going to be a star: it seems probable that her dislike of that term stems from those times; if a reluctant star is not a contradiction in terms, surely Doris Day exemplifies that rare species.

The shoe was on the other foot during this impassioned discussion: with Al Jorden it had been he who pleaded for another chance to save their marriage – this time it was Doris who tried all she knew how to convince her husband their union could be made to work. He insisted that stardom was there in the sky, waiting to grab her. And so it was – with a little help from her agent – in fact two agents, one right there on the spot, the other waiting his turn in the wings. True to pattern, that night ended in lovemaking, and, if nothing else, reassured her that his physical desire for her was as strong as ever.

The heart-searching that went on after this second débâcle threw up some conclusions indicating that her romantic view of marriage had unsurprisingly received substantial dents: the rose-coloured spectacles were off, with some deductions that gave the lie, even then, to the myth of 'the Constant Virgin'. It is Doris's firmly stated conviction that no one should enter into the married state before having lived together – not just slept together; whether her two unhappy experiences had taught her that at this early stage of her life is debatable. Living together would surely have revealed Al Jorden as the pathological sadist he was, and no one, other than an equally pathological masochist, would have dreamed of walking down the aisle with him, for better, for worse. There was only worse in Al's case and she could have saved herself much physical and mental pain had she been able to find out about this before. As for George Weidler, he seems to have been a good and essentially pragmatic man, with whom the friendship they later were able to find with one another could have come to pass had they moved in together before seeking the benefit of clergy.

The most successful romantic novelist of them all, the pink and candyfloss *grande dame* Barbara Cartland, with her insistence that virginity is the only state for a young lady of quality to enter into marriage – only hussies and tarts taste the fruits before wedlock – might perhaps postulate that, even if a couple do live together in unmarried bliss, only time and experience tell, in the long run. Doris's third marriage seemed to be built on rock-firm foundations, with both her husband and herself mature and experienced adults – but, would she have wed again if the future could have been revealed? Given her unshakeable optimism, and her faith in predestination, probably she would have.

After George left to go back on the road with Stan Kenton, Doris decided to shake the dust of Hollywood from her jodhpurs and head on back to her mother and son in Cincinnati, which, at least was home. And so little dust appeared to have settled, in any case, that there seemed no point in staying, even though the thought of going back to WLW radio was as dreary as any of the alternatives. Al Levy did his best to help and cheer her up, with roses sent to her hotel and by taking her out to dinner. This seems to have been a period of constant tears for Mrs Kappelhoff's unambitious young daughter, a state of mind out of which Al did his best to jolly her. He enlarged again on the glittering future she had ahead, but unfortunately could not propose anything immediate. He did, however, manage to sell her trailer for a good price and three days after her parting from George rang to invite her to a party. Doris objected that she was in no party mood and Al said that was just why she had to get out of her hotel room for a change of

atmosphere and to meet a few new people. He over-
ruled her objections, said he would pick her up at eight
and hung up the phone.

The party was at the Beverly Hills home of composer
Jule Styne on Elm Drive, and among the guests were his
partner, lyricist Sammy Cahn and several other musicians and singers, so it was inevitable that people would
get up and entertain. Doris did all she could to get out of
singing, but Sammy Cahn propelled her over to the
piano, where Jule Styne was tinkling the ivories. Much
against her will she sang a chorus of 'Embraceable You',
perched on Styne's piano: later her agent Al, Jule and
Sammy took her aside and told her about the score they
had written for a new musical, *Romance on the High Seas*.
They explained about Judy Garland and then Betty
Hutton being unavailable and how the director, Michael
Curtiz, was testing other girls, including Betty's sister
Marion, a band singer, who had appeared in a couple of
movies. They then asked Doris if she would like to go to
Warner Brothers for a test. She was very unenthusiastic
and said she was on the point of returning to New York
to play her second month at the Little Club. Al's response was to undertake to get her to the studio in the
morning.

The audition was set for 1 p.m. in Michael Curtiz's
office bungalow on the Warners lot. Sammy Cahn says
in his autobiography *I Should Care*, 'Doris showed up
just as she was: no special hairdo, no pretty dress. I said
"Okay, let's rehearse. Let's do the first two choruses of
'Embraceable You'". She did two bars, and then threw
herself, crying, onto the couch. I turned to Al and said
"Do you want to explain that?"' After Levy had told
him about Doris's marital situation, Sammy told Al to
get her on her feet and they went on with the rehearsal. Cahn goes on, 'After a bit I told her "Mr Curtiz

is expecting a Betty Hutton sort of singer, kind of bouncy." Doris, to her credit, said "I don't bound around. I just sing." So I tried to think of a bouncy song to give her and finally settled on "What Do We Do on a Rainy Night in Rio?" – a Latin song by Leo Robin and Arthur Schwartz that might make her move a little bit. She sang it, but just standing there, with perhaps a little finger snap. I said, "Look, you've got to move at least a little." She said, "Betty Hutton moves because she doesn't sing".

'At that point we had to go in to see Curtiz, who looked at her and says: "You sing, Dolling." She did "Embraceable You". Michael Curtiz looked at me as if to say, "This is very very good," but said, "You move a little, Dolling." She did "What Do We Do on a Rainy Night in Rio?" and you could detect a tiny sway. At that – I swear to you – this eminent Hungarian got up from behind his desk and walked over and put his hands on her hips and moved her as she sang again. And then he finally said the fateful words, "We make film test." At least I knew I'd done my part.'

'One day they screened the tests of the three girls. First came Marion Hutton who was not earth-shaking. Then came Janis Paige – by comparison, excellent. Then came Doris Day – and the projection room, when they ran the film, exploded.'

It says a great deal for the pertinacity of Al Levy and the patience of director Curtiz that the test got made in the first place. When he asked if she'd like to be in his film she said she didn't really know because she had an engagement in New York, then told him about her depression and its cause. After a few bars of 'Embraceable You' she burst into tears and asked to be shown to the Ladies' Room. On her return the same thing happened again and she apologized to Curtiz and prepared

Doris, aged three, on a Cincinnati pony, with her beloved brother Paul, who was to die in early adulthood after an injury incurred in a baseball accident.

Right: Doris as an adolescent after an accident to her leg in a car crash put paid to her ambition to be a dancer. During her convalescence she was inspired to take up singing through enforced days of listening to the radio.

With Barney Rapp, band leader from Cincinnati, who first employed her as a singer and Joseph Cheriavsky, MD of radio station WLW, who gave her her first break on the air.

First grooming in an important step up the ladder, as vocalist to Bob Crosby and his Bobcats.

Doris Day – early Hollywood version, with Lee Bowman in her second movie *My Dream Is Yours* (1949).

Below: With Eve Arden in *Tea for Two* (1950).

Left: With son Terry, born of her first marriage to Al Jorden, trombonist to Barney Rapp, 7 February 1942. After Doris married Marty Melcher Terry adopted his stepfather's name.

On the set of *Storm Warning*, her first film without song and the only one in which she dies at the end, as Ginger Rogers's younger sister, married to Ku Klux Klan member Steve Cochran. This was the realization of a dream; Rogers had been her childhood ideal of a film star. Ronald Reagan first left, Steve Cochran next to Doris (1951).

Wedding to Marty Melcher, Burbank City Hall, 3 April 1951.

Recording sessions with Johnnie Ray and Frankie Laine.

Below: A domestic moment with her mother, Alma Kappelhoff, captured by the studio publicity department.

With Danny Thomas in the Gus Kahn biopic *I'll See You In My Dreams* – Doris as his wife Grace LeBoy and Elsie Neft as Mrs Kahn (1952).

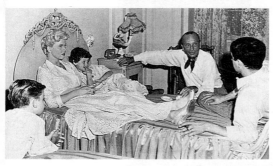

Above: On the set of *I'll See You In My Dreams* with director Michael Curtiz (centre), Danny Thomas (right), Robert Lyden, Mimi Gibson.

A lunchbox for Terry on the way to school.

With Ray Bolger (seated) and Claude Dauphin in *April in Paris* – her most unsuitable leading men and 'the worst musical she ever made' (1953).

Below left: One of several kooky moments from *My Dream is Yours* (1949)

Below right: As *Calamity Jane* – her favourite film (1953)

Above: With Frank Sinatra in *Young At Heart*, a musical version of Warners' *Four Daughters*, a hit of 1938 for John Garfield in the Sinatra role and Priscilla Lane in Doris's part. Sinatra acted up, had Marty Melcher barred from the set, but the partnership was an effective one (1955).

Above: As Thirties' singing star Ruth Etting in *Love Me or Leave Me* with James Cagney as her husband and would-be Svengali Marty 'the Gimp' Snyder – her first film for MGM after seven years with Warner Brothers and a highlight of her career (1955).

Love Me Or Leave Me – with director Charles Vidor.

Directed by Alfred Hitchcock with James Stewart (foreground), Bernard Miles, Brenda De Banzie in *The Man Who Knew Too Much* (1956).

With James Stewart in *The Man Who Knew Too Much*, filmed in Marrakesh, London and Hollywood.

to leave. To her astonishment he handed her the script of the film, told her, 'You're very sensitive girl. To be good actress is to be sensitive,' and that she was to go away and study the lead part. She argued that she hadn't any experience and didn't know how to act. He said, 'You let me decide that.' He did, and to coin another cliché, the rest is film history.

She had three scenes to memorize and two songs, which posed no problem after the practice she had learning material for Les Brown. At the 6 a.m. make-up call she fell asleep under the hair dryer and when she came to was dismayed to find they had tried to make her look as much like Betty Hutton as possible, with thick make-up to disguise her freckles, long false eyelashes and stiffly lacquered hair piled on top. Again, at rehearsals Curtiz tried to move her around à la Hutton, but when it came to the take Doris did it her own way: she says, 'To thine own self be true. Don't imitate. Don't try to imagine how someone else might feel. Project your honest response to your movie situation, quite the same as you would respond honestly to a life situation. I have never been one for artifice. It is a characteristic I despise. I am always exactly what I am. I always show exactly how I feel. If I am happy, I bloom with it. If I am depressed or grouchy everyone around me knows it.' She felt no nerves, because the outcome, either way, did not worry her.

Doris enjoyed making the test, but believing she hadn't a hope in hell of getting the part went ahead and booked her return ticket to Cincinnati. Al took her out to dinner at the Brown Derby and tried to talk her out of leaving, without success. The next day she was in her hotel room packing when Jack Carson, the star of the film, phoned to tell her he thought she had the part: first she refused to believe it was he, then she doubted what

he'd said and insisted she would be leaving for Cincinnati that evening. Minutes later Al Levy rang, making it
official.

4

The Warner Years

Sammy Cahn and Jule Styne's best song for *Romance on the High Seas* was 'It's Magic', which ideally suited Doris Day's mellifluous style of delivery and became such an enormous hit – her single recording of it topped the million-seller mark – that the title was adopted for the film's release in Britain. Doris was fourth billed, after Jack Carson, Janis Paige, and Don DeFore: Paige, whose screen test had so impressed Sammy Cahn, had the secondary role of a wealthy socialite, Elvira Kent who suspects her husband (DeFore) is having an affair with another woman. She books a ticket to Rio on her own, persuading nightclub singer Georgia Garrett, a poor girl who yearns to travel but cannot afford it, to impersonate her. So Elvira's plan is to stay behind in New York to keep an eye on her husband. He, in his turn, becomes suspicious of his wife and hires private detective Peter Virgil (Jack Carson) to trail her on the voyage. Georgia, expensively gowned by Elvira to aid the deception, is naturally mistaken by Peter for her, and, even more naturally, he falls for Georgia. To add to the complications Georgia's admirer Oscar Farrar appears aboard the luxury liner – enter Oscar Levant, with his sardonic humour and way with a piano. The mistaken identity theme is the most familiar of all musical comedy plots, and the Garrett part a symposium of hundreds of blonde working-girl roles, longing for the adventure and romance she finds beyond her pocket and travelling vicariously with the aid of brochures from a sympathetic travel agent (William Bakewell). She tells him she's had seven passport pictures taken, but never as a blonde. Her gum-chewing Honky-Tonk singer persona is reminiscent of Alice Faye in her brasher days, the blue satin gown, cascading flowers in her hair as she sings her first jolly Betty Hutton-type song 'I'm in Love' on her very first day on the set, conjure up memories of Grable, June Haver or whoever, but the utter sincerity and truth in her voice and eyes when she sings 'It's Magic' are uniquely Doris Day, a quality which shines through all those early Warner production-line musicals. For the first of many occasions she transcends her material, as if biding her time to emerge from the chrysalis of the standard Hollywood blonde mask imposed on her. She hated the way she looked, referring to herself as a 'pancaked, lacquered Hollywood purse made out of a Cincinnati sow's ear'! Hard words, indeed, but at least Curtiz had the wisdom to put a stop to the lessons Doris had started to take from Sophie Rosenstein, the Warner Brothers acting coach. He told her that lessons would be a mistake, imposed on her strong individual personality which was going to make her a big important star. He pointed out that the Carole Lombards, Humphrey Bogarts and Gary Coopers were always themselves, playing different parts, but with the same strong personality coming through. The character actors, who submerge themselves in the roles they played could be great performers, but never stars.

Doris found that acting for the movies came to her with greater ease and naturalness than anything else she had ever done before. Nerves were unknown to her, and she felt for Jack Carson who would often be sweating with apprehension before a take. If she had faith in a director – and Michael Curtiz was one of the best – she would take to direction like a duck to water.

She became very fond of Jack Carson and they started an affair. He was kind and considerate, but something of a loner and not good at communicating his feelings, although his sense of humour, which came across so well on the screen appealed to hers. He had come to films from vaudeville in 1937 and played scores of supporting roles, from villains in Westerns to back-slapping bores in comedies before becoming one of Warner Brothers' most reliable stars. He lived in Longridge, in the valley, and two ex-vaudeville colleagues kept house for him, where Doris often visited and frequently stayed overnight, but when he began to talk of marriage she withdrew from a relationship which she wanted to prevent becoming too serious. They teamed well and made three musicals together. Sadly, Carson died of cancer at fifty-three in 1963: his last film, in 1961, was *King of The Roaring Twenties* – he was a heavy drinker and in later years put on weight alarmingly – there were signs of this eventuality in his films with Doris.

Of the other stars in *It's Magic* Don DeFore and Janis Paige were an unappealing couple – she was to come into her own some ten years later as an amusing singer-comedienne with Astaire and Cyd Charisse in *Silk Stockings* and had a big success on Broadway in *The Pajama Game* in 1954, three years before Doris made the film. The supporting cast was sprinkled with the familiar faces with which the Hollywood of those days proliferated, many of whom would show up in Doris Day movies for the rest of her career: the best known was S. Z. Sakall, 'Cuddles' – he of the wobbling jowls and hand-wringing distress signals, emitting long-drawn 'phews' and clapping his hands to his cheeks. He was

Uncle Lazlo; then there was Eric Blore as the ship's doctor, all gentlemanly double takes and outrage, so well-remembered from the Astaire–Rogers musicals, the bleakly camp Franklin Pangborne, the prissy hotel clerk *par excellence*, explosively Italian fatherly Fortunio Bonanova – the list is endless: they were salt of the earth and of the cinema, people whom Doris admired and had a good deal of time for – never stars, but always greeted with anticipatory chuckles by regular filmgoers.

Soon after the making of the film Doris was delighted to hear from George Weidler: they had a happy reunion over dinner and a weekend at Balboa, where he was playing with the Stan Kenton band: she found him changed, very much for the better and with a sense of inner peace and emotional security she had not evidenced before. He explained that he had found a way of life that had changed his whole attitude, a way that was contained in Mary Baker Eddy's book *Science and Health with Key to the Scriptures*. From it Doris gleaned undreamed-of disclosures that have formed the basis of her philosophy ever since and which supported her through some traumatic periods of her later life, the essence of which lay in Mrs Eddy's tenet, 'Man is not material: he is spiritual.' These revelations were more than welcome at a time when her life had moved conclusively into a new orbit with a success the like of which she could never have envisaged and certainly did not consciously set out to discover. This brought its own stresses and her emotional life had lately developed unwelcome complications. But the new friendship with George, from whom she was now divorced, and her own voyage of discovery of forces in herself that would change her way of thinking completely were positive factors from which she derived substantial comfort: although she still felt a strong physical attraction for her ex-husband and they had become lovers again, the thought of re-marriage was far from her mind and in its place they shared an *amitié amoureuse* of comforting stability.

At this time she needed all the support she could muster. She had made light of a warning from Michael Curtiz that Al Levy's attention to her was beginning to border on the obsessional. As she was dating Jack Carson she persisted in regarding Al as a best friend, but no more, but after it was brought to her notice that he was actually spying on her, studying her from the gantry during the filming, then sitting in her hotel lobby, often hiding behind a newspaper – at the start she was unable to bring herself to mention the matter to him, but there came an evening when she could ignore it no longer. He followed her up in the lift and into her bedroom, where he turned off the lights, forced her onto the bed and hurled himself on her. They had dined together and Al was due to drive her to the country to spend a weekend with a girlfriend of Doris's called Lee Levine, who had herself discovered the values of Christian Science.

That such a close friend, whom she trusted so implicitly, could subject her to an attack that amounted to attempted rape, was shattering in itself: it also meant that their close business relationship could not continue. After she had talked him out of his bizarre and distressing onslaught he cried uncontrollably, declaring his deep love and affection, and offering her marriage: he could not bear the thought that she would prefer to spend a weekend with Lee Levine rather than with him. He suggested that if Doris slept with him she would alter her mind, and nothing she could say seemed to convince him that physical love and, least of all, marriage, was totally out of the question. The spying on her continued: it was almost a replica of the behaviour of Al Jorden at the time their marriage was well and truly on the rocks, and in the end, sick and tired of not even being able to visit restaurants with friends without the spectre of Al Levy ever-present, Doris went to lay her problem before his partners at Century Artists, Dick Dorso and Marty Melcher.

There and then Marty agreed to become her agent: he told her that, in any case Al was going to New York to run their office on Broadway, so he would be out of her way. The arrangement seemed an admirable one: Doris had always found Marty pleasant and efficient. He was at that time married to Patty Andrews of the Andrews Sisters, whose fame on radio after their first big record hit *Bei Mir Bist Du Schöen* in 1937 became so popular that they appeared in several films during the Forties, their last actual appearance on screen being in the Crosby–Hope–Lamour *Road to Rio* in 1947, the year before Doris ignited the cinema firmament with *Romance on the High Seas*. I personally could never understand their appeal: at the local Odeon where I worked such brash and tinnily tuneful musicals as *Give Out, Sisters* turned up with distressing regularity, but their following was considerable, including, oddly enough, among the gay community – drag shows were seldom without their own version of LaVerne, Maxine and Patty. In fact, the two latter Sisters, with a 'borrowed' third, after the death of LaVerne, did enjoy a Broadway comeback and a brief British tour in the Seventies.

Riding high on the overwhelming success of *It's Magic* – the song received an Academy Award nomination, as did the film's original score – Michael Curtiz was eager to hurry into production with a follow-up film, to be called *My Dream Is Yours* with the same Jack Carson–Doris Day team and himself at the helm of the second production for his new agreement with the studio which gave him an independent unit as well as a share in the profit of his films, which yielded his star 500 dollars a week.

Before the second film, however, Doris was committed, at last, to a tour with Bob Hope, for which Les Brown claims Hope had to pay her ten times the money for which he could have got her first time round, when she had just completed twenty weeks with Frank Sinatra in his New York radio show *Your Hit Parade*, an experience she seems to have cordially disliked, not because of Sinatra, whom she claims to like and admire, but on account of her aversion to working on radio. Bob Hope's concert and radio troupe entailed flying to a different city every night, in the depth of winter; when they played matinées they often landed in two different cities in one day. Several of the flights were scary, due to the weather conditions, and her dislike of flying received sharp impetus during those experiences. They did two 15,000-mile concert tours and since that time she will go to extreme lengths to avoid going up in an aeroplane. Singing in the circumstances did not come easily, after the fear of the flight and being pushed out of the way by Bob Hope's clamouring fans every time they disembarked from the plane: what she did enjoy were the sketches with him, from which she learned invaluable lessons about comic timing. From the brief glimpses we have been able to catch on television of those shows, they were an admirable team, although Doris does not retain a high opinion of the quality of some of the writing, usually on the lines of Bob's supposed meanness, already over-worked, one might think, by Jack Benny. What is there about avarice that always gets a laugh? What made it sure-fire, she remembers, is the all-embracing warmth of Hope's personality: she found that just watching him work made her feel good. After the tour the Lever

Brothers Swan Soap radio show from Hollywood represented sheer purgatory for her: she started with a song, almost inevitably 'It's Magic', then a sketch, often dire, but rendered humorous by Hope's comedy genius: Doris used to marvel that such a genuinely funny man and experienced performer could take as holy writ the assurances of his yes-men about the quality of the material his writers kept dishing up for him.

For his part his admiration for her is boundless: he rates her as one of the great singers, whose ability to put across a ballad proves her to be a mistress of superb timing. He was less than pleased when her new agent, Marty Melcher, outlawed ballads for Doris and said that henceforth she would sing only bouncy numbers. It seems that Betty Hutton image continued to haunt her, and Hope says, so truly, 'It's a crying shame that Doris has this thing about not appearing before live audiences, because on a stage, I can tell you, she lights up the house. She has that rare quality of making people feel good by just walking on – whatever she radiates lifts them. And when she sings a ballad, and you're there, she can break your heart.'

Doris was relieved to return to the time-clock schedule of working on a film, also that Jack Carson was to be with her on the next two subjects. He seems to have been uncharacteristically generous for a comedian in teaching her how to make the best of herself in every shot, the intricacies of camera angles and little subtleties of technique of which the director was too often unaware, or for which he did not have time. Her close relationship with Jack at this, crucial stage was a godsend, as they could work with each other after hours, and Doris, always in need of warmth and affection could feel buttressed by this gentle giant with his intricate knowledge of the ins and outs of acting for the cinema. He was thirty-eight when she was twenty-four, an equable balance for the time and the place. She speaks of acting for the camera being an 'immediate love affair', and, in this instance it was comforting to have someone to share it with. She also enjoyed recording for films, because of the assurance that it could be repeated until it turned out right, whereas on radio and stage it was a one-take affair, and if you were not at your best, hard cheese.

My Dream Is Yours suffered from having the abrasive Lee Bowman as Gary Mitchell, conceited idol of the bobbysoxers in virtually the male lead, with Carson as talent scout Doug Blake having to work overtime to atone for his client's on-screen addiction to the bottle and to get young widow Martha Gibson launched on a singing career as a replacement when Mitchell is fired after one binge too many. When she becomes a big success for grateful sponsor Felix Hoffer (S. Z. Sakall) she persuades the good-hearted Blake to arrange a comeback for Mitchell, for whom she has fallen: in the meantime Doug has persuaded his colleague Vivian Martin (Eve Arden) to take in Martha and her young son as lodgers, much against her better judgment. But she, too, has a heart of gold, as well as a witty tongue, and all ends with the scales falling from Martha's eyes on finally realizing what a conceited bore the singer is and turning back to her long-suffering discoverer.

Casting Doris close to her real-life persona as an aspiring singer with a little boy takes this film a step towards integrating her public and private images and away from the Hutton replacement. Though Al Dubin and Harry Warren's cheerful 'I'll String Along With You' is delightfully handled, there is no song as right for Doris as 'It's Magic' was, but there is compensation in the casting of the marvellous Eve Arden as Carson's bright-as-a-button associate in her first teaming with

Doris. She had the ability to make dud lines sound witty and bright ones sparkle like diamonds: warmth and asperity make strange bedfellows but Arden married them brilliantly. Sadly, she died in November 1990 a week after I wrote to her via her agent for reminiscences about filming with Doris. Heading the team of character actors, is the ever-reliable Adolphe Menjou, with his waxed black moustache, as Thomas Hutchins. After starring as a sleek drawing-room sophisticate in Chaplin's *Woman of Paris* in 1923, he specialized in that type of role until the early talkies – he even made an excruciating gramophone record to put over his heart-throb image, called 'Two White Arms' – then eased into character roles as high-powered executives, newspaper editors, ageing wolves and assorted uncles. S. Z. Sakall, as the sponsor and Franklin Pangbourn, 'Sourpuss' manager of the shop where Doris is recording her jingles, fusses and fumes as only he could, while, lower down the cast list were two girls who epitomized the brash and brassy shop-cum-showgirl type, Bronx-voiced Iris Adrian – who even made the London Palladium later in her career, in the same role, and soulfully angelic-faced dumb blonde Marion Martin. Serene-faced stage star, Selena Royle, played Sakall's wife, Freda.

In the third and last of her films with Jack Carson, *It's a Great Feeling*, also made in 1949, Doris is billed above him – evidence of her growing popularity – and Dennis Morgan top-billed: in this, the first of six films in which she was directed by David Butler, he appears as himself, a plump, cheerful man, who refuses to direct the film-within-a-film because he, like every other director on the lot, is unwilling to work with Carson. That is the running gag of the movie; when producer Arthur Trent (Bill Goodwin) assigns Carson to direct the film himself, star Dennis Morgan threatens to withdraw: to trick him into changing his mind Jack persuades Doris, as Judy Adams, a movie-struck waitress in the studio commissary, to pose as his pregnant wife, in need of money towards this eventuality, thus causing the tender-hearted Morgan to relent and agree to star in the film.

All this is an excuse to introduce almost every star and director on the lot as 'guests', and for Doris herself to embark on a number of impersonations and disguises, including Bette Davis (one of the few *not* in the film), a French chanteuse called Yvonne Amour (reminiscent of Mae West's burlesque in *Every Day's a Holiday* in 1938, but not half as hilarious), a waitress, lift attendant, cab driver and dentist's assistant. There's some more harking back to Betty Hutton in her song 'That Was a Big Fat Lie', and Doris's most charming moments are her reflective singing of Jule Styne and Sammy Cahn's 'Blame My Absent-Minded Heart'. This kind of film invariably proves a *bête noire* to the critics; for myself I find it amusing and entertaining, with some good-natured self-ribbing from the Warner stars, including Edward G. Robinson helping Doris to get past the studio guard, Danny Kaye believing he's a train, Jane Wyman throwing a faint, Ronald Reagan getting his hair cut and a quaint little scene with Joan Crawford, who overhears Morgan and Carson discussing getting the waitress into movies. She reacts as only Crawford could react, to 'We'll take off her clothes' by telling them they should be ashamed of themselves – 'That poor child' and administering a back-hander to both actors, saying, 'I do that in all my movies,' before she exits dramatically. Doris looks after her admiringly and says, 'I just *love* Miss Crawford!' The feeling seems to have been mutual, according to my conversation with her several decades later. Other stars briefly on call were Gary Cooper, Patricia Neal, Eleanor Parker and directors Michael

Curtiz, King Vidor and Raoul Walsh. Crawford was in England in 1967 filming the circus thriller *Berserk*, in which, resplendent in scarlet ringmaster's outfit she had Ty Hardin as her youthful trapeze artist lover. She and I had corresponded since my 1965 study of her in *Films and Filming*: discussing the current stars she admitted to admiration for the talent of Barbra Streisand, but said of Doris 'There's one girl who became a big star after appearing in one of my Warner movies: Doris Day's the name – what a sweet girl, and such a fine actress; she deserves all her success!'

The pay-off is a neat one: the little waitress decides against going on pursuing a film career and books a ticket back to her home in Gurkey's Corners, Wisconsin to marry her fiancé, Jeffrey Bushfinkle. Morgan and Carson hot-foot it after her and arrive at the church just as she is about to exchange marriage vows: her fiancé raises her bridal veil to kiss her and the camera moves in on Errol Flynn no less. The title tune was nominated for an Oscar, Dennis Morgan got his tenor tonsils round 'Give Me a Song with a Beautiful Melody', helped Doris out on 'Absent-Minded Heart', joined her and Jack Carson in 'There's Nothing Rougher Than Love' and the *New York Times* summed up the songs as well as 'It's a Great Feeling': 'it may not be great precisely but it is pleasant.' The only sour note was struck by the *New York Herald Tribune*: 'Doris Day made this reviewer uncomfortable by insisting that she couldn't act throughout the proceedings. This sort of confession is too close to the truth for comfort.'

Unjust, indeed, though one writer blames director Butler for some outrageous mugging in which she indulges to obtain the attention of producer Bill Goodwin throughout her various disguises: a curious effect of speeding up the camera as she flashes her eyelashes up and down, making a Bugs Bunny grimace while the soundtrack emits weird tweeting sounds. Whoever's idea this was – and it was unlikely to be the star's – it was most definitely not a good one.

The style of these three first Doris Day musicals demonstrated clearly what was lacking in Warner's showcasing of their brightest new discovery, she who ousted Janis Paige, originally their stand-by singing star of the period, and put paid to their borrowing June Haver, the studio's second-string Betty Grable, from Twentieth Century-Fox. Warners' most successful musical movies had been the Busby Berkeley spectaculars of the Thirties, like *42nd Street*: while the nominal stars were Bébé Daniels – her playing of a star on the wane had the uncomfortable ring of truth, till she shook the dust of Hollywood from her heels with husband Ben Lyon and headed for England and an enduring new career on radio and in musical comedy – Warner Baxter and the juvenile leads crooner Dick Powell and hoofer Ruby Keeler. However, the real triumph belonged to Berkeley's kaleidoscopic geometrical patterns of 'les girls', shot from every which way but straightforward. Berkeley was credited with the musical numbers in *It's Magic*, but they were routine Technicolored crowd scenes.

Michael Curtiz was not in his element directing musicals: like the studio itself he excelled in gritty, real-istic drama, escapist thrillers, action movies of the *Casablanca* genre, for which he won an Oscar in 1943: the year later his *Mildred Pierce* did the same for Joan Crawford and brought her career back to the forefront – he was always happy directing 'tough' stars like Craw-ford, Davis, Bogart, Flynn. So, while he was a kindly and encouraging helmsman for Doris in her first two films, and, indeed, without him and his patience it is likely she would never have had a film career, what wonderful music she might have made under the direction of the geniuses of MGM – the top studio in the field – like Vincente Minnelli and Stanley Donen. It is significant that her best part, in *Love Me or Leave Me* for Charles Vidor in 1955, the first film she made after her release from the Warner contract was at Metro, where seven years later she appeared again in her last for the studio *Billy Rose's Jumbo*, directed by Charles Walters: although enchanting, it failed at the box office – the era of the successful Hollywood musical was over.

In her fourth movie and third for Curtiz, the best of Curtiz and Doris came together, in her first dramatic role and the kind of film at which he excelled, Carl Foreman's script with Edmund H. North for *Young Man with a Horn* – a title which still evoked sniggers in the Britain of the Nineties, demonstrating conclusively why it became *Young Man of Music* back in 1950. Based loosely on the life of the great jazz musician Bix Beiderbecke, changed to Rick Martin for Kirk Douglas's character in the film with Mary Beth Hughes as his sister Margo, the story is narrated by Hoagy Carmichael as Smoke Willoughby, a pianist, who traces Rick's career from his orphaned childhood, when he attracts the attention of the great jazzman Art Hazzard (Juano Hernandez), who teaches him all there is to know about being a trumpet player. Rick becomes obsessed with hitting that unattainable high note, and is disillusioned with his life, even though he becomes a name player: his two best friends are Smoke and the Doris Day character, Jo Jordan, a band singer who loves him in her own quiet way, until she introduces him to her friend, a neurotic 'intellectual' playgirl Amy North (Lauren Bacall). The billing for the film, above the title is Kirk Douglas, Bacall and Doris Day, in what is an almost peripheral role, which keeps disappearing from the story. But it is one which she plays with a quiet sympathy which contrasts well with the angst-ridden Beiderbecke role played to the hilt by Kirk Douglas and the sultry temptress Amy, who marries him as a casual experiment in man-catching, then is unable to come to terms with competing against his love for his music. Bacall, as ever, is mesmeric, Hoagy Carmichael as sympathetic as always in the kind of role he made his own and there is a deeply moving study of the old jazzman, who started Rick as a trumpeter and in the end leaves him to die on his own after an accident, by Juano Hernandez.

The actual trumpeting was done by Harry James, who acted as musical adviser on the film, with the musical direction by Ray Heindorf, who creates a rich jazz flavour entirely appropriate for the smoky atmosphere of the band's sessions. Doris's songs are perfectly in keeping with the band singer character she plays, mellow and right from the heart, and her few dramatic scenes touching in their sincerity. 'Too Marvellous for Words', 'I Only Have Eyes for You', 'With a Song in My Heart', 'The Very Thought of You' all carry through her feelings for the man she loves, who has set her aside to satisfy the momentary whim of the society girl, who in the end leaves him to go off to Paris with an artist – a lady friend who 'understands' her. The way Bacall and her new friend play, it seems highly probable that Amy, with her philosophy of 'How do you know about anything until you try?' is about to embark on some trial diversification with her new friend. Michael Curtiz was nothing if not a sophisticate, and there is a highly insinuating scene with a young lift boy who gazes at Amy with unabashed admiration, of which she is fully aware. She pauses in the hall, looks back and returns to the elevator, as the doors close. Next shot she has returned to Kirk Douglas's apartment on the top floor.

The actual filming of *Young Man With a Horn* turned out to be an upsetting experience for Doris, particularly in her scenes with Douglas as the trumpet player, reminding her as they did of her association with Al Jorden, and some of the songs she sang were ones from her band days – even her name in the film, Jo Jordan, has an eerie echo. The realism of her performance may well have been accentuated by these factors. The film and the album she cut of the songs were both highly successful.

There was a total change of pace in her next movie in that busy year of 1950, with the musical *Tea for Two*, in which she was top-billed for the first time – another first was her teaming with Gordon MacRae, her clean-cut and charming, if somewhat bland leading man in five musicals, most of them sure-fire successes. Doris thought of her Warner years and, particularly the people she appeared with as her 'Repertory period'. Many of the supporting players went from film to film, and she was in four movies with Gene Nelson – also in *Tea for Two* – and three with Ronald Reagan. *Tea for Two*, one of the biggest hits of the year, was her second with David Butler, who in all directed her in six, then there were the four with Curtiz and three with Roy Del Ruth. Similarly, various producers kept coming up again and again in her career at Burbank.

No, No, Nanette was the original title of the stage show, whose Vincent Youmans–Irving Caesar score included the new title song and 'I Want to be Happy', the only ones included in this new screen version, which was something of a hybrid, as was the previous remake in 1940, starring Anna Neagle, and the 1930 original. Neagle's husband, Herbert Wilcox, also retained the above hit tunes and more of the play's storyline, which concerned Nanette's attempts to save her philandering uncle from the results of his complex assignations with various showgirls et al and from detection by his suspicious wife. In the 1940 movie the uncle was the splendidly hesitant Roland Young, his intimidating wife memorably sardonic Helen Broderick, a stalwart of the Astaire–Rogers musicals, and the most notable threat to their married bliss none other than Eve Arden, with a fractured French accent. Doris's *Nanette* was a dollar millionairess, whose uncle, (S. Z. Sakall), managing her financial affairs, tries to keep from her the news that her fortune has been wiped out in the Wall Street crash of 1926, although she has decided to invest a large sum of money in a Broadway show starring herself. To stall her he makes a bet that she can only be given the money if she can say 'No' to every question for twenty-four hours. She moves the entire company of their proposed musical into their palatial home, and, after the inevitable complications, though she wins the bet and learns that she is penniless (who footed the bills for turning the place into a grand hotel?), the lawyer comes up with the money and *No, No, Nanette* opens triumphantly on Broadway.

So it's eventually a play within a play within a film with the story of how it came to be put on told in flashback by Uncle S. Z. Sakall to the offspring of Nanette and Jimmy Smith (Gordon MacRae) who got hitched, presumably after their Broadway hit. Doris particularly enjoyed working with 'Cuddles' Sakall and it seems that everyone on the set felt the same way, because they all called him by the same sobriquet: she found him a 'delight' and as funny off screen as on. Maybe more so. Coincidentally, Eve Arden, to whom Doris's biographer George Morris referred as 'a star's best friend', was also in this up-dated *Nanette*, this time as Doris's secretary, Pauline Hastings, giving the scenario a lift whenever it was in danger of sagging, and looked quite unchanged in the ten years that had elapsed since her 'French' *femme fatale*. Gene Nelson was there, on hand to partner Doris in her first dances for the screen, showing how completely she had recovered from that near fatal accident back in Cincinnati. Here Nelson was Tommy Trainor in the plot within the plot, or was it the plot within the flashback? – as usual in his films, with a motiveless part, presumably just waiting to leap into the dance: he was a superbly athletic tapper and a graceful partner for Doris, though noticeably lacking a positive personality. In one of his films when a lady enthusiastically called him the 'world's greatest dancer' he reminded her, maybe somewhat ruefully, that Fred Astaire got there first: he had the grace, agility, originality *and* personality.

Doris found a new friend in Billy De Wolfe, as Larry Blair, the producer of the show, brimming with character, albeit the type herein designated 'eccentric' – 'camp' in those days signified West Point, at least on the screen – and it was at this point he christened her Clara Bixby. A further *Nanette* coincidence: some fifteen years on Billy was set to dance a Charleston with Anna Neagle in the Charity Benefit 'Night of a Hundred Stars' at the London Palladium: his illness stepped in and the partnership never happened, but *Nanette* seems to keep cropping up every decade or so. In the Seventies a stage version at The Theatre Royal Drury Lane starred Neagle in the Helen Broderick part of Jimmy's Smith's wife – kind of an updating of Doris Day at the end of her movie, in which she plays her first 'mature' wife and mother – and inherited the tap-dance scene to 'I Want to be Happy' from Ruby Keeler who did the part in the tremendously successful Broadway version the previous year.

Bill Goodwin, Doris's would-be producer in *It's*

A Great Feeling, became her wealthy lawyer-backer, William Early, in *Tea for Two* and Patrice Wymore, who was to become the third Mrs Errol Flynn the same year, in her first film played Beatrice Darcy, a kind of composite of all the avaricious showgirls of the previous versions – a beautiful girl, talented singer and dancer, whose career suffered as she tried to help her husband through his subsequent problems.

Doris's career reached an early nadir in her third film for 1950 with a footling part in *The West Point Story*, starring James Cagney and billed third, after Virginia Mayo, who played Eve Dillon the long-suffering show-girl fiancée of Cagney's down-at-heel Broadway director Elwin Bixby. He is persuaded by a producer with whom he had clashed to stage a show at West Point, written by his nephew Cadet Tom Fletcher (Gordon MacRae). His inducement is a starring role for Eve, who is tiring of her on-again off-again engagement: Bixby agrees, is inducted as an honorary officer at the Academy, rebels against military red-tape, punches a few noses, is demoted, tries to persuade Tom to quit West Point, on his uncle's orders, so that he can take the show to Broadway. Tom refuses, and is only keen to leave after Bixby has introduced him to film star Jan Wilson, and they have fallen in love. Enter Doris Day, in the most negative role of her career. All she is called upon to do is look fresh-faced and keen, in contrast to Mayo's dis-illusioned Eve, a part in which Virginia is excellent. Doris also carols some Jule Styne–Sammy Cahn songs, including 'By the Kissing Rock' with Gordon MacRae and 'Long Before I Knew You', dances 'The Military Polka' with Gene Nelson – another best friend-of-the-hero role as Cadet Hal Courtland and persuades Tom back to his Army career: West Point Must Come First. Tom is arrested for defecting, Bixby persuades the

French President to grant him an amnesty (in fairly fluent French) by virtue of a French decoration he, Bixby, earned during the war, the show goes on, and is a success – natch – Joe and Tom swear eternal fealty, he signs the Broadway rights over to Bixby, and Eve gets to do her big song and dance 'It Could Only Happen in Brooklyn' with Cadet Gene Nelson.

This was the kind of film Doris went with her agents to protest to Jack Warner about. The result was that he roared at her, 'So you're a big star already' and bawled her out for telling the front office how to run the studio 'after a coupla pictures.' Later she became friendly with Warner and learned that his bark was worse than his bite: however, she was not happy about being barked at – except by four-legged friends – and resolved never to suffer rudeness again. Indeed, her last film for that year was, experience-wise, a distinct up-surge and, in one respect something of a dream come true. In *Storm Warning* she starred with Ginger Rogers and Ronald Reagan, and though she took third billing again, and her role as Ginger's young sister was subservient to that of the long-established star, she was delighted to do the part, which called for her to die in the end, for the one and only time in her career. It was producer Jerry Wald who approached her to ask if she thought she could handle a dramatic part and when she heard that Rogers was already cast Doris accepted without hesitation.

The director was Stuart Heisler, who excelled in the thriller genre and had made one of the most exciting Alan Ladd–Veronica Lake films, *The Glass Key* in 1942. Like *The West Point Story*, *Storm Warning* was in black and white, which suited the subject, whereas the military musical would have benefited from the addition of colour. There are undertones of *A Streetcar Named Desire* in Daniel Fuchs's and Richard Brooks's script –

no one has ever been able to ascertain whether it was intentional or not. From the beginning the mood is heavy with menace, as Martha Mitchell, a fashion model from New York (Ginger Rogers) arrives in a bleak Southern town on a late night bus to visit her sister Lucy (Doris Day) and witnesses a man being dragged from the county jail and shot by men wearing Ku Klux Klan masks. Her horror is compounded when she recognizes Lucy's husband Hank Rice (Steve Cochran) as the man who did the shooting. Everyone in town is too frightened to give evidence, but the district attorney Burt Rainey (Ronald Reagan) soon deduces that Martha knows more than she is prepared to admit. Unwilling to destroy her sister's happiness it is only when her brother-in-law tries to rape her after a drunken celebration with the Klansmen that Martha decides to tell what she has seen. The Klansmen abduct her and after a mock trial she is sentenced to be punished. As the whipping starts D. A. Rainey arrives with the police and Lucy, who dies from a bullet aimed by Hank at her sister – or at the Imperial Wizard in his robes, the action is all too quick to be quite sure what has happened. Joan Crawford told Jack Warner he must be joking when he offered her the part of Martha: 'No one would ever believe that I could have Doris Day for a sister!' she said.

The casting of Steve Cochran as Hank, sullenly resentful of Martha's encroachment into his love-nest with Lucy, who is pregnant, his unwilling acknowledgment of attractions as he spies on her undressing and his subsequent attempt at rape, all add to the *Streetcar* analogy, though, compared with Vivien Leigh's Blanche du Bois, Rogers's Martha, although ripely glamorous, is a positive pillar of rectitude. Her dramatic portrayal is finely etched, and it is quite in accord with her character as a fashion model, that Carl Guthrie's atmospheric camerawork should favour her rather than Doris, whose matter-of-fact haircut and housewifely clothes are just right for her devoted wife and mother-to-be role. She is believable and touching, making an under-developed character, where the script is concerned, the most sympathetic in the overall gloom. Cochran is broodingly effective as her husband; a quality he deployed to good effect in all his films, whether light-hearted Danny Kaye romps or the grim realism of Antonioni's *Il Grido* (*The Outcry*) in 1957. The year of Doris's film début Steve was hand-picked by Mae West for her Broadway revival of *Diamond Lil* and at the time of his mysterious death aboard his yacht in 1967, at the age of forty-eight, Mae, who liked them tall, dark and handsome, had announced him as her co-star in one of her many comeback projects which never materialized. Another early choice to play Martha was Lauren Bacall, though whether that would have worked as well as the Rogers–Day combination is a matter for conjecture.

The Reagan district attorney character is as under-written as Doris's Lucy, with just a tiny hint of a possible happy ending for him and Ginger, but his spare and laconic playing again points to his having been a much better actor than his detractors will allow. *Variety* voted *Storm Warning* 'a rip-roaring, spine-tingling film that keeps the customers on the edge for a fast ninety-two minutes . . . Miss Rogers and Doris Day as the sisters wangle every thespic value out of their melodramatic lines.' This side of the Atlantic, *Picturegoer* sniffily commented: '*We* were the first to hail Doris Day as a scintillating new discovery . . . was the experiment to put her into *Storm Warning* really necessary?'

Doris's admiration for her co-star increased at close quarters: Ginger's persona – chauffeur-driven limousine, secretary in attendance etc – contrasted with her friendly manner with everyone on the set, although she was in no doubt over who was the boss. Furthermore, when Miss Rogers wanted script changes she simply sent for the writers, in marked contrast to the reception Doris had had from Bossman Warner over her mild objection to a scenario. The time was not far away when the same omnipotence would be hers, though her exercise of her prerogative would be sparing, in accordance with her character. Sammy Cahn amusingly quotes an instance which probably did not fill him with hilarity at the time:

'I was trying to make another picture, not getting anywhere, and facing the judgment day called "option time" – to be or not to be renewed. Doris Day had by now made it to queen of the Warner Brothers lot [NB Joan Crawford had abdicated and gone on to pastures new], which meant all she had to say was "Of course Sammy will produce my next picture." The late Steve Trilling, knowing my sentiments, came and begged me, "Sammy, she's the only musical star we've got. Go see her." [Steve Trilling was Jack Warner's assistant and alter ego . . .] So I went to see her on the set. "Doris, could I see you for a moment?" "Of course." Shining and radiant. Only twice have I asked someone for a job. Once was Doris Day . . . "Of course," she said, "are you kidding?" This to the accompaniment of hugs and embraces. So I went dancing back to Steve's office, telling myself it's sometimes worthwhile to humble yourself. She was so *warm*. The moment I entered his office Steve said, "They really don't want you, Sam." I felt my stomach open up.'

And so, where Doris's progress towards the Warner throne is concerned, to the 1951 *Lullaby of Broadway*, which is where I came in, so it is likely to be a film to engender nostalgic prejudice. But, viewed again, it was delightful on its own merits, and never before had Doris had such a pick of classic songs by ace composers. The title song and 'You're Getting to be a Habit with Me' – Bébé Daniels's hit from *42nd Street* – both by Harry Warren and Al Dubin, Cole Porter's 'Just One of Those Things', Gershwin's 'Somebody Loves Me', charmingly duetted and danced with Gene Nelson and the Dick Powell hit 'Zing! Went the Strings of My Heart' by James F. Hanley: she brought new verve and style to every one of them. Her dancing, too, on her own and with Gene Nelson, elevated for once to leading man status, also had a new sense of style. Of course, the 'Shanty in Old Shantytown' honours went to Gladys George as in 'Please Don't Talk About Me When I'm Gone': she shared the more mature acting hand-outs with the ubiquitous S. Z. Sakall and Billy De Wolfe as, respectively, Adolph Hubbell, a kindly old millionaire, who allows Billy as Lofty Mack, a dancer friend of Melinda Howard (Doris Day's) mother in her palmy days, to persuade him to pretend he is renting his mansion from the once famous Jessica Spencer (Gladys George). They throw a party for Jessica and Melinda to be reunited, but the alcoholic nightclub singer gets too drunk to attend. Lofty, posing as a butler in the Hubbell establishment contrives for Melinda to be able to go on living there; in the meantime she has fallen for star dancer Tom Farnham (Gene Nelson, second-billed to Doris above the title); his producer engages her to co-star with him on Broadway. However, both Tom and grouchy Mrs Hubbell (Florence Bates) mistake her husband's altruism towards Melinda as something more personal: a divorce suit impends, but, again through the intervention of Fairy Godfather Lofty, is called off in the nick of time for the Hubbells to sit hand-in-hand in a box to witness the triumph of Melinda and Tom in – guess what? – *Lullaby of Broadway*.

It is easy to dismiss this as improbable rubbish, but the always underestimated David Butler zings the whole thing along so you've no time to disbelieve: Doris, whether in top hat and tails for her opening number or the usual peaches and creamy confections costumier Milo Anderson swathed her in, is a musical comedy dream come true. Despite the still heavily made up and lacquered Betty Grable look, Doris's freshness of appeal and straightforward sincerity in even the most improbable situations were as marked as those of the young Deanna Durbin some fourteen years before: they both looked their audience in the eye, as it were, and sang out from the heart, although Durbin's pure soprano and Day's jazz-inspired phrasing were as different as sleigh bells from the saxophone. Come to think of it, Deanna's 'It's Foolish But It's Fun' from the 1938 *Mad About Music* nicely sums up the appeal of *Lullaby of Broadway*. Interestingly, Warners had planned to borrow June Haver to star, but by this time had obviously become aware that Doris's name meant immeasurably more at the box office.

Way down the cast, but worth her weight in entertainment appeal, was the redoubtable Florence Bates, with her unassailable water-buffalo persona, as 'Cuddles' Sakall's jealous and dominant wife, and right at the bottom of the list, as a passenger on the boat carrying Doris from London to New York, Bess Flowers, a lady who had played leads in Westerns and numerous silent movies. She had graduated – as she herself regarded her position – to 'Queen of the Hollywood Extras', always *soignée*, always in demand as 'classy' well-dressed adornments to hundreds of talking pictures, sometimes billed and with dialogue, more often not. Because she had been around so long she knew most of the big names, and was to be seen in the background of stars like Dietrich, Jean

Arthur, Myrna Loy – Bess actually had a speaking part in *Song of the Thin Man*. She was also to appear again (uncredited) in many more Doris Day movies such as *Calamity Jane*, *Please Don't Eat the Daisies* and *Move Over, Darling*.

Hollywood had moved, in its own glossy Technicolored way a few paces towards realism since the heyday of Busby Berkeley at Warners. Though the studio's dance and musical directors have had their detractors – Doris had a particular antipathy, seemingly with good reason, towards LeRoy Prinz, who put her through her paces in the dire *April in Paris* – at least Al White and Eddie Prinz created a believable Broadway stage musical *Lullaby of Broadway* for Doris and Gene Nelson to appear in as a finale. No longer did the stage dissolve into a gargantuan display of revolving girls reflected in 'By A Waterfall' as in *Gold Diggers of 1933*; nor was Dolores Del Rio, a graceful and accomplished dancer, made to disappear after a few steps with Ricardo Cortez into a nightmare mirrormaze, to materialize several hundred geometric patterns later back where they started, as in the 1934 *Wonder Bar*.

As far as dancing was concerned *Lullaby of Broadway* was the most intricate Doris had tackled. She had come through *Tea for Two* with credit, due to her own determination and considerable help from Gene Nelson, the film's overall choreographer and his wife Miriam, who undertook to put Doris through her dance steps personally. She learned the hard way, through endless hours of rehearsal, both physical and mental, as she had the knack, carried on from the way she ran through her songs in her mind, of monitoring her dance routines in her head. Her powers of visualization must have been considerable. The most testing of the *Lullaby* dances was one with Gene, calling for spins and turns up and down a long flight of stairs, à la Fred and Ginger – even the gold lamé evening gown was evocative of one worn by her in the 1949 *Barkleys of Broadway*. Between them the Nelsons encouraged, cajoled and tricked Doris into accomplishing what was really a very perilous exercise. The trick was that Miriam did not actually attempt the turns on the stairs; by sleight of hand and foot she kidded Doris into thinking her mentor had, in fact, done steps she later confessed were quite beyond her. It was this power of concentration, this striving towards perfection, that singled Doris Day out from the other exponents of song and dance of her era.

Her friendship with Ronald Reagan, whom she had met through mutual friends before her teaming with him in *Storm Warning* – in the storyline of which he and she were on opposite sides of the fence as she persisted in believing in husband Steve Cochran – ripened in large measure as a result of their shared interest in dancing and the fact that Doris was a good listener, Reagan a good talker. He was divorced from Jane Wyman in 1948 and moved into an apartment on Sunset Strip with a magnificent view of Hollywood from his rooftop eyrie. Doris herself was deeply attracted to this spectacular idyll, so enamoured of the view that she loved going up there to gaze down at the twinkling lights and dream that one day she would have her own room with a similar view – a dream that to date has never materialized.

In view of Reagan's predilection for politics – he was an ardent Liberal Democrat in those days – it is remarkable that he did not become actively involved earlier: at this stage of his acting career he was president of the Screen Actors' Guild, a position he took over in 1947, held until the year he made *The Winning Team* with Doris, 1952, and assumed again in 1959. She was in accord with most of the views on which he held forth to her and prophetically told him he should be touring the country making speeches. His powers of persuasion came from his believing in what he was saying or, as she says, 'making you think he believed, which, for a politician, I suppose, is just as good.'

She had lived in a house belonging to her hairdresser, with whom she had built up a friendly relationship during the filming of *It's Magic* – despite the long blonde wig she so disliked but which was the way Mike Curtiz envisaged her – and the home which she shared with the hairdresser and her husband happened to look out onto the back of Marty Melcher's house. He had become a sympathetic confidante to his client, besides having gradually managed to raise her salary from five hundred dollars to two thousand, so she was able eventually to buy a house she could live in with son Terry, who was nearly eight and had lost none of his early exuberance. Their new home by Toluca Lake cost 28,000 dollars and Marty helped them move in. Doris was concerned when he admitted that his marriage with Patty Andrews was reaching a dead end, and more concerned after he left her and went to live in a house on his own that Patty and Al Levy were among the people who jumped to the conclusion that the break-up was due to the fact that she and Marty were having an affair. It was not so at that time, although perhaps inevitable, due to the closeness of their business relationship and Doris's own loneliness – she has reiterated, time and again that success in her career meant little when measured against a meaningful relationship – that they would end up by sleeping together.

Doris has stated that she liked Patty and felt bad about the whole affair. Although Alma Kappelhoff and her grandson had come to regard Marty Melcher with real affection there were others who did not share their enthusiasm. It is impossible, in view of later events, to judge impartially Marty's motives. Harsh things have been said, but never by Doris herself, and she was the one most cataclysmically affected, in the long run. Through thick and thin she has held to her belief that he loved her, despite all the wheeling and dealing in which he became involved. One of those who thought otherwise was the head of music at Warner studios, Sam Weiss. Patty Andrews was a client of Century Artists when Marty joined the firm and they were married soon after. Weiss, who was fond of Patty, has stated that Melcher ditched her when Doris came on the scene as Warners' hottest new property. Weiss was involved when Patty went to the house where Alma was alone one evening while Marty and Doris were out on a publicity excursion. Alma rang the music chief to say she was scared out of her wits because Patty had a baseball bat and was yelling blue murder, vowing to get Marty. Mayhem was avoided and eventually she went away, but the incident demonstrates how violent were the feelings being engendered over the situation at the time. Weiss states flatly that the only thing Marty loved was money. 'He loved Patty's money until Doris's money came along and then, because there was more of it, he loved Doris's money more.'

It is hard to believe it was that simple: if he had been motivated entirely by avarice it is unlikely that Doris, despite her nature, trusting to the point of naïvety, would have been taken in, in the first place, or continued to be duped for so long, in the second place. He did great things for her career, and for a long time, for her peace of mind: doubtless his ambition was overweening, but it is hard to draw the line between how much of it was for himself and how much for her own betterment. He had a real understanding of her talent, and if, later on, his understanding became blinkered enough to stand in the way of potential growth in her stature as an actress or had he not been instrumental in manoeuvring her out of her commitment to Warners it seems very probable that her career would have reached stalemate as did Betty Grable's, her only female rival at the box office in this year of 1951. Her reign was coming to an end, after ten record-breaking years as the movies' Number One Box Office Star, a position to be challenged by Doris Day between 1959 and 1966, her seven years of predominance in the polls. In 1952, Doris, when the *Motion Picture Herald* announced its annual selection, had shot to top position and her popularity remained reasonably steady from then on, with the five consecutive years between 1959 and 1963 as Number One at the Box Office. Grable's career came to a full stop in 1955 after two standard Twentieth Century musicals, *Three for the Show* and *How to be Very Very Popular* – both very very undistinguished, by which time the public palate had become sated with the sameness of material repeated over a period of fifteen years. Conversely, that was the year that the Day career, freed of the shackles of Warners', 'safe', repetitive fare, took off, thanks to Marty and his stage-managing, with the major gamble of *Love Me or Leave Me*.

Marty Melcher and Doris Day were married on her twenty-seventh birthday, 3 April 1951, at Burbank City Hall by J. P. Leonard Hammer, with a young stranger as witness. By that time Marty and Doris were very close, mentally and physically, although she did not hear those mythical bells that movie heroines used to believe signified that the Big Romance had come along. They had reached comfortable compatibility through shared interests, such as their deepening involvement with Christian Science. Melcher was born an Orthodox Jew but it was not difficult for him to learn to relate to the teachings of

Mary Baker Eddy: in fact, his enthusiasm became even more intense than his wife's – another factor which makes it improbable that his sole motives in life were materialistic. Shock waves reverberated around Doris's Cincinnati relatives when they heard of her marriage to one of the 'Chosen People': most of the family were devoted bigots, as her father had been – only Alma seems to have been a free spirit, for all her devotion to Catholicism, and it is surely from her that her daughter inherited her liberalism of outlook.

The Melchers' honeymoon took the form of a motor trip to the Grand Canyon and she approached her new marriage with confidence and a serenity perhaps born of their joint commitment to Christian Science. They felt better for having followed the precept to avoid alcohol and smoking, something that used to place considerable strain on Doris's singing voice. They had bought another house at Toluca Lake from Martha Raye, that rumbustious embodiment of raucous humour, whose film career had started at Paramount with Bing Crosby and Bob Hope in such physical, not to say frenetic farces as *Rhythm on the Range* and *Give Me a Sailor* in the late Thirties when, for all her youth, she was the owner of the biggest bust and mouth in town. Neither grew smaller with the passage of time, as can be verified by her felicitous teaming so many years later with Doris in *Billy Rose's Jumbo*. Martha sold her house for 40,000 dollars and Alma moved into a small apartment near by, so she was on hand to cook the newlyweds their first dinner in the new home. Terry was clearly happy – he seemed to have found the father he had never had, and everything appeared to be coming up roses: a happy home and a burgeoning career, in that order, were something that had proved elusive to his mother but at last were there to be accepted and enjoyed.

On Moonlight Bay, Doris's third film that year of her marriage, now tends to be decried as sentimental pap and an attempt to jump on the bandwagon of the Vincente Minnelli–Judy Garland *Meet Me in St Louis*, but it is unfair to dismiss *Moonlight Bay* so summarily. For one thing, the Booth Tarkington stories on which it is based have a home-spun charm that even the un-imaginative direction of Roy Del Ruth cannot entirely dispel, and for another, it is a positive step towards that streak of the tomboy in the Day persona that would emerge so rewardingly two years later in *Calamity Jane*. Doris's Marjorie Winfield is an entirely credible teenage role model for the Twenties independent girl, holding her own with a baseball bat among the boys, enthusias-tically asserting that she does not believe in marriage, but gradually succumbing to femininity, pretty dresses and such to marry the 'Boy Next Door' (Gordon MacRae) – he it was who first proposed the 'marriage is slavery for a man' thesis. The good old respectable middle-class values are reasserted after some titillating dalliance with radical thinking, and what is so different in its exposition is the delicate shading of Doris's compromise of her free-thinking attitudes for love and marriage when the 'right man comes along'.

The film confirmed Doris's growing popularity with the Photoplay Gold Medal Award for the year's number one female star and proved again that her teaming with Gordon MacRae pleased the public, even if he, personally, left the critics shading from indifference to downright hostility. He had, nevertheless, an essential 'nice-ness' that blended with her wholesome qualities and acquitted himself creditably in the mid-Fifties in the film versions of such musical comedy blockbusters as *Oklahoma!* and *Carousel*, which provided meatier roles than the cardboard cut-out leading men of his early days at Warners.

The story-line of *On Moonlight Bay* casts MacRae as college student Bill Sherman, a next-door neighbour of the Winfield family, who earns the disapproval of father Winfield (Leon Ames) by announcing his contempt for banks and tearing up a five dollar bill in front of him. Father, of course, is a leading banker. Gradually Marjorie Winfield's interests shift focus from baseball to dancing: her young brother, an unrepentant tearaway escapes punishment by putting it about that his father has become an alcoholic – as young Wesley Billy Gray does an unconscionable amount of scene-stealing, with Ellen Corby more than holding her own as his acidulous school teacher Miss Stevens and the archetypal dominant housekeeper Stella – Mary Wickes in full rasp, smashing more crockery than Arthur Lucan's Old Mother Riley in a benefit night at the old Holborn Empire. After further infuriating George Winfield by arriving to save Marjorie from an imagined drunken beating, Bill has a change of heart, drops his radical opinions and with the final approval of all the family, heavily influenced by mother Alice (Rosemary DeCamp) gets ready to walk their daughter down the aisle.

The sequel, with the same leading players, came two years and five films later and had a little something the other hadn't got, probably due to David Butler having taken over the directorial reins. Bill returns from World War One seeking to postpone his marriage until his prospects are more settled: Marjorie, at first dismayed, then has her own reason for putting off the marriage, due to a misunderstanding that her father is having a liaison with a glamorous French actress Miss LaRue (Maria Palmer) who wishes to lease the local theatre. It's all to do with part of a script which father Winfield, as the theatre's trustee, has to approve and which in turn causes Bill to think has been sent to Marjorie by Wesley's infatuated music teacher, Chester Finley (Russell Arms). All misunderstandings are cleared up in time for Bill and Marjorie to be reunited at a skating party to celebrate her parents' twentieth wedding anniversary.

Doris Day's Marjorie has changed her hair from auburn to platinum blonde under the stresses of wartime – or is it simply further evidence of her growing up? There's a new spontaneity in the presentation of some of the musical numbers, including 'Ain't We Got Fun?' as Doris, Gordon and Mary Wickes indulge in a little house-cleaning and the Day–MacRae 'Just One Girl', while their other duets, 'If You Were the Only Girl' and 'Your Eyes Have Told Me So' have an extra warmth and tenderness in this their fifth and last film together. Donald Saddler's staging of the musical numbers is cheerfully inventive, especially in the big production 'Chanticleer', which features some of Doris's most athletic and zestful dancing.

The relationship between George and Alice Winfield is more sharply in focus, due to his supposed liaison with the French actress and the imminence of their twentieth wedding anniversary, and here the charming Rosemary DeCamp comes into her own, playing the kind of role she excelled in – that of mother, friend, sister or sympathetic confidante. She played the first quite splendidly in two bright and breezy Universal musicals of 1944, *The Merry Monahans* and *Bowery to Broadway*, as the trouper mother of Donald O'Connor and Ann Blyth. She wrote to me during the preparation of this book, giving permission to quote from her talking book for Cambria Recordings *Tales from Hollywood – Fifty Years in the Great American Dream Factory*.

The best fun I had during the Warner years was playing in the two Doris Day musicals *On Moonlight Bay* and *By the Light of the Silvery Moon*, both based on Booth Tarkington's *Penrod* stories.

Again the director was Dave Butler. He had been a romantic star in silent pictures and then went on to have a long and successful career as a director in sound, specializing in comedies and musicals. He lacked the inherent conceit of many male stars, and yet knew actors' problems from the other side of the camera. A big man with a Francis X. Bushman kind of head, X-ray eyes, he had a rat-a-tat-tat tempo when he was in the cage with the big cats. And we had some big cats on those pictures, at least we thought of ourselves that way. There was Gordon MacRae with his warm golden voice, and Leon Ames, who was a skillful veteran, plus Doris Day. Even smaller parts were played by fine talents with well-known names: Mary Wickes, Russell Arms, Maria Palmer and Merv Griffin. Both the casts were full of favourites.

Dave could handle us all, even getting along with Marty Melcher, Doris's producer-manager husband. When we had too many games and tricks going, Dave would swell up and play the martinet over delays and too many takes; but even when he screamed and swore, we knew he was one of us, an actor before he became a boss. He was a dear, funny man, and one of the greatest storytellers in Hollywood, both on film and in conversation.

One long scene, with Leon Ames in bed and the rest of us twittering around him, took forever. The set was hard to light, and there were camera delays, as well as equipment failures. When we finally neared the end of a good take, Leon was sound asleep and missed his line. On the next take we tied a thread to his big toe and yanked it on his cue. He let out a howl, Dave yelled, the cameraman went to the toilet and the front office phoned down a curse.

I always wonder how the news got around that studio so fast. It was as if Jack Warner had a console of peepholes to spy on every stage. He knew instantly if an actor blew his lines, or held up production. More than likely he had his own little CIA network of assistants with walkie-talkies.

Knowing Doris Day during those years was a door to light and fun. She is not only amazingly talented, but honest and invigorating. Her dancing, and that vibrant voice, made everyone around her alive. Her religious faith inspired and awed us.

Towards the end of one of the 'Moons', Harvest, Silvery, or whatever, a whole sound stage was converted into a woodland snow scene with trees and ice and skaters. Doris, Leon and I (her parents) had to come circling into a long boom shot in an old-fashioned sleigh. The top of the boom was way up in the catwalks to catch the hundreds of extras, who were costumed for the year 1918 in furs, boots and woollens – all very expensive. The long-shot opened wide, and then zoomed in on us, for a close three-shot.

This was during the first Adlai Stevenson campaign for the Presidency. I think Doris and I were the only Democrats in Burbank. We had some big coloured Stevenson buttons which we kept hidden. As soon as Dave yelled, 'Cut! Print!' and climbed off the boom, we pinned our buttons conspicuously on our chests and waited for him to come up to the sleigh. His eyes, which missed nothing, saw the buttons immediately. Doris assumed an innocent look, and I kept my face blank. Dave began to rant and rave about, 'the cost of the shot' and 'idiot actresses', and went on to what he thought of 'God-damned politicians', until his face became a dangerous purple. Then we told him his shot was OK. I don't think he believed us until he checked the dailies.

When I see those two pictures on television, I realize it is the only period in my long career that I would like to live over again. We were all part of a lovely reproduction of an age of innocence that may never really have existed, except for us, at Warner's in 1953.

Interestingly, the photos of Rosemary DeCamp of those days bear a striking resemblance to some of Doris's mother, Alma Kappelhoff.

Of the four films between the two Booth Tarkington fables, there was little to write home about, except Doris's moving performance in the Gus Kahn musical biopic *I'll See You in My Dreams* with Danny Thomas as the lyricist and Day as Grace LeBoy, who writes the music for his first song hit, marries him after various misunderstandings, mainly over the way he takes her devotion so completely for granted, and is finally reunited with him at a lavish Hollywood musical gathering following further emotional complications involving a glamorous star, Gloria Knight (Patrice Wymore). Frank Lovejoy plays Kahn's collaborator, Walter Donaldson, the songs are a joy, all the lyrics being by Kahn, including the title song and Walter Donaldson's 'Love Me or Leave Me' – a happy signpost for the future, and Doris's warmth and depth of characterization overcame the liability of the extraordinarily unattractive Danny Thomas, who makes a chauvinist character quite unbearably boorish. It takes all her subtlety to make us believe in this attraction for her, a feat she brings off triumphantly in the moving reconciliation scene at the end, presumably authentic, as Grace

Kahn wrote the original story on which Jack Rose and Melville Shavelson's script is based. Michael Curtiz's caring direction almost overcomes the handicap of his leading man and reminds us that he made one of the finest biopics of all time, *Yankee Doodle Dandy* with James Cagney.

Mary Wickes is on hand again, abrasive as ever, in her 'Minder' role as Anna – she has been likened to Marjorie Main after a crash course in dieting, but she has her own distinction, and other good actors include James Gleason, sympathetic as ever as Fred Thompson, Jim Backus, the immortal voice of 'Mr Magoo' – more abrasiveness as Sam Harris – and Minna Gombell, one of the classic faded blondes of the screen, as Doris's mother. Patrice Wymore again excels as the actress who comes between the Kahns – her scene with Doris is nicely balanced – and she crops up again briefly in *Starlift* as one of many 'Guest Stars' who entertain the Forces about to board ship for the Korean front.

Roy Del Ruth jollies along a plot about two soldiers, Sergeant Mike Nelson (Dick Wesson) and Corporal Rick Williams (Ron Hagerthy) who set out to contact a school friend, Nell Wayne (Janice Rule) who has become a movie star. Surprise, surprise, she gets her starry friends to put on a show at Travis Air Base, and they all troop on as themselves, including Doris Day, who gets her silver tonsils around ''S Wonderful', Gordon MacRae, Gene Nelson, Virginia Mayo, James Cagney, Gary Cooper, Phil Harris, Frank Lovejoy, Randolph Scott, Jane Wyman, Ruth Roman and Louella Parsons, who writes a story about the childhood sweethearts. Definitely a No-No.

It was during the making of *I'll See You in My Dreams* that the *Motion Picture Herald* announced that Doris Day had made it into the top ten most popular movie stars, a singular achievement after making only nine films. This was early in 1952, not long after her marriage to Marty Melcher. For the next seven years she remained *in situ*, despite the quality of some of the films into which she was put. Her next biopic, *The Winning Team* dealt with the life of the great baseball player Grover Cleveland Alexander, with Ronald Reagan as the hero and Doris as his wife Aimée, who leaves him after he has started suffering from double vision due to epilepsy – a hangover from a childhood accident, but a complaint about which he tells no one. People assume he has become an alcoholic, and that includes Aimée, who returns to him when she discovers the real cause of his blackouts and helps him fight his way back to the top. This is the one Doris Day movie which has proved impossible to find in video form, at least in England, and there seems to be no record of its having been shown on television here.

An interesting cast included Frank Lovejoy, Eve Miller, who was to suffer through another dire film with Doris, Gordon Jones and Rusty Tamblyn as Alexander's brother Willie: he was just three years away from his triumph as Russ in *Seven Brides for Seven Brothers* when his acrobatic dancing lit up the screen. Later successes were the title role in *Tom Thumb* in 1958, as the tiny son of woodsman Bernard Miles – later Lord Miles – and Jessie Matthews, in her last important screen role, and, in 1961, *West Side Story*. The director of *The Winning Team*, Lewis Seiler, was more at home with action films – this, considering the subject, could be considered one – than with handling major female stars, though he did pilot Dietrich through *Pittsburgh* in 1942 and Gracie Fields in *Molly and Me* in 1945, of which Gracie commented, 'He didn't seem to know quite what to do with me, so in the end he wrote in a pub scene with a few songs, and called it a musical!' She had been, as England's number one singing star of the Thirties movies, the clogs and shawl version of what Doris Day became to American films a decade later – the cheerily carolling working girl spreading a little happiness among her companions.

Critics' opinions of *The Winning Team* could safely be called 'mixed': at one end of the scale the *Hollywood Reporter* called it, 'a moving semi-biography of a man who lived through the glamour of fame and the degradation of the gutter . . . Reagan is excellent as Alex . . . Miss Day gives her finest dramatic performance to date, playing Aimé with sensitivity and understanding.' At the other end the *New York Herald Tribune* wrote, 'Reagan's performance of Alexander consists of being bland or troubled according to the turns of the plot, plus imitating a pitcher's windup on many occasions. Miss Day is a straight and narrow version of a fretful but loving wife . . .'

Doris, by this time, was seeing Reagan less frequently, but she enjoyed acting with him again and she got the opportunity to reprise the festive favourite 'Ol' Saint Nicholas', which she had recorded previously in 1949 for Columbia.

Friendship was not on the cards with her next co-star, Ray Bolger, though her nature was such that she managed to get along well personally with him, despite the friction his behaviour was to engender on the set of *April in Paris*. By a rare coincidence Doris's next subject for the studio was to have been a re-make of the musical comedy *Sunny*, which had been filmed with Marilyn Miller, ex-Ziegfeld Follies star dancer, in 1930, and again with Anna Neagle in 1941, in which Ray Bolger was the choreographer and they danced a sensational version of the hit of the show 'Who'. Bolger was the clown in this story of circus life with Anna as the bareback rider for which role Doris had been cast – in the event, her bareback exploits had to wait several years, until *Jumbo*. Oddly enough, in view of subsequent events, Bolger displayed quite a lot of charm in *Sunny*, though he was not the male lead: that role fell to John Carroll, and there is no record of Bolger having tried to upstage the star, which would have been difficult with her husband Herbert Wilcox directing. Eleven years later, by the time it came to Doris Day's turn to be partnered by Ray Bolger, it was a very different story. Interestingly, early publicity stills of her bear an uncanny resemblance to the Anna Neagle of those Hollywood musicals: they both exuded the same 'sunny' ambience, though Anna was, incredibly, thirty-six at the time.

David Butler, whom Doris, like Rosemary DeCamp, found urbane, considerate and witty and always genial and understanding in his dealings with his actors – except when they pinned Democrat badges to their lapels! – accused Bolger, in the middle of a take, of upstaging Doris, which apparently everyone on the set but she had noticed. A heated argument broke out, with Butler threatening to take action to redress the balance in the cutting room and Bolger to 'fix' him with Jack Warner, and the atmosphere from then on was anything but genial. Given these circumstances, the general miscasting and the footling storyline, it is perhaps not surprising that *April in Paris* has been called 'a disaster for all concerned and the worst film in which Doris ever appeared.' Almost everything about it was wrong, starting with the casting of Ray Bolger as a Washington diplomat, S. Winthrop Putnam, and as her leading man he was ludicrous. The scene where she (as a chorus girl Ethel Jackson, mistakenly chosen to represent the American theatre at a Paris Festival when the invitation was intended for Ethel Barrymore) has to do a double take, indicating her sudden falling for the Bolger charms, is risible! Danny Thomas, charm-wise, was bad enough, but at least he was an actor able to invest his scenes with pathos, but Bolger, cocky and parrot-like was a distinct turn-off.

Then there was the choreography. Doris was anxious for Gene and Miriam Nelson to put her through her paces as they had done so brilliantly in *Tea for Two* and *Lullaby of Broadway*. After twelve successful films for the studio she thought her word might now carry some weight, but she was saddled with Eddie Prinz, the brother of Warner's leading dance director LeRoy Prinz, and she hated the choreography from the word go. She was now number two in the box office ratings and still with no say on the running of her movies; from then on she could not wait to work out her contract, which had a year to go. The next bone of contention was the score: apart from E. Y. Harburg and Vernon Duke's lovely title song, which she invested with touchingly wistful nostalgia, the other songs were among the most banal ever penned by Sammy Cahn and that same Vernon Duke, of whom Cahn wrote, 'I don't think he could write a bad song.' How wrong he was.

Cahn describes the *April in Paris* debacle in his usual satirical manner. 'Came the day when we went to Doris Day to audition the songs for *April in Paris*. She expressed delight and joy over each of them, and I danced away from that audition. A few days later we were told she'd hated every note, every word. Frenzy and panic. We started to rewrite, and I would stake Vernon's reputation, much bigger than mine, that the rewrites, no matter what Doris Day thought good or bad, were inferior to the originals.'

The nadir of both choreography and songs, was surely

reached in an unbelievable scene called 'That's What Makes Paris Paree', when Ethel Jackson has reached the Gay City, having apparently been married by the ship's captain on board the ocean liner to Bolger as Putnam (Love at first sight!) and is suddenly starring in a revue with a *melange* of poodles, dyed every colour of the rainbow, wandering, with understandable bewilderment through Eddie Prinz's extraordinarily muddled choreography. This wild scene in the Gay City, found its way onto the front cover of *Gay Times* in May 1990, with Doris in a kind of drum majorette outfit, with bare midriff and aigrette-topped pillbox hat, cheerfully holding six of the multi-hued poodles on leads. It seems incredible, at this remove that Doris, with her regard for her animals, could have countenanced, even in 1952, such a demeaning display, quite apart from the fact that they must have been both confused and unhappy wandering in and out of the scene, which reached a new low in taste even for LeRoy Prinz who gets the 'credit', though his brother Eddie perpetrated it. And what about the aigrette? It is interesting to speculate what today's Doris would have said if asked to wear such an excrescence.

She could hardly have foreseen the echoes that would be reverberating through the corridors of time nearly forty years later after taking part in that tasteless charade, and if she could have gazed into her crystal ball it seems likely that she would have been as insistent about 'That's what Makes Paris Paree' being excised from the *April in Paris* script, as she was that Cahn and Duke rewrite the score of the film. In an article called 'Gay aspects of Fifties pop' Kris Kirk wrote:

'Gay people have always had clever little ways of finding aspects of culture they can relate to, no matter how straight and narrow that culture is . . . although the gay counter-culture and the aesthetic that gays invented – the irony of the camp point-of-view – were very well hidden, if you look hard enough you can find plenty of examples of the gay/pop/Fifties continuum peeping through. Take Doris Day . . . Not that there was ever a breath of sapphic scandal about Doris Mary Anne von Kappelhoff from Cincinnati . . . who embodied the decade by always being, as Alexander Walker described her "confident, upbeat and absolutely sure of her destiny".' And in a sense Doris was some kind of example of the new woman. 'To many women in an era when man was still the boss as well as the breadwinner,' says Walker, 'Doris looked an ally, a girl who not only wouldn't take their man away from them but was well-equipped to make a man keep his distance till she was ready for him.' And therein lies the rub.

Gay Times continues: 'For as well as appealing to musical queens, Doris Day was *the* big heart-throb of Fifties dykes. Partly, one presumes, because of that husky voice and the boyish crop she wore so often, and no doubt the tomboy energy she conveyed so well as the pistol-packing slapping, two-fisted *Calamity Jane*. But it wasn't just sex; it was image too. All great icons have a dual personality, and the other side of Doris's homely as apple pie/good sport/perfect wife image was the girl who always says no till the right man comes around, the foremost practitioner of prolonged avoidance of sex. 'I knew Doris Day before she was a virgin,' was Oscar Levant's best-known joke, but it seemed funnier in the Sixties than it does now. Doris was a "new woman" before even the "old woman" was invented. A potent brew for all those dykes who looked beyond the freckles and saw Sex on Legs.'

Who would have thought that vapid film *April in Paris* could have unleashed so much philosophizing? The ultimate in charades, the plot rested heavily on 'will she lose her virginity?' because we knew, which she didn't, that the ship's captain who had carried out the marriage ceremony was, in fact, debonair ladykiller Phillipe Four-quet (Claude Dauphin), out of funds and forced to work his way home as a waiter, masquerading as the captain, so Ethel and Putnam were not 'married' at all. He upsets his fiancée Marcia by telling her their marriage must be kept a secret – Eve Miller plays this role in a state of perpetual flounce – and off she goes; Ethel pretends to fall for Philippe and goes on a whirl of Paris nightlife with him, making Putnam jealous, so he whisks her off to the Eiffel Tower for a final gay song and dance, though perhaps, in the circumstances, the word 'gay' is best avoided – more a case of out of the frying pan into the fire. Claude Dauphin's frying pan has lots of Gallic charm, but is really too mature for Doris, so she loses out all round.

It was only a light trip 'By the Silvery Moon' before Doris's best film of the era, *Calamity Jane*, the start of all that serious analysis of 'Doris Day – role model for people of all persuasions', and the film with which she was to be identified for future generations.

5

❋

The Road to the Top

The year in which Doris Day made *Calamity Jane*, in 1953, was a watershed year for her in several ways. Where her home life was concerned everything in the garden seemed lovely. Marty Melcher had legally adopted Terry the previous year and the two were very compatible. The boy was ten and happy to be Terry Melcher. Doris's brother Paul had joined the rest of the family in Los Angeles and moved his wife and children out: he started work for the company, started by Doris and Marty, called Arwin Productions, and her earnings were now, thanks to his astuteness, around 5,000 dollars a week. He had left Century Artists and was now concentrating on managing her affairs and the music company they had established to handle general music publishing besides Doris's songs and records.

She loved filming *Calamity Jane* – the pistol-packing cowgirl who gets involved with Wild Bill Hickok, and threw herself enthusiastically into the characterization, which was the most physical she had ever been called upon to play – the leaps onto horses, moving wagons and the rest seemed to come naturally. In the words of Betty Hutton's hit song, one of many by Irving Berlin from the previous year's *Annie Get Your Gun*, which not only had a similar theme, based around another famous cowgirl,

128

Annie Oakley, but the same leading man in Howard Keel. Both these gals, historically, were butch and very plain, with little in common with the blonde pulchritude of Hutton or Day – someone like Marjorie Main would probably have been nearer the mark, but where would the box office have been then, poor thing? Doris, admiring Jean Arthur's husky 1935 'Jane', compromised by lowering her voice and sticking out her chin a little. Sammy Fain and Paul Francis Webster's score was a pippin – every one a gem and 'Secret Love' earned Doris her third million-seller, besides winning the Academy Award as Best Song of the Year: it was her last film with David Butler and together they hit the jackpot. The film was one of the top hits of the year, and as a result Marty was able to negotiate a lucrative new deal for her with Warners. She loved working with Howard Keel, and it is regrettable that they never filmed together again. On every level the movie worked marvellously, opening with a bang as Doris literally hurls herself into 'The Deadwood Stage', establishing the *Calamity Jane* character right away, clad from head to toe in buckskin, wearing boots, six-shooters around her waist, a Confederate cap on her tousled blonde locks and a red kerchief round her neck. The singing voice is zestful, and the speaking tones somewhere down near her boots. The parallels with *Annie Get Your Gun* are, of course, obvious, especially in her first 'antagonistic' duet with Keel's Wild Bill Hickok 'I Can Do Without You', a dead ringer for 'Anything You Can Do', but, by and large, the score is as varied and rich, the acting as energetic, and where *Calamity* succeeds is in Doris Day's performance: she establishes a real character, shading from the rough, tough frontierswoman of the beginning, through varying degrees of adapting to the feminizing influence of her love for a soldier and her friendship with a 'buttons and bows' actress to the realization that her real affections lie with Bill Hickok and the final blossoming into radiant womanhood in her tender and inspired singing of 'Secret Love'. By contrast Betty Hutton's Annie, engaging tomboy though she was, lacked subtlety: Judy Garland, had she been able to carry on with the filming, might have been something again. The eminent Paul Dehn summed it all up perfectly, 'Doris Day, emerging in a stinging temper from the honeycomb of sickly sweet pictures that have recently been her lot, gives the performance of her life as a wild Western shrew magnificently worth the taming . . . by the end, she is within hailing distance of Ginger Rogers and Judy Garland.' He refers to real stardom and in this I think he underestimates Doris Day's potential.

Howard Keel, as tamer, relied mainly on his easy charm and splendid baritone: the part was not too well defined in terms of character, but he and Doris were delightful together, in contrast to the pasteboard Lieutenant Gilmartin (Philip Carey), an even less sharply drawn individual. Allyn McLerie is a vivacious and likable contrast to Doris in the role of Katie Brown, dresser to a singing star, Adelaide Adams (Gale Robbins), with whom Calamity travels to Chicago to bring back to save the Golden Garter, a dance hall owned by her friend Henry Miller (Paul Harvey), from bankruptcy. Katie impersonates Adelaide, breaks down on stage, but Calamity persuades the customers of the saloon to let her continue in her own breezy style. The girl is a success, Calamity moves her into her log cabin with her, where she adds a much-needed feminine touch until Jane finds her embracing the officer Gilmartin. A jealous scene ensues, Calamity orders Katie out of town, but Bill Hickok intervenes, realizes he loves Calamity, they switch partners and the film ends with a double wedding.

Calamity Jane was enjoying a record-breaking run at the Radio City Music Hall in New York when Doris was laid low with a mysterious malady, against which she fought with the help of her Christian Science Practitioner, Martin Broones. Initially she had turned to the writings of Mary Baker Eddy, with their forceful Mind over Matter message, but found little relief from an increasingly agonizing difficulty in breathing. Martin Broones was the husband of Charlotte Greenwood, who Doris wrongly thought was English. In fact, she was born in Philadelphia and enlivened many musicals with her eccentric comedy dancing, of which the high spot was an incredible kick over whatever or whoever happened to be in the vicinity. She was still doing this, as Aunt Eller, in the film version of *Oklahoma!*, in 1955, at the age of sixty-two, having jollied along several of the wartime Technicolor Alice Faye–Carmen Miranda–Betty Grable musicals at Twentieth Century-Fox. Like her husband, Charlotte Greenwood was also a Christian Scientist.

Both Broones and Marty Melcher tried to help Doris's condition by reading to her from *Science and Health*, but to no avail. The condition worsened and was compounded by an inability to swallow and, in the middle of all this physical torment she was driven almost out of her mind by a sadistic sex caller on the telephone of the kind that she would have to relive years later in the filming of *Midnight Lace*. In the early hours of one morning, many weeks after she had tried to deal with her illness by sticking to the tenets of her faith, she was convinced she was about to experience a heart attack. Fear had been added to all her symptoms, fear that a small lump she had discovered in her breast was cancerous, fear that she had a collapsed lung, fear that the mysterious night caller on the phone would appear in person.

She persuaded Marty to call Mr Broones, although it was two o'clock in the morning, and when he did come she fainted. A doctor who lived nearby was by her bed when she came to; contrary to general belief that no practising Christian Scientist may under any circumstances consult a doctor, it is permitted in cases of emergency when the person concerned finds himself or herself totally unable to combat the mental condition at the root of the physical distress. The doctor diagnosed that she was hyperventilating, brought on by the stress and tension of overwork, which caused her to breathe too deeply, taking an excess of oxygen into the body, at the same time expelling too much carbon dioxide, which caused the faint through having a surfeit of oxygen in the system and too little carbon dioxide. The doctor showed her how to regulate her breathing by putting her lips to a paper bag and only breathing in the air she had exhaled into the bag, so that she would assimilate some carbon dioxide.

The doctor booked her into hospital – the starting date for a new film, *Lucky Me* was fast approaching – the lump in her breast, which turned out to be a cyst, was excised by minor surgery, and she was visited by a neuropsychiatric specialist, Dr Karl von Hagen, who confirmed that she was on the brink of a complete nervous breakdown. He explained that whereas Christian Science is a general application of the philosophy of the dominance of mind over matter, the medical approach is the practical application of knowledge to a specific bodily function.

She was allowed to go home and told to note down every physical manifestation that worried her, together with her thoughts on the matter, and to follow a strict regime of quiet, with as few outside distractions as possible, talk kept to a strict minimum, as much reading of uplifting books as possible – and, above all, no film scripts. Dr von Hagen prescribed swimming three times daily, with particular emphasis on the 'dead man's float' – floating, totally relaxed, on one's back. The only drug he gave her was a liquid sedative to be taken before sleeping.

With these aids allied to the wisdom of her Christian Science reading she very gradually fought her way back to health and peace of mind. The doctor visited every day for discussions on what she had written down on her notepad and minutely analysed the cause of every distressing physical symptom. She dwelt much upon two quotations from *Science and Health* – St John's 'Ye shall know the truth and the truth shall make you free' and Shakespeare's 'There is nothing either good or bad, but thinking makes it so.'

Doris believes in predestination, and the conclusion she reached, over and beyond the Christian Science which formed an invaluable stepping stone to her own personal religion is described in her book: 'I feel that God is my very being and God is the life of everything around me. So I don't have to seek God. He's right here. I don't pray. I just realize God.'

There was a price to pay for her enforced withdrawal from public life during her slow and painful recuperative period. The new peak of popularity brought about by *Calamity Jane* called forth ever greater demands upon her for interviews, which she had, *faute de mieux*, to decline. The alternatives were to let it be known that she was combating the effects of a severe nervous breakdown, which could have led to endless speculation and to her being branded every kind of self-indulgent neurotic or to suffer in silence and hold her peace. Whichever course she followed at that time was open to severe misconstruction, but maybe the first might have been wiser when dealing with the press, who can be understanding when presented with the facts. Much was made of her declining to sing 'Secret Love' at the Academy Awards ceremony.

What happened was that the Hollywood Women's Press Club voted her their annual Sour Apple Award – that ultimate in journalistic bitchiness – as the most unco-operative actress in movies. That hurt her terribly: previously she had been noted for her willingness to co-operate in every way in the promotion of her films and such. When the time came for her to accede to Warners' increasing pressure that she start work on the new film, and the go-ahead was finally given by the invaluable Dr von Hagen, she was appalled by the banality of the script, of which the principal writer was James O'Hanlon, whose *Calamity Jane* had had so much going for it production-wise and due to the dynamism of the central characters had come through with flying colours. Doris discussed the matter with Martin Broones, with whom she had consulted during her recuperation. His attitude was, 'A deal's a deal' and rather than take a suspension she should honour her contract. So she gritted her perfect teeth and got on with it, with the proviso that if the shooting was likely to over-run she insisted the director, Jack Donohue, shorten it. He had landed the commission after his good work on the staging and direction of the musical scenes of *Calamity Jane*.

Lucky Me was the opposite of that for Doris, despite the chirpy 'Blue Bells of Broadway', and the romantic 'I Speak to the Stars', sung with Robert Cummings on a moonlit beach scene. Sammy Fain and Paul Francis Webster could not be expected to come up with a winner every time – Cummings played a songwriter, Dick, who allows Doris's Candy to think he is a garage

employee. She is one of four stranded theatrical enter-
tainers reduced to paying for a meal in an expensive
restaurant by working in the kitchen. The other three
are Flo (Nancy Walker), Hap (Phil Silvers) and Duke
(Eddie Foy Jr), and the plot involves Dick trying to put
on a show with help from a wealthy backer, Thayer (Bill
Goodwin) whose daughter Lorraine (Martha Hyer)'s
designs on Dick are far from platonic. When she learns
that Candy, who has fallen for the songwriter, despite
her initial fury at his deception, is the prospective star of
her father's show she tries to sabotage the proceedings,
but the four professionals all don various disguises at the
party given to celebrate Thayer's birthday and also to
hear the numbers from the show, and the proceedings
end with Lorraine thrown into her own swimming pool,
Daddy coming up with the money and Candy and Dick
going on to star on Broadway. Where have we heard
something like that before?

Thanks to Doris's charm and expertise and enthusiastic support from the butch and raucous Nancy
Walker – sort of a cross between Martha Raye and
Cass Daley – Phil Silvers (devotees of Sergeant Bilko
will love his act – I wish I could join their number) and
Eddie Foy Jr, plus Bob Cummings's hard-worked-at
boyishness that resembled a rather pretty ventriloquist's
dummy, there is quite a fair amount of humour and
entertainment to be milked from the situations and
Doris does an amusing English 'Grande Dame' act –
much more successful than her earlier 'French Cabaret'
star – as partner to Eddie Foy's Leon Errol-like 'Lord'
impersonation.

Robert Cummings was another casualty of the Grim
Reaper during the writing of this book – surprisingly he
turned out to be eighty – like Eve Arden he looked so
young for so long – reputedly he took so many rejuvenat-

ing pills he turned into a walking pharmaceutical cabinet. Martha Hyer, coolly blonde and beautiful, suffered in her career from being dubbed, 'the poor man's Grace Kelly': an interesting debut in this 1954 comedy was Angie Dickinson as one of Hyer's guests.

One of the few happy factors connected with the movie's production was the warm friendship Doris formed with Judy Garland, making *A Star is Born* on the same lot. When not actually filming they were together a great deal; observers say they seemed to share the same sense of humour and always appeared happy in each other's company, maybe in sympathy over the pressures of their lives.

Although *A Star Is Born* was perhaps the peak of Judy's later career, the traumas of her life were to multiply, though she battled on with films, television spectaculars, theatre and cabaret shows until her tragic death in London from an overdose of sleeping pills in 1969. The coroner's verdict was accidental death. Devastated, Doris said 'Judy was one of the funniest, wittiest ladies I've ever known.'

It was after the filming of *Lucky Me* that Doris felt able to invite the press to her home to make her peace – something that simply had to be done, both as a caring human being whose natural inclination was to be courteous and friendly to the world at large, and, from a practical point of view, as a working actress who recognized that the 'gentlemen of the press' – and the ladies too, very much so where the Hollywood gossip columnists were concerned – had a vital part to play in keeping her image before the public. This was very much Marty Melcher's angle, and at first he attempted to parry the writers' questions towards his own view of what his wife should be answering – an act she gently but firmly detected in making a candid admission that she had suffered something very near to a complete nervous breakdown and she hoped they would bear with her now that she had been able to come to terms with her life and career again. It was just not in her nature to make a life's work out of shunning the press, as Garbo had and Katharine Hepburn always has done, and that was a fact the press appreciated, to a man – if not always to a woman.

Doris was in need of all her new-found strength and returning resilience during the filming of her last film for Warners, *Young at Heart*, filmed in 1954 and released at the beginning of the following year. Marty, divining from the fall in box office receipts of *Lucky Me* that the potential for musicals along the old pattern was being lessened by the increasing hold of television specials and the like on the public, had incorporated his wife into their newly formed company, Arwin Productions, now that her annual income was reputed to have reached five million dollars a year, including her average of a new single record release monthly, with annual sales of up to five million. It was through this company that he arranged to release her new film under the Warner Brothers banner: a remake of Michael Curtiz's *Four Daughters*, which brought stardom to John Garfield in the 1938 version, based on Fanny Hurst's *Sister Act*: this time Frank Sinatra played the moody and self-pitying young pianist, Barney Sloane, with Doris in the Priscilla Lane role of Laurie Tuttle, living quietly with her sisters Fran and Amy in a small Connecticut town, where their father is a music teacher. Dorothy Malone and Elisabeth Fraser inherited the parts played by Rosemary and Lola Lane in the original, when the leading ladies really were a sister act. Fay Bainter had played their wise and understanding aunt, for which Ethel Barrymore, a born 'theatrical dame' if ever there was one, was a natural in the 1954 version. Curtiz had directed with heart and his natural flair for realism, for which the sullen virility of 'boy from the wrong side of the tracks' Garfield was ideally suited.

Director Gordon Douglas, a technically efficient and always polished director somewhat lacking in personal distinction, was up against a Sinatra who had fought back to the top with his Academy Award-nominated performance in the 1953 *From Here to Eternity* after a period of being virtually ostracized by the profession which had once placed him on a pedestal, and he was behaving, despite all the soft focus Doris Day brings to bear on the matter, outrageously. She had no very happy memories of working with him on the *Your Hit Parade* radio show shortly after she made *Romance on the High Seas*, not, she insists, because she did not get on with him, but because she hated that kind of radio programme performed live before her *bête noire*, a big audience in a large theatre. This was at a time when they were both going through a self-protective phase and she claims not to have been able to get to know him, despite the long periods they spent together professionally, yet says they had a 'pleasant, easygoing relationship'. Sinatra is one of the many stars who did not respond to my letter about working with Doris, yet, when asked about his relationship with Deborah Kerr, he replied by return with a panegyric which Deborah joked brought a blush to her cheek, and, by contrast, said she found him a delight to work with: 'We had a ball – it was so much fun.'

From the word go, Doris had the opposite of a ball. At a pre-production conference at which Marty Melcher, representing Arwin Productions was present, Sinatra sat with a paper in front of his face, reading; later he refused to go on the set if Melcher was anywhere on the lot. Music publisher Sam Weiss states that Marty made an approach to Frank Sinatra to do with some of the songs in the film, after which he said to Jack Warner, 'I refuse to work on this picture if that creep Melcher is anywhere around.' So he was barred, but, in addition it appears that Frank caused massive delays by being late on the set, something that features high on Doris's list of cardinal sins. At the outset of the filming he insisted he would walk off the picture if cameraman Charles Lang – one of the Hollywood greats, who had won an Academy Award for his cinematography on the Helen Hayes and Gary Cooper version of *A Farewell to Arms* in 1933 – was not fired. Such was Sinatra's power, even on a film nominally under the aegis of Doris and Marty Melcher, that Lang was replaced by Ted McCord. Finally, Frank refused categorically to die at the end of the film after crashing his car in a suicide attempt, which had been the original logical ending for as self-destructive a character as Barney Sloan, played so brilliantly by John Garfield – all of which Doris defuses and almost excuses by putting her co-star's behaviour down to 'expediency', and 'there is no right or wrong when a picture is in production'.

Despite these very severe set-backs they teamed charmingly together, the songs were a delight, including the duet 'You My Love' written by Jimmy Van Heusen and Mack Gordon, 'Hold Me in Your Arms' sung by Doris and penned by Ray Heindorf, Charles Henderson and the ubiquitous producer – composer – M. D. Don Pippin, whom I met in London when he was Constance Bennett's pianist at the Café de Paris, two years after this film. Cole Porter's 'Just One of Those Things' and 'One for my Baby' by Harold Arlen and Johnny Mercer were sung by Frank, who really did seem to have the lion's share of the best songs. He also, of course, had the showiest part, but some writers seem to have read 'a thinly veiled animosity' into their relationship, which admittedly allows them no real love scenes together.

Doris conveys a desperately caring feeling towards the man she elopes with rather than hurt her sister Amy, who is in love with songwriter Alex Burke (Gig Young), to whom Laurie had announced her engagement. If her pep talk to Barney in hospital is strongly reminiscent of the one she gave the despairing Kirk Douglas in *Young Man With a Horn*, she still conveys a passionate sincerity, even though it does end in the ridiculously contrived finale scene with the whole family playing and singing happily round the piano. In this Sinatra was a fool to himself with the *Saturday Review* declaring: '*Young at Heart* proves that Hollywood has not lost its knack for making indifferent new pictures out of good old pictures', while *Films and Filming* pulled no punches with, 'The cadaverous and undernourished Sinatra, pairs oddly with Doris Day, whose rosy-cheeked tomboy vitality affords the only lively relief in two hours of pedestrian sentiment and platitude.'

The interesting supporting cast suffered from somewhat underwritten characters, none more so than Dorothy Malone as the frustrated sister Fran: a year or so away from her supporting actress-Oscar for her role of a frustrated nymphomaniac in *Written on the Wind* with Rock Hudson and Lauren Bacall; her peak was to come as star of the TV soap *Peyton Place* from 1964 to 1969. Gig Young as the brash young composer Alex, understandably lusted after secretly by all the sisters, whether overtly or not, had only just recovered from playing Joan Crawford's exhausted toy boy in her return-to-MGM and last musical *Torch Song*, the previous year. 'You're no good,' she snapped, 'but you're beautiful!' The *Young at Heart* ladies were of gentler persuasion, but that kind of role seemed to haunt him, even after his Academy Award nominations for *Come Fill the Cup* in 1951 and Doris's *Teacher's Pet* in 1958. Eleven years later he finally won the Oscar for *They Shoot Horses, Don't They?* with Jane Fonda and Susannah York. He died tragically, police said by his own hand, in a Manhattan apartment next to the body of his German actress-bride of three weeks: He was still clutching a gun. At one point he was married to Elizabeth Montgomery, daughter of Robert, and star of the eternally popular TV series *Bewitched.* with the formidable Agnes Moorehead.

The gallant side of Frank Sinatra was evidenced by the surprise party he threw for Ethel Barrymore's seventy-fifth birthday, at which Doris could not, as usual, restrain her tears. Someone threw her a box of Kleenex tissues which hit her on the forehead: the thrower was lucky to get away without having his teeth rammed down his throat by Frank and for evermore it seems she could not reach for a Kleenex without thinking of Sinatra, so she obviously does have a soft spot for him some-where!

It was not without considerable heart-searching that Doris Day tackled the part of marcelled radio and recording star Ruth Etting who, as she survived until 1978 must surely have been well content with the glamorized version of herself that came across in MGM's Eastman-coloured version of her life *Love Me or Leave Me*, the title taken from one of the most popular Etting recordings of her day by Walter Donaldson and Gus Kahn. The lady certainly had a plethora of great songs at her command, including 'Shaking the Blues Away' by Irving Berlin, 'It All Depends On You' by Buddy DeSylva, Les Brown and Ray Henderson and, what was perhaps Etting's theme song from her early days in speakeasies, Rodgers and Hart's infinitely touch-ing 'Ten Cents A Dance'. It was one of those 'tarnished angel' songs that include Noel Coward's 'Half Caste Woman' and 'Mad About the Boy' and the way that the matchless Elisabeth Welch can sing 'Love for Sale' in her eighties still makes it fresh and movingly acceptable. Doris's record album of the songs from the film stands today as one of her all-time great achievements, singing songs associated with Ruth Etting, whose style, manner and way of life were the direct antithesis of everything Doris Day stands for.

This was the reason why it took all of Joe Pasternak's powers of persuasion to get her to play the most con-troversial role of her career: he was the Hungarian-born genius who had saved Universal from financial disaster by launching the fourteen-year-old Deanna Durbin with her spontaneously happy personality and incredible soprano singing range into a series of smash hit musicals, starting with the 1936 *Three Smart Girls* and revitalized Dietrich's wilting career by changing her image to that of a raunchy bar singer in the 1939 *Destry Rides Again*. There it is again – that word 'image'. Like it or not – and Doris Day has always claimed she couldn't understand what it meant – the great stars have achieved that because they *do* have a recognizable image, and if they can act as well, so much the better, which is something that Doris has recognized in her own way.

Apart from the score of the MGM musical, there was the inducement of working again with James Cagney in the pivotal role of Martin 'the Gimp' Snyder. They were together in *The West Point Story*, a real low spot of her early career, when his romantic interest in the film was Virginia Mayo, but now, in the authoritative screenplay by Daniel Fuchs and Isobel Lennart the relationship between Etting and 'the Gimp' was set out in a way that gave both stars an opportunity to portray a passionate and combative partnership. The real tension starts when Ruth achieves stardom on Broadway in *The Ziegfeld Follies* and he finds himself on the outside looking in.

She marries him out of pity, and his jealousy flares up again when the pianist Johnny Alderman (Cameron Mitchell), who loved her at the start of her rise to stardom, turns out to be the musical director on her first film. 'The Gimp' shoots Johnny and is put on trial for attempted murder: Ruth bails him out, he appears to be chastened and sets her free to marry Johnny on his recovery – all of which appears to have followed the true storyline of the Ruth Etting story, which the *Saturday Review* called, 'Probably the solidest, strongest, most credible film biography yet . . . a musical with a more than generous complement of nostalgic "oldies" neatly wrapped up by Doris Day'. She sings them in a quiet, smoky voice that is always reminiscent, but never an imitation, of Ruth Etting's, and with orchestrations and settings that capture the feel of the period.

Many have counted the Etting role as the best acting performance of her career – or at least, the one in which she extended herself the most. The *Hollywood Reporter* said, 'Doris Day comes through as a subtle and sure emotional actress . . . she makes every sullen glance, every cautious smile and every murmured commonplace speak volumes. A great popular star has become a great actress.' Doris was the only actress to be billed above James Cagney in his thirty years of Hollywood stardom. Their admiration was mutual: he compared her work with that of two of America's greatest stage actresses, Laurette Taylor and Pauline Lord, and said she had the same qualities, the 'Same capacity, same understanding of what's required and how to communicate it . . . an almost naive quality of innocence and trust. As an actress she perfectly illustrates my definition of good acting: just plant yourself, look the other actor in the eye, and tell him the truth.' Cagney also saw the parallel between the relationships of Ruth Etting and Martin

Snyder and Doris Day and Marty Melcher: he thought that both lived vicariously through their wives. The similarity was to become painfully obvious later, though Melcher did manage his wife's business career in a way Snyder would never have been capable of.

Director Charles Vidor had an undoubted flair with musicals, as had been demonstrated in two of Rita Hayworth's best, the 1945 *Cover Girl* with Gene Kelly and the following year's *Gilda*, which Ephraim Katz, the definitive film encyclopaedist, calls 'the evergreen of American screen erotica', in which the drama outweighed the musical content, especially as Hayworth's singing voice was dubbed. But whereas the drama in *Gilda* was sheer high camp melodrama, that in *Love Me or Leave Me* was the stuff of real life, albeit seen through the Hollywood glamourizing lens. The scene where Snyder rapes Ruth after she has told him she doesn't love him any more was played for real and took a great deal out of Doris – she called it 'one of the most fully realized physical scenes' she had ever played – so much so that she was disappointed to find when she finally saw the film in the cinema that most of the scene had been cut. Unlike most stars she never watched the daily rushes.

Dubbing and realism bring us to the star originally chosen to play Ruth Etting – Ava Gardner, as strange a choice as Katharine Hepburn in *Mary of Scotland* or Kay Francis's Florence Nightingale in *The White Angel* – to elevate the social stratum a tidgeon. Gardner's dark, passionate intensity was light years away from Etting's sub-nightclub queen persona, besides which, her songs would inevitably have had to be dubbed, as was evidenced when she gave her touching performance as Julie in the second re-make of *Show Boat* in 1951. The 1936 version had the tragic blues singer Helen Morgan reprising her Broadway role of the girl ostracized because she is found to have a strain of Negro blood in her and takes picturesquely to the bottle. 'Bill' and 'Can't Help Lovin' that Man' were the classic songs Kern wrote for her and Gardner wanted to have a go at them herself. That she could hold a note was proven the following year when she played a bar-room singer in *Lone Star* with Gable, but probably not up to the standard required for *Show Boat*. More to the point, Lena Horne who could have played and sung Julie magnificently was not allowed to do so because she *was* coloured. Hollywood, with that same Production Code which refused to pass the Cagney–Day rape scene, was a funny old place in the Fifties.

Ava Gardner was a prime example of a real star who consistently underestimated herself. She 'started' with a bang in the 1946 *The Killers* with the also newly 'discovered' Burt Lancaster: in fact, her MGM debut was in Norma Shearer's *We Were Dancing* in 1942, after which she played over a dozen small parts on the studio's contract roster. She went on to succeed Rita Hayworth as the Hollywood love goddess in the late Forties, until Marilyn Monroe claimed the position in the mid-Fifties. Gardner abdicated to pursue the gay (as in lively) life among the matadors of Madrid following her divorce from Frank Sinatra in 1957 after six tempestuous and highly publicised years. On her return to the screen some three years later she did some of her best work in such films as *On the Beach* with Gregory Peck, Tennessee Williams's *Night of the Iguana* in 1964 with Richard Burton and Deborah Kerr and *The Devil's Widow*, filmed as *Tam Lin* opposite the mean, moody and magnificent Ian McShane (now associated with his successful television series *Lovejoy*) directed by Roddy McDowell in 1968 in the UK, by which time Gardner had settled in London near Hyde Park. Running to swim in the Serpentine in the Eighties I often passed her walking her Corgi, Carré. She was given an open invitation to join the Swimming Club boys in the Lido for their après-swim 8 a.m. cup of tea, but though she seemed intrigued, alas the invitation was never taken up. She retained much of her beauty and magnetism through cameo roles in international films and television until a couple of years before her death, following a stroke, in 1990, the year of the posthumous publication of her autobiography.

A lovely and exciting lady, certainly – Ruth Etting, never! My first sight of Doris Day's mesmerizing performance was cycling back from a publicity date at the Birmingham Hippodrome, at a small cinema on the outskirts and I stayed to see the performance twice. The lady I had just left was the other Day in my life, the blonde and peppy Jill, leading TV glamour girl of the time and one of the loveliest faces and forms to grace the screens of the Fifties and Sixties. Like Doris, of whom she was a confirmed admirer, Jill started as a band singer, was signed without noticeable previous experience to star in a Technicolor comedy with music *All For Mary*, this same year – and there the matter rested. Since the days of Jessie Matthews and Anna Neagle, international stars of the genus female simply have not been built in this country: they have always had to cross the Atlantic to find fame and fortune. Jill took herself to Hollywood to seek a part in MGM's *Les Girls* in which our own Kay Kendall distinguished herself opposite Gene Kelly: the role she sought went to Taina Elg, who could neither sing nor dance, and Jill went on to the usual British destiny of summer shows, pantomimes and TV spots to retire, all too early, in 1970, following the tragic death of her son Douglas, named after her husband, one of the country's greatest living alto sax players, from leukaemia at an early age. She died, sadly and suddenly, days before her sixtieth birthday at the end of 1990 – another example of a bright musical talent allowed to languish unseen in the country of her birth through lack of the right opportunities.

The right opportunities were lining up for Doris Day in that year of 1955, as never before. The next year, her star ascending ever higher in the box office firmament, Alfred Hitchcock offered to make good his promise to her when they had met at a party six years previously: he had said he would like to work with her one day. The film was to be a remake of his own *The Man Who Knew Too Much*, previously shot in London in 1934, starring Leslie Banks and Edna Best, who went to Hollywood to make *Intermezzo* – a love story – with Leslie Howard and Ingrid Bergman in 1939 and stayed there for the rest of her career. The story was updated and Americanized to suit the stars, Doris and James Stewart, and the young daughter kidnapped in the first version played by four-teen-year-old Nova Pilbeam, our leading child star of the time, was transposed into a boy, Hank, son to American doctor Ben McKenna and his wife Jo, a retired musical star.

Once again, Doris was reluctant to accept the part, however intrigued and flattered she was over having been offered it by the great Hitchcock. Her main ob-jection was the travel involved, including locations in London and Marrakesh. She had never been out of the country before and her dread of flying, engendered by her tour with Bob Hope, had abated not one jot. It was Marty who talked her into it – one more positive reason Doris's admirers have for being grateful to him. So much has been written about his lack of taste and judg-ment, but he was instrumental in persuading her to take on another challenging acting role and one so different to her last, in a film that could hardly fail to be a world winner and thus advance her star status even further. He suggested they go by train and boat and take young Terry, aged fourteen, with them. Marty countered her objections to leaving her two beloved standard poodles behind by pointing out that her mother could move in to look after them, with the help of the housekeeper.

As the filmgoing world knows Marty Melcher won the day. After *Love Me Or Leave Me*, when Doris's fans were disappointed she lost out on an Academy Award nomination to two other stars of real-life musical biographies, Susan Hayward as Lillian Roth in *I'll Cry Tomorrow* and Eleanor Parker as the crippled opera star Marjorie Lawrence in *Interrupted Melody*, several interesting propositions were turned down. Whether Marty did this on behalf of Doris or she of her own volition is presumably difficult for her to elucidate after all these years. The musical remake of *The Women* opposite Howard Keel she would have liked to have done, but filming with Hitchcock assumed priority and June Allyson took the Norma Shearer 'Good Wife' role – not nearly as rewarding as the 'claws out' bitch role played by Joan Crawford and later Joan Collins. It seems the Melchers were not eager for Doris to do the remake of the Irene Dunne–Charles Boyer *Love Affair*, so Deborah Kerr stepped in to one of her most popular films ever, and the one most often repeated on television, with the possible exception of *The King and I*, *An Affair to Remember* opposite Cary Grant. Nothing came of a plan to remake *Stage Door* with Carol Channing, though the thought of either of Doris or her in the Katharine Hepburn–Ginger Rogers roles is a trifle difficult to visualize.

Another hesitation over the Hitchcock project was the

song Jay Livingston and Jay Evans had written for Doris to sing in the film. She thought it had limited appeal and saw it as primarily a children's song. Marty argued with her again and said that Hitchcock also thought it would be a hit. The name was 'Que Sera, Sera' and of course it turned out to be the most popular of all her songs when she recorded it for Columbia. Furthermore she soon realized that 'Whatever Will Be Will Be' summed up her life's philosophy of predestination.

In the event she enjoyed the trip to London, with two days and nights on the Santa Fe Super Chief to Chicago, then another luxury train to New York before boarding the *Queen Elizabeth*, where she enjoyed inordinately the peace, rest, dining at the captain's table and, above all, the privacy. The scene was very different on their way by car to their suite at Claridge's, where Doris was mobbed by crowds and they became virtual prisoners at Claridge's, with crowds camping outside and so many flowers inside that it reminded her of a funeral parlour. Terry thought it all great fun and loved getting signed photos from his mother, brought up for the occasion by a Paramount publicity man, which the boy lobbed down to the waiting crowds beneath. They had to leave the hotel secretly in the early hours to fly to Paris for dress fittings with an assistant of Edith Head's, the studio's top designer, from whence they drove to the South of France and became caught up unwillingly, as far Doris was concerned, in the Cannes Film Festival. After pleasant meetings with old friends Van Johnson, who went into a decline over the reception of his film with Deborah Kerr *The End of the Affair* from Graham Greene's novel, and Peter Ustinov, who gave them an enjoyable beach picnic, they drove to Marseilles and from thence took the boat to Morocco.

There she found nothing pleasant; the sight of the

emaciated animals physically sickened her when they arrived in Marrakesh, where the filming was to take place; she insisted Marty tell Hitchcock to send for Grace Kelly to replace her, and when that ploy failed to work she refused to go ahead with the filming until all the animals in the scenes were fed and watered. A special feeding station was set up for the horses, cows, dogs, goats, lambs, cats and any other stray animals who, had they been of a religious turn of mind, must have thought they were present for the 'Second Coming'.

Food from the community pots was something she understandably could not stomach, so she lived on hard-boiled eggs, and, even worse, she became quite desperate over the way Alfred Hitchcock not only did not give her any direction but never spoke to her after or before the scenes. Again she asked Marty to suggest to Hitchcock he send for Grace Kelly: her husband reminded her she had made a deal, which had to be honoured; this, of course, she knew, and the net result was a strong Tom Collins over dinner in the courtyard of their hotel La Menara. Christian Science or no Christian Science she had to find some release from her frustration and the predictable sequence was almost instant inebriation, with son Terry walking her round and round the fountain, until she finally retired, defeated, to oblivion on her bed.

After filming in Marrakesh she was so eager to get out of the place she accepted the proposal they fly to make up for lost time with some relief. The same mobbing took place at the Savoy, with people pitching overnight tents and calling 'We want Doris!' in the early morning, to the fury of Clifton Webb and his mother Mable, who were staying in the suite above theirs. During all the filming in London the director continued what seemed to Doris like his conspiracy of silence, and when she spoke to James Stewart about the matter, he just shrugged and said, 'That's the way he is!' As it appears that when they all dined together Hitchcock would be socially chatty and charming, it does seem somewhat singular that Doris was unable to bring herself to talk to him direct, or that Stewart, who had worked so success-fully with him in the past could not have been more reassuring.

What actually happened was that when the unit returned to Hollywood she called her agent to set up a meeting with Alfred Hitchcock for a frank discussion. He explained to her that the reason he had not given her any direction was that he was content that what she had been doing was right for the film. From then on every-thing came up roses; her over-active imagination had clearly gone into overdrive; a little consideration from him and plain speaking from her would have spared her weeks of anguish, especially as they were obviously on the same wavelength all the time. For one particularly emotional scene involving the kidnapping of her son, Hitchcock suggested that after a rehearsal before lunch they try and get it on one take in the afternoon. With her in-built self-confidence as a performer and what Cagney called 'her ability to project the simple, direct statement of a simple, direct idea without cluttering it,' the scene was achieved in the desired one take, just as she was able to do on most occasions for her recording sessions.

Her Hitchcock experience was to leave a lasting im-pression on Doris's confidence and her knowledge of film-making: she considers him a genius – maybe the only one with whom she had the privilege of working, and a 'lovely man'. Out of the doubts and uncertainties of the start of their working relationship came an affec-tion born of mutual respect.

Presumably the experience of working with Hitchcock

is what induced Daniel Gélin, one of the brightest stars of French films to play the smallish part of Louis Bernard, an intelligence agent whom the McKennas (Stewart and Day) have encountered on their holiday in French Morocco, and who is stabbed before their eyes in Marrakesh market, virtually before the unravelling of the plot. As a young romantic he had starred in such classics as *La Ronde*, *Edward and Caroline* and *Adorable Creatures*, and only the year before *The Man Who Knew Too Much* had played the title role in *Napoleon*. Other interesting players in the international cast were Brenda de Banzie and Bernard Miles (now Lord Miles), both stage actors of renown, as the seemingly nice and ordinary English couple, the Draytons, who actually kidnap Ben and Joe's son Hank (the likeably natural Christopher Olsen), assorted British stage stalwarts in Ralph Truman, Richard Wattis and Noel Willman. There were also Hollywood 'B' stars Carolyn Jones, at her best the following year as Elvis Presley's leading lady in one of his most acceptable movies, *King Creole*, famous in the Sixties as Morticia in the TV series *The Addams Family*, and Hilary Brooke, who retired when she married MGM's general manager Ray Klune in the following year, 1957.

The plot thickens as the McKennas follow the Draytons to London but are powerless to rescue Hank, who is being held hostage to ensure they do not reveal Bernard's dying message to the police that an assassination attempt is to be made on a leading statesman's life – in fact this is planned during a concert at the Albert Hall and the target is a foreign Prime Minister, due for despatch at the clash of a cymbal during Arthur Benjamin's 'Storm Cloud Cantata'. As Jo's realization of this had dawned during the symphony she screams at the crucial moment, thereby saving the life of the Prime

Minister and ultimately of her son, whom Ben rescues after a struggle with Drayton when they have found Hank at the Embassy of the Prime Minister who was to have been killed.

This is one of the Hitchcock's classics, although the critics of the day snootily rated it inferior to the 1934 version, perhaps because of the presence of Doris Day whom they tended to dismiss as a 'pop star'. In fact her performance is superb and the perfect reply to the jibes about her inability to portray anything other than a 'superannuated virgin' which persisted from the late Fifties right up to *Where Were You When the Lights Went Out?* released by MGM in 1968. The layers of subtlety were revealed by her ambivalent feelings after the kidnapping of her son to whom her attitude had been inordinately possessive and the revelation that her over-dependence on tranquillizing pills had not only imposed a strain on her marriage but had brought her to the verge of a nervous breakdown. This represents acting of the highest order: the hysteria that overtakes her as she realizes that on her lies the balance between saving her son's life and that of a perfect stranger is truly distressing to watch and something that no other of Hitchcock's 'cool blondes' could have come anywhere near conveying. Again she was pointedly overlooked by the Academy Awards nomination board. *The Hollywood Reporter* considered, 'Stewart gives one of his best performances'.

Doris, who had made Billboard's Top 100 Chart, started in 1955, with her recording of 'I'll Never Stop Loving You' by Nicholas Brodsky and Sammy Cahn, written for *Love Me Or Leave Me*, had two more hits in 1956, after 'Que Sera, Sera' which was among the top best-selling records for twenty-seven weeks – 'The Party's Over', which appeared for eleven weeks and the title song of her next film *Julie*, in for ten weeks. This was one she had personal reasons for not wanting to do. The subject of a jealous husband plotting to kill his wife was far too close to her own experiences with Al Jorden, and the excessive jealousy of Al Levy.

When she suggested to Marty that he should have shown her the script before committing her to this subject which he had felt would be fine for him to produce under the banner of MGM, with whom he had signed on her behalf a five film contract for a total of 900,000 dollars, he flew into a rage and, as usual, Doris gave in. He signed Andrew L. Stone and his wife Virginia who specialized in small-budget films shot on the actual locations, with Stone as director and his wife editor. As usual Andrew L. Stone had written the screenplay.

The story concerns Julie Benton who discovers that her new husband, Lyle (Louis Jourdan), a concert pianist, murdered her first husband to clear the way for marrying herself. She decides to leave him and he announces that he will kill her next. He is insanely jealous of anyone for whom she shows friendship, especially the sympathetic Cliff Henderson (Barry Sullivan); Detective Captain Pringle (Frank Lovejoy) is sympathetic, but the police are unable to offer her official protection, so she flees and returns to her old job as an airline stewardess. Benton tracks down Cliff, attacks him and discovers Julie's whereabouts, boarding her plane as a passenger. In the ensuing gun battle both Benton and the pilot are shot dead and Julie is left with the task of landing the plane.

Doris starts the film on a note of hysteria which she has to sustain throughout most of the footage. The whole thing was a nightmare for her from start to finish, not least in subtle changes in Marty's attitude towards her and her son Terry. As producer of the film he was showing a new tyrannical side of himself which was far from pleasant, and as Terry grew older his stepfather became less friendly and easy-going. Physically, too, the filming took its toll: not only did Doris have to take flying lessons so that she could convincingly pilot the plane to a safe touch-down at the climax, but on her way to her first lesson in the new Cadillac which was a present from Marty to her they were struck amidships by a young man in a hot-rod racer who had just driven through a red light. Miraculously, neither Marty nor Terry was injured, but the Cadillac was demolished and Doris was taken to hospital for an X-ray of the bumps and bruises incurred in the crash.

She had more emotional things to worry about: the location took in the Monterey coast from San Francisco to Carmel – her introduction to the charming coastal resort which was to become her home was the one positive benefit that accrued from the film, apart from her successful recording of the title song by Leith Stevens and Tom Adair. Doris found Louis Jourdan a sympathetic and attractive companion with whom it was far more congenial to converse than her husband, whose conversations tended to be limited to shop talk about films, profits, record albums and the like, or discussions about their Christian Science sessions.

Marty convinced himself that Doris was having an affair with the handsome French star, who was a couple of years away from his most famous film *Gigi*, but she insists that this was not so. More seriously, soon after the start of the filming of *Julie*, Doris began haemorrhaging quite seriously. Marty opposed her suggestion that she go to see her gynaecologist in Los Angeles and insisted they call their Practitioner, Martin Broones. She agreed and talked to him every day, trying to put into effect what he suggested she should relate to in the Christian Science book. She followed the advice religiously, but the haemorrhaging continued. As she featured in practically every scene going to Los Angeles would have meant closing down the film. Marty insisted that the reason her lessons were not conquering the bleeding was that she was not concentrating sufficiently on studying *Science and Health* – instead she was, 'gabbing with that Frenchman'. So she finished the film – surely a prime example of mind over matter – then disregarded Marty's orders and drove immediately to see her gynaecologist, Dr Willard Crosley; he diagnosed a tumour the size of a grapefruit growing into her intestines and insisted she be operated upon immediately at Glendale Memorial Hospital. During a four-hour operation they removed the tumour, performed a hysterectomy and rebuilt her intestines which had been seriously damaged by the giant tumour.

Her ten days in hospital and the weeks that followed were a period of intense agony, both physically and mentally. At thirty-two the thought that she could never have another baby caused her considerable anguish and the pain inside her made it difficult to walk and impossible to stand up straight. The nurses encouraged her to let the tears flow, as they did frequently, rationalizing that she had indeed plenty to cry about.

As for the film delivered of those months of painful endurance, *Julie* emerged as an entertaining variation on the husband-out-to-kill-wife theme that was not new when Frank Vosper's *Love from a Stranger* brought that intensely patrician star Ann Harding from Hollywood to Britain to be terrorized by Basil Rathbone as the lethal husband. After that ordeal she returned from the screen for five years upon marrying symphony conductor Werner Janssen, returning in 1942 in *Eyes in the Night* to play gracious character roles from then on. The slight twist at the end of *Julie*, with Doris bringing the pilotless plane down to a safe landing, manoeuvred effectively with all the intensity at her command – and that is *some* intensity. This was later emulated with additional harrowing factors by stewardess Karen Black in a plane that was literally falling to pieces; among the passengers she restored triumphantly to terra firma were Myrna Loy playing an alcoholic, singing nun Helen Reddy and Gloria Swanson, as herself dictating her memoirs, in her last film *Airport 1975*. With all these stars, plus Charlton Heston and Technicolor the *Airport* film had the edge over *Julie* for sheer arcane absurdity. However, apart from Jourdan's Gallic charm which added an extra dimension to his menacing husband that was not there in the script, the dependable Frank Lovejoy in his first film with Doris since the 1951 *I'll See You in my Dreams*, Barry Sullivan provided a stalwart pair of arms for the beleagured heroine to fall into when all her traumas were disposed of. Mae Marsh played 'Hysterical Passenger', a great star discovery of D. W. Griffith's, for whom she made one of her most notable successes in his classic 1915 *Birth of a Nation*. Like Lillian Gish she was one of the first 'perpetual virgins', until that commodity lost its marketable value, to sleep the good sleep for some three decades until a kiss from 'Prince Charming', Rock Hudson, on the cheek of our heroine restored it in a glorious Eastman-coloured, CinemaScoped and, dare we say, sophisticated version with a wave of the 'Dream Factory' wand from 'Fairy Godfather' Ross Hunter. But that is three long years away.

In the meantime Doris had a couple of happy events to cheer her out of her pain and sadness. During her recuperation she signed a new contract with Columbia Records for one million and fifty thousand dollars – the highest of its time – and she and Marty spent 150,000 dollars on a new home on North Crescent Drive in Beverly Hills, in which she lived until she moved on to Carmel. She says it was modest by Beverly Hills standards, and what appealed to her most was a giant sycamore tree which overshadowed the house. The only real shadow on the horizon was the fact that Marty would not let her invest in a new ceiling, saying that all her surplus cash had to go to Jerry Rosenthal's investment programme, to form what he called 'tax shelters'. Rosenthal was the lawyer who was officially in charge of their company's business affairs. Doris, though naturally disappointed and a little puzzled, in view of the lucrative recording contract she had just entered into, let the matter rest, as she always did, with the reflection that Marty knew better than she about such matters.

MGM wanted to hold the premiere of *Julie* in Cincinnati with special junketings to welcome their most famous daughter home, and she went along with the plan, as the film was Marty's first as actual producer. Governor Frank Lausche declared that from 8 October 1956 it would be 'Doris Day Week' throughout Ohio and the Melchers travelled there by train. Terry included Doris's public relations man, Warren Cowan, among the welter of MGM personnel who were *de rigueur* in those days. A familiar face in the crowd turned out to be that of the father she had not seen in so many years. He had, not surprisingly, aged, and she did not recognize him. When he came up to her they were unable to talk properly and she invited him to her hotel, the Plaza, for breakfast the next morning. The only sign of life she had had from him was a glass jar he had sent as a wedding present, and although she had heard he had bought some property in the black ghetto as an investment, knew nothing of his present circumstances, though she had guessed at some radical change through a new gentleness in him she sensed at their brief meeting at the station.

When he turned up for breakfast her father was, understandably, tense, but one of Marty's qualities was the ability to put most people at their ease, so the meeting was a pleasant one, though fragmented, with phone calls and the business of a day about to be devoted to publicity matters already making it difficult to have any in-depth conversation. She gathered he had given up the music that meant so much to him, but he soon made an excuse to leave and they promised to visit his home when the business side of the day was over. A liveried chauffeur drove Doris and Marty to the heart of the black ghetto in the gleaming MGM Cadillac: Warren Cowan was with them and Doris felt terribly out of place and embarrassed by such a show of ostentation contrasted with the abject poverty and squalor into which they had come. She had not yet acclimatized herself to her father's change of heart: that he, who had always been the epitome of a racist bigot, could have chosen to live there in Avondale, was quite incomprehensible to her. There was bunting festooned over the bar and grill into which her father led them; the street outside was crowded with welcoming black people.

The bar was a handsome German one and the drinks served were all German beer: Christian Science rules were set aside for the evening as she, Marty and Warren Cowan accepted the foaming steins passed to them throughout the evening. She was touched that all the records on the jukebox were of Doris Day, and delighted the company by going behind the bar to help draw the beer. Her father explained that he had gone one evening to the property which he had bought as an investment to help out the man who ran it when he was taken ill. He lost his heart to the place and the people on sight; the feeling was mutual and he had thrown in his lot with them ever since. It was then that he introduced the black lady to whom he was engaged to be married, Luvenia Williams Bennett, whom Doris greeted warmly, grateful for the vital change she had helped to bring about in her once remote and austere father. When the MGM Cadillac drove them back to their hotel she reflected that was the best party she could ever remember having been to, and the happiest time she had ever spent with her father.

She only saw him once more, several years later, when she was on her way to New York with her mother and Marty and stopped in Cincinnati to visit her aunt and uncle. To their horror she phoned her father and asked him to come round. He arrived with his wife Luvenia and another black woman, left the car and came in on his own, with the barest of perfunctory greetings to his ex-wife, who soon left the room. The meeting was terribly strained: Doris's Uncle Frank and Aunt Hilda served beer and cheese while it was all too apparent the two ladies sitting in the car outside were not going to be invited in, something Doris regretted fervently, but about which she could no nothing, and when her father left she merely waved to the ladies from the porch as the car drove off. This has evidently caused her a great deal of soul-searching through the years: it is easy to be wise after the event as she has been in saying she wished she had gone out to them, but regrets are vain, *que sera sera* and so on: what is unthinkable is that her relatives could have submitted her father and herself to such an ordeal. When he died some years later she sent flowers to the funeral but did not attend; it is a rule of hers never to go to funerals. Nor has she ever heard from Luvenia again, which perhaps has not surprised her too much, though she was grateful that he ended his life among the friends with whom he was happiest, and who called him 'Mister Bill' from the time he settled among them.

Doris returned for the last time to her old alma mater, Warner Brothers for her next film *The Pajama Game* in 1957. I am at a loss to understand the euphoria with which it was received at the time and which continues up to the present in any serious assessments of Doris Day's work. It has been called, '*the* definitive musical version of a Broadway stage hit' and Doris's performance the perfect fusion of her star persona and the character of Babe Williams, tough union representative who first feuds with then falls for John Raitt as Sid Sorokin, the new workshop superintendent of the Sleep Tight Pajama Factory. She is, indeed, excellent and fetching in her uniform, playing the role as well or better than one can imagine anyone else doing, although Janis Paige, the nominal lead of *Romance On the High Seas*, ironically ousted from the part by directors George Abbott and Stanley Donen, presumably to supply box-office appeal to back up the original stage cast including Raitt, Carol Haney and Eddie Foy Jr, drew equally ecstatic press notices on Broadway. But the suspension of disbelief called for to accept this blonde, bubbly, tuneful, agile bundle of feminine pulchritude as a rasping 'Everybody out!'-type union rep is something quite beyond me. Miriam Karlin would have been just the ticket! I have a natural aversion, anyway, to the factory system, as a result of a month's enforced labour in one, but I still find the scene hard to envisage. Possibly I hit the wrong factory.

The storyline has the union pressing for a 7½ per cent rise in wages, which Hasler, the factory manager (Ralph Dunn) refuses to countenance. After Sid and Babe have fallen in love at the annual union picnic and the boss again refuses to compromise, Sid breaks up a 'Go Slow' ordered by the union and Babe sabotages her sewing machine, causing a blow-out in the factory's electrical system. He is forced to fire her, until he discovers that Hasler has been allotted an increase for the workers which has been going into his own bank account. Naturally he yields to pressure, and as in all the best pantomimes is reunited with the happy workers, while Sid and Babe climb into the latest spotted pyjama wear for the finale.

Carol Hanley (Gladys Hotchkiss), an Olive Oyl-shaped comedienne with a distinctive style, is un-accountably in love with Eddie Foy Jr as Vernon Hines, a jealous maniac with a penchant for knife-throwing, but she does get to give splendid account of herself in Richard Adler and Jerry Ross's exciting 'Hernando's Hideaway'. She leads her factory worker friends into a joyous song and dance – their 'Once A Year Day' at the company picnic imaginatively choreographed by Bob Fosse. Doris, naturally, gets the lion's share of the splendid Adler-Ross score, with 'Hey There', as she sings to herself in a mirror, at the same time celebrating and questioning her love for John Raitt. This kind of example of acting through song is a rare gift and one I can only remember equalled, many years before by Gracie Fields in the 1936 *Queen of Hearts* when she sang 'Why Did I Have to Meet You?' to a photograph of John Loder playing a film star whom she, as a poor working girl, pines for. At the end, in a gesture of resignation, she tears the picture into fragments. Doris's duets with Raitt, 'Small Talk' and 'There Once Was a Man' are by turns evocatively tender, sexy and raunchy, both stars teaming in effortless accord.

Despite the general acclaim *The Pajama Game* was not the financial success its makers had expected. 1957 was the year when musicals, including Stanley Donen's other musical, the exquisite *Funny Face*, with Fred Astaire and Audrey Hepburn, and Astaire's *Silk Stockings*, a remake of *Ninotchka*, with Cyd Charisse in Garbo's part, were failing to hit the jackpot at the box office. Marty Melcher was astute enough to recognize that a change of pace was necessary if his wife was going to maintain her peak box office ratings and the first film that reflected this metamorphosis was the 1958 *Teacher's Pet*, a black and white comedy with Clark Gable as a bombastic newspaper editor, a character in which he had excelled before, notably in the 1935 *After Office Hours* with Constance Bennett as his female oppo, with whom he first fights, contemptuous of what he considers her limited mental abilities as a journalist. In Doris Day's case his contempt is over the fact that she teaches journalism courses at a night college. As Professor Erica Stone, Doris plays an intellectual for the first time and modifies her natural vivacity accordingly, teaming charmingly with Gable's Jim Gannon, despite the obvious disparity in their ages: his first sight of the pretty teacher he had assumed would be an acidulous blue-stocking is played with the kind of Puckish bafflement that had become one of his most successful stock-in-trades through the years. He enrols in her classes, amazing her with his quick grasp of the essentials of journalism, the truth comes out inevitably and their mutual animosity turns, of course, to love.

Gig Young is on hand again, as a suave admirer of Erica's, Hugo Pine, with a penchant for the bottle, and it was presumably for his over-long and over-played hangover scene that he was nominated for an Oscar. Then there's Mamie Van Doren as burlesque queen Peggy DeFore to whom Jim Gannon has evidently related in the past. She certainly puts her all into her act, and then some, as she bumps and grinds her way through 'The Girl Who Invented Rock n' Roll' watched by Jim, Hugo and Erica in a nightclub, which of course is where Mamie claims she was slighted by Doris Day, provoking her indignant rebuttal in Christopher Frayling's documentary 'I Don't Even *Like* Apple Pie'. Mamie Van Doren wrote to me about this. 'I have not seen Miss Day's documentary, but might force myself to sit through it just to see her reaction. As you will recall from my book, I described her unpleasant behaviour toward me and her childish tantrums on the set of *Teacher's Pet* – behaviour which annoyed Clark Gable and director George Seaton. I can offer no explanation to her reaction to Professor Frayling's mention of my book – except that the truth hurts.' There the case rests. Her actual words were: 'I had looked forward to meeting Doris Day. A mutual friend of ours Charlotte Hunter, a dance coach from Universal, told me what a warm, friendly person Doris was. Doris had always been one of my favourite singers, with hits like "It's Magic". I had also become a fan of her movies after seeing *Love Me Or Leave Me*, in which she played opposite James Cagney.

'Nevertheless, our first meeting on the *Teacher's Pet* set was far from what I expected. Doris ignored me when we were introduced and proceeded to conduct herself like a spoiled star. George Seaton and Gable had to stoically bear her tantrums and disagreeable attitude.

'Her dislike for me became most apparent when it was time to shoot reaction shots of Doris, Gable and Gig Young watching a dance number I did while singing "The Girl Who Invented Rock n' Roll". Doris failed in take after take to smile radiantly while watching me dance. Finally Seaton called for my Double to be positioned off-camera so that Doris could watch someone who could produce the required reaction. Doris's cold attitude toward me never improved, and mercifully we saw little of each other during the film.'

Teacher's Pet drew the biggest audiences to a Doris Day film since *Love Me Or Leave Me*, and the title song stayed in the charts for twelve weeks. This, like the Mamie Van Doren number, was written by Joe Lubin, and later that year she had another huge hit disc with 'Everybody Loves a Lover', a front-runner on Billboard's Top 100 for fourteen weeks. The popularity of *Teacher's Pet* pointed the way for the role model Doris was to assume, with variations, from the next year's *Pillow Talk* through some of her biggest successes, that of that confident, successful 'virgin' businesswoman – an equal to any of the males in repartee, mental acumen and all the attributes of the macho male represented by the likes of Gable, though he did meet his match in a number of strong leading ladies like Colbert, Crawford, Harlow and Rosalind Russell. By the end of the film Gable and Day have agreed that there is something to be said for each other's point of view – his original thesis that the only way to learn journalism is by practical hard graft being modified finally by his consenting to deliver a series of guest lectures at her classes. The screenplay of Fay and Michael Kanin neatly wraps up the compromise in the editor conceding that, 'experience is the jockey, but education is the horse', while the professor admits that everything about journalism cannot be learned from a text-book. Q.E.D.

She seems to have had considerable affection and respect for Gable's inner strength and utter simplicity. She must have suffered for him when it became known what a toll the perpetual lateness and unreliability of Marilyn Monroe took of his stamina during the last film that either of them made, John Huston's *The Misfits* in 1961, and this may account for the perceptible coolness Doris had displayed when talking about Monroe.

A sad blow just before the start of the filming of

Teacher's Pet was the sudden death of Doris's brother Paul. He had been working on the publicity for the musical side of Arwin Productions, having moved with his wife and children to Los Angeles and had been very proficient at his job, but the baseball injury of his youth finally took its toll after a lifetime of combating the seizures to which he was prone and he was a regular drug user. Sam Weiss has gone so far as to say that he feels that Marty Melcher's attitude to Paul was a contributory factor to his death. He says that his brother-in-law treated him shabbily and demeaningly, not paying him a decent wage to keep his wife and children, although he was working so hard on Doris's behalf. Paul never complained, so she never found out: if she had it would have been one more distressing circumstance in the changing relationship she had with her husband, who was getting even deeper in his business involvement with the lawyer Jerry Rosenthal, instead of concentrating on producing his wife's films. After *Julie* he let others do the actual producing, while he was billed as co-producer, with a 50,000 dollar fee. Then his attitude to Terry had moved far away from the chummy relationship they had in the beginning. Eventually he took him away from the Christian Science School where he was happy and sent him to Harvard military academy in Beverly Hills, which he hated. Doris tried to remonstrate, but Marty insisted that Terry was associating with a bad element among the local youth where they were living in Toluca Lake and that boarding school from Monday to Thursday would be just the ticket to keep him out of mischief: he would come home for the weekends, Friday to Sunday. She regretted, as always, that she had not stood her ground where her son was concerned, but as she was working studio hours all week, and on Sundays preparing for the next week, the bulk of the decisions always rested with

Marty, though later she was to say that Terry was not the type to submit to the rigorous discipline of a military school, into which 'love has never found its way'.

One of the most ruinous and expensive projects in which Jerry Rosenthal involved Marty, and through him, the totally unwilling Doris, was a garish hotel in Palo Alto, near San Francisco, where she found herself committed to attending a gala opening of a hotel she loathed and of which she was the nominal owner. She argued with some bitterness, but in the end Marty had his way and Doris had to content herself with glaring at Rosenthal at the next table, with a group of Hollywood rowdies swigging champagne at her expense. 'I just looked daggers at him, hoping one of them would pierce his gizzard,' she wrote.

The same year as *Teacher's Pet* Marty made an altogether unfortunate decision to star Doris in an adaptation of the stage play *Tunnel of Love*, which was a total flop, despite some surprisingly enthusiastic reviews in the American press: the *Hollywood Reporter* praised Gene Kelly's 'expert direction' and 'Miss Day's clean playing of sexy situations. She's as wholesome as wheatgerm, as bubbly as champagne.' This conjures up some kind of detergent – the kind with which the whole tasteless concoction should have been swilled down the plug-hole. Joseph Fields, the official producer, also wrote the script, based on his own play with Peter DeVries, with, of course, Marty Melcher as co-producer. The film was in CinemaScope, but photographed in black and white, with Doris as Isolde Poole, who longs for a baby of her own, so she and her husband Augie (Richard Widmark) try to adopt one. Their next-door neighbours Dick Pepper (Gig Young, again an alcoholic lothario) and his wife Alice are prolific in producing progeny – this role reunites Doris with Elisabeth Fraser, her sister from *Young at Heart*. Due to some improbable plot peregrinations, the drunken Augie takes the at first po-faced adoption rep Estelle Novick (Gia Scala) to dinner and passes out at a motel to which they had driven. When he receives a letter months later asking for a loan as Estelle is going to have a baby he assumes it is his, and so later does the suspicious Isolde. But of course it's not, and, surprise, surprise, as the credit titles roll she finds she is going to have a little one of her own.

The constant repetition of the same stale joke about the hilarity of being unable to conceive, or, conversely, being unable to stop conceiving, is wearisome in the extreme, and Widmark is far from being a natural comedian, although he throws himself with gusto into the absurd situations, with expert backing from Gig Young. There's an intriguing parallel to the *Teacher's Pet* situation at a dance where a very sexy young actress-model, played by Vikki Dougan, makes heavy play for Augie and receives one of her 'daggers' looks from Doris, putting one in mind of the line spoken by June Havoc in a Rosalind Russell comedy, 'I'm liable to throw you a dirty look, and where I throw dirty looks no grass grows – ever!' This dirty look is accompanied by a song from Doris, 'Runaway, Skidaddle, Skidoo', which didn't make the charts, but neatly fitted the occasion.

The 1959 *It Happened to Jane* was also, and more understandably, enthused over by the press, as was Doris's part as a 'free spirit' – a homespun version of the independent type of young woman who cropped up in so many of her movies. This time she is a mail order lobster dealer – Jane Osgood, a young widow with a small boy, Billy, played by Teddy Rooney. When a shipment of lobsters is ruined through the inefficiency of the railroad company she becomes involved in a prolonged battle with Harry Foster Malone, chairman of the railroad, with the backing of her lawyer, George Denham (Jack Lemmon). The to-ings and fro-ings of the plot include Jane winning her action for damages and when Malone (Ernie Kovacs) appeals, she legally seizes one of the company's trains which brings her much publicity and support until he counteracts by cancelling all train stops at Cape Ann, the small town where she lives. Denham talks the townsfolk back into supporting her, and he and Jane decide to take their lobsters to market in the train they commandeered from Malone. He craftily sends them on a cross-country route through New England, until George Denham persuades him to relent. Jane finally makes up her mind to marry George – she literally forces him to propose while he is shovelling coal into the old train engine – a scene which highlights the happy rapport between Lemmon and Day, who has, not without regret, rejected the offer of marriage from Steve Forrest as Larry Hall, a smart and attractive young newspaperman who has espoused her cause.

Richard Quine's subtle direction has been compared with that of Capra, in the updated 'common man' (woman in this case) comedy against the forces of tycoonery. Doris's performance – from her first appearance as a dungareed lobster farmer to the scene where, clad in a pristine white dress, she climbs aboard the train and helps George furiously stoke up the boiler in a frantic race against time to get her crustaceans to market, thereby putting paid to the machinations of the demonic Ernie Kovacs – is a joy to behold. Her teaming with Jack Lemmon is so felicitous it makes one regret it was to be their only film together, to date. The townsfolk, headed by the redoubtable Mary Wickes, are all recognizable small-town stereotypes, and young Billy, as played by Teddy Rooney, is entirely natural and engaging.

Despite all these assets and the plaudits of the critics the film was, unequivocally, another flop. Reasons for this have been advanced, including the choice of title, which during the filming was *That Jane from Maine*. Later it was re-released as *Twinkle and Shine*, which suggests a Twenties British musical comedy. Unsurprisingly that did nothing to help the box office. Jack Lemmon thought a lot of the film and even more of Doris Day. He blames the title for its failure, and his experience of working with her is the direct antithesis of Mamie Van Doren's. He found her always good-humoured and caring for her colleagues as if they were her family, and to him acting with her was an elevating experience making those who played with her want to rise to her level in bringing the best possible quality to a scene. He felt in her 'an enticing sexual quality that is there but subliminal. She doesn't lay it out there, like a Marilyn Monroe, but it's there, nevertheless – the difference between a nude and a woman in seductive clothing.'

What Doris needed now if she were to maintain her pre-eminent status at the box office was an important new production. Twentieth Century-Fox were readying a screen version of the smash hit Rodgers and Hammerstein musical *South Pacific* and they thought she would be ideal to play Nellie Forbush, the part to which Mary Martin had brought such éclat on Broadway. Doris agreed and was as excited over the prospect as over anything she had done to date. The fly in the ointment was the vast salary Marty Melcher was asking for his wife's services: in the event the studio passed and gave the role to their contract player Mitzi Gaynor. The film was an inevitable success but lacked Doris's own special potent brand of magic, which could have made it one of the greatest musical classics of all time.

6

Pillow Talk and a
New Deal

Ross Hunter had a theory for which many stars have
had cause to be grateful: 'There's no such thing as a
dated actor'; already in 1959 the big movie chains that
book the pictures were telling him Doris Day and Rock
Hudson were things of the past, who had been overtaken
by the newer stars, just as, in the Thirties Dietrich,
Crawford, Hepburn and West were all written off as
'Box Office Poison'. Every one of them went on to scale
new heights in the succeeding decades. In 1959, a year
after Lana Turner had been the subject of worldwide
denunciations after the scandal of her teenage daughter
Cheryl Crane stabbing her mother's lover, Johnny Stom-
ponato to death, Hunter showed his faith in her by
starring her in the remake of Fanny Hurst's *Imitation of
Life*, which had been a big success for Claudette Colbert
in the Thirties. Turner again gave the lie to those who
claimed she was just a manufactured MGM commodity, elevated to stardom after her original *Sweater
Girl* publicity, and unable to act her way out of a body
stocking. She was magnificent in the 1946 version of
The Postman Always Rings Twice opposite John Garfield
and Oscar-nominated for *Peyton Place* in 1957: she gave
another creditable performance for Ross Hunter in

Portrait in Black in 1960 and six years later in the perennial *Madame X*.

He felt that it was essential for Doris Day to change her image if she was to survive as a top star. She had been the girl next door for too many years, and now at thirty-five needed to catch up with her moviegoing public, who had grown more sophisticated with the passing of the decades, and who would appreciate a new Doris even more sophisticated than they. They needed someone whom they could look up to and emulate. For her part she felt the same: she recognized that the wholesome standard 'Doris Day movie' was becoming an anachronism and the box office returns reflected that fact. Of course, *Love Me Or Leave Me* and *The Man Who Knew Too Much* were giant strides in the right direction, but the films since then had been of uneven quality, and now a whole new deal was called for, a complete metamorphosis into the persona of the 'Girl Who Didn't Even Like Apple Pie'.

Sex was the name of the ingredient and that was something vital to box office even before Mae West thought she had invented it. Doris, of course, had always had sex appeal, but, as Jack Lemmon said, subliminal, hidden behind the freckles, the chintzy dresses and the down-to-earth no-nonsense personality – an amalgam of which was last on view in *It Happened to Jane*. As Ross Hunter so picturesquely put it, 'No one realized that under all those dirndls lurked one of the wildest asses in Hollywood'. So he sent her the script of *Pillow Talk* and she was attracted by Stanley Shapiro's screenplay instantly, as the humour came from characterization and situation rather than gags. However, being genuinely unaware of her own potential as a sex symbol, which surely lay at the base of her appeal from the beginning, she had difficulty visualizing herself as a chic interior decorator. It would have been no good her suggesting Hunter send for Grace Kelly, because this time she had moved to a loftier stratum of society, so after a slight argument Doris allowed him to persuade her that she wasn't just an old-fashioned girl and that he would get Jean Louis to create some sensational gowns to show off her 'wild fanny' (sic), his make-up department to evolve a new-look maquillage and coiffure and she would end up looking like every modern woman's dream of perfection.

That agreed, there was the slight problem of Marty Melcher wanting to use his co-producer's prerogative to change the title to *Anyway The Wind Blows*, which by a rare chance was the title of a song he was about to publish. Ross must have had his own kind of quiet strength to have dealt with so many high-powered lady stars and the title remained the way it had started out. From the word go Doris was happy and everyone around her was happy. She loved the producer's evident taste and his lavishness in spending money where it really mattered. The gowns Jean Louis executed for her made her euphoric and she adored everything he created for her. She felt they enhanced her body and the part she was playing, and the make-up and hairdos were of the kind she had dreamed of but never experienced before. She has pulled no punches about, 'the Warner Brothers embalmers who posed as make-up men', and felt that at last the contemporary modern girl struggling to get out from behind the apple-cheeked façade was making her way into a new era.

Some things remain a constant in Doris Day movies, before and after 'the new deal', including a title song for the star: this time Buddy Pepper and Inez James composed the peppy 'Pillow Talk'. Apart from the elegance of the sets by Alexander Golitzen and Richard H. Riedel and the Jean Louis gowns, the new element was Rock Hudson as leading man, playing Brad Allen, a philandering songwriter, who shares a party line with Doris's Jan Morrow, a self-sufficient and successful interior decorator. She despises the kind of 'who's for the next lay?' attitude that is Allen's stock-in-trade, especially as he is always on the line dating his girls when she, Jan, wants to use the phone for business purposes. Never having met him she is taken in by his impersonation of a simple Texan, Rex Stetson, which he uses when he is surprised to find himself attracted to the angry neighbour, with whom he has had several altercations over the phone line. His friend Jonathan Forbes, a rich impresario who is also in love with Jan is played by Tony Randall: he is unable to persuade Brad to disclose his real identity, which she inadvertently discovers during a romantic idyll in the country. Hurt and angry she returns to her interior decorating business, and when Brad commissions her firm to redecorate his apartment she revenges herself by furnishing it to look like a bordello. She wins game, set and match after registering with satisfaction his rage and discomfiture and his intention to leave the place to her when she replies that she intends to stay there with him.

This, for a start, gives the lie to the 'eternal virgin' gibe: after at first strenuously opposing his assumption that she will be a pushover like his other girls it is she who makes the running after admitting to herself that she has been with a lot of men in her life, but it is he who represents the prime catch, to be savoured at her leisure after she has established with him her integrity as a woman. No virgin, she, and it is he who capitulates in the end in this role reversal of *The Taming of the Shrew* situation.

She has two desirable leading men to choose from: the

highly dishy Rock Hudson, giving a good account of himself in his first comedy role, which the persuasive Ross Hunter had assured him he could do, and the suavely understanding Tony Randall, that superbly adroit pointer of comedy lines, as her millionaire suitor. Both men evidently loved working with Doris: Hudson said that he received good advice from the director Michael Gordon, who told him, 'Comedy is the most serious tragedy in the world. Play it that way and you can't go wrong. If you ever think of yourself as funny you haven't got a chance,' but the best acting lesson came from his co-star, whose sense of timing and instincts provided a wonderful blueprint for comedy. He thought she was an actor's studio all by herself: 'When she cried,' he says, 'she cried funny,' a quote that has gone round the world, and one she has been happy to repeat in interviews. Happily for teamwork, Tony Randall worked with her again in the 1962 *Lover Come Back* and two years later in *Send Me No Flowers*, also with Rock Hudson: their contrasting comedy styles blended admirably – Hudson admired what he called Randall's deliberate, 'holding back kind of comedy' but said it would never work for him.

Despite all the signs that they had a comedy which worked like magic, with the additional bonus of the popular gravel-voiced comedienne, Thelma Ritter as the alcoholic housemaid, Alma and practised support from comedy veterans Allen Jenkins, Lee Patrick as a client of Doris's Mrs Walters and Marcel Dalio, Ross Hunter had great difficulty getting anyone to book it. Everyone told him that sophisticated comedies like *Pillow Talk* went out with William Powell and Myrna Loy. Eventually he persuaded Sol Schwartz, owner of the Palace Theater on Broadway, to book it for a two-week run. It struck oil immediately, romantic comedy became the in-thing again and theatre owners who had turned him down had to close their deals on his terms. Not only was Doris at last nominated for an Academy Award, but by the end of 1959 she had shot up to number one at the box office, a position she maintained for five years.

Her next film, in 1960 was a complete change of pace and with another new leading man, the debonair David Niven in *Please Don't Eat the Daisies*, a screenplay by Isobel Lennart, based on Jean Kerr's best-seller, Doris plays Kate Mackay, the wife of Larry Mackay, a former professor of drama who is launching his career as a New York drama critic by reviewing a musical produced by his friend Alfred North (Richard Haydon). He lets his friend down as gently as possible – the show is a stinker – North is outraged and leading lady Deborah Vaughn (Janis Paige) slaps his face. Larry finds himself a celebrity due to the resultant publicity and Kate, worried that his success is affecting his judgment, forces a move to Hooten, seventy miles from New York, where they acquire an old house, while he stays in an hotel to try and meet a publishing deadline. Kate busies herself with refurbishing the house, looking after their four children and shaggy dog Hobo, and plunges herself into local amateur dramatics. In the meantime the musical comedy queen Deborah has forgotten her fury and followed Larry to his hotel in Hooten. Plot ramifications galore emphasize the episodic nature of the storyline involving Alfred North submitting a play which turns out to be one written by Larry at college: Larry permits a benefit performance but prematurely pans the play, thus re-affirming his integrity as a drama critic. Kate and he resolve differences and life returns to normal after her spirited attempt to establish her own identity by involving herself in local dramatics and by spiriting the family away from New York to the country.

Previously unreleased shot of Doris as the virtuous advertising executive
Carol Templeton in *Lover Come Back* (1962).

Previously unreleased shot of Doris with Cary Grant, taken
during the filming of *That Touch of Mink* (1962).

As the wife terrorized by an unknown killer, with Rex Harrison in *Midnight Lace* (1960).

Right: With her other favourite co-star, James Garner and, left to right, Casey Adams and Fred Clark in *Move Over, Darling* (1963), the film she 'inherited', with a title change from *Something's Gotta Give*, after the tragic death of Marilyn Monroe.

One of the more bizarre moments from *Move Over, Darling*.

Previously unreleased shot from 1964 of Doris admiring the roses in the garden of her previous [Beverly Hills] home in Los Angeles.

Previously unreleased shots. *Above:* Doris being kissed by her co-star and friend Rock Hudson, in their comedy movie, *Lover Come Back* (1962). *Below:* Doris having fun trying hats in a Beverly Hills milliners (1964).

Left: Pause for a laugh with Rod Taylor between sessions with the script of *The Glass Bottom Boat* (1966).

Below left: Waiting to be called before the camera for the third series of *The Doris Day Show* (1970). *Below right:* With mother Alma at a Seventies Animal Rights Meeting.

Left: With Guest Star Perry Como on *The Doris Mary Anne Kappelhoff Special* (1971). *Below:* Doris cycling – her favourite form of relaxation (1980). *Bottom left:* At home in Carmel, with two of her dearest friends.

Doris Day Animal Foundation and
      Doris Day Animal League
Suite 100
227 Massachusetts Avenue NE
Washington
DC 20002 USA
www.ddaf.org   www.ddal.org

Top left: Photo call with Rock Hudson – his last appearance – for *Doris Day's Best Friends* (1985). *Top right:* With Clint Eastwood at the Golden Globe Awards, accepting her Lifetime Achievement award (1989). *Above:* With Pierre Patrick, the producer of musical *My Doris Day*, at her home in Carmel (2000).

Joe Lubin wrote the title song, and Doris sings a reprise of 'Que Sera, Sera', the teaming of Doris and Niven is delightful, with a real feeling of their genuine affection for each other despite their identity clashes; Hobo the dog is a splendid affirmation of her always great love for shaggy animals, and the four boys, with baby Adam taking special pleasure in dropping water bags out of the window, constitute an entirely convincing family mix. For all his sophistication David Niven is entirely at ease as a paterfamilias with a nicely easy platonic relationship with the admirable Janis Paige as the sexy actress – now well into her stride as a comedienne with a touch of the camp. Comedy proliferates: the supporting cast are the adorable Spring Byington, as dithery as ever, rasping Patsy Kelly as the maid, Maggie dropping pearls of wise-cracking wisdom as she had done during the decades, with Richard Haydn's deadpan British drollery splendidly to the fore as the pompous playwright, Jack Weston, making bricks without straw to get laughs, and ex-leading lady Margaret Lindsay as pretty as ever in the peripheral role of Mona James.

The film cleverly pinpointed Doris Day's versatility – from sexpot interior decorator to warm and loveable housewife and mother in one stride – she renders the title song delightfully, capering round the garden with the children and the faithful and boisterous Hobo in attendance, the whole making a great contrast to the sophisticated elegance and dialogue of *Pillow Talk*. *Please Don't Eat the Daisies* was released for Easter 1960 and was so popular it consolidated her position as number one box office attraction. Statistics show, as far as can be ascertained, that her profit for each of her films at that time was in the neighbourhood of one million dollars.

It was back to Ross Hunter and opulent settings for

her next film of that year, *Midnight Lace*; the gowns were as glamorous as those in *Pillow Talk*, only this time they were designed by Irene, one of Hollywood's greatest, who created the costumes for MGM stars from 1938 and during the Forties, after she formed her own company. Constance Bennett in *Merrily We Live* was the first, Katharine Hepburn in *Without Love* and *The State of the Union*, Claudette Colbert in *The Palm Beach Story*, Greer Garson in *Gaslight* and *Mrs Parkington* were among the top ladies who were delighted with the designs she did for them, and Doris Day enthused about Irene's elegant American look, a contrast to the French ambience of Jean Louis, but every bit as stunning. During the two films on which they worked together they became close friends and Irene, a sad woman who drank heavily, confided to Doris that the love of her life was Gary Cooper, although she never made it clear whether they had actually ever been lovers, or if it was an entirely one-sided romance. She had an unhappy marriage to a man she saw only occasionally. The last film Irene designed for Doris was *Lover Come Back* in 1962: Gary Cooper had died from cancer the previous year and Doris was at the studio getting her hair done when she heard on the radio the announcement that Irene had jumped to her death from her hotel room at the Knickerbocker after booking in under an assumed name.

The content of *Midnight Lace* was as different from Doris's most recent films as could possibly be imagined – a fact that critics of the last and most successful part of her career ignore when they complain of the 'sameness' of her films between 1959 and 1968. It was a psychological thriller based on Janet Green's play *Matilda Shouted Fire*, with a script by Ivan Goff and Ben Roberts that impressed Doris as so well-written that she yielded again to Marty's insistence that she do it, although it was in the genre of *Julie*, which she had hated so much: she was once more being trailed by a killer, only this time the interest lay in who the unseen but very much audible menace could be.

Doris plays Kit, married to a rich English business-man, Tony Preston (Rex Harrison); the film starts with her walking through the fog of a London park when a sing-song voice assails her from the enveloping pea-souper – very rich in EastmanColor – and from then on she is the victim of repeated obscene phone calls which invariably end with a death threat. The police clearly think she is hallucinating and even Tony and her glamorous Aunt Bea (Myrna Loy), visiting from Amer-ica have their doubts, until Bea picks up the telephone and takes the call intended for Kit. Only the dishy young building contractor on the site next door, Brian Younger (John Gavin), offers her sympathy and appears to believe her, and it is he who is on hand to play Sir Galahad at the dénouement, when Tony, apparently using his best endeavours to help her track down the hidden terror, turns out to be the villain. He has been plotting with his mistress Peggy Thompson (Natasha Parry) to arrange a murder which can be passed off as suicide. Brian rescues Kit after a chase round the top of his scaffolding, and he and Aunt Bea help the distraught heroine away from the scene.

Making all allowances for a very bizarre Hollywood conception of London the interesting cast supply the Britishness, from the suave Rex Harrison down to the small part players. There's Herbert Marshall, the British stage star who became something of a romantic team in early British talkies with his wife Edna Best in films like *Michael and Mary* and *The Faithful Heart* before settling in Hollywood after going there to appear with Marlene

Dietrich in *The Blonde Venus* in 1932. He played opposite such stars as Claudette Colbert in *Four Frightened
People*, Norma Shearer in *Riptide*, Constance Bennett
in *Outcast Lady* (*A Woman of the World* in the UK,
from Michael Arlen's *The Green Hat*) and Garbo in
The Painted Veil, all in 1934, when he enjoyed a well-
publicized affair with Gloria Swanson. After *The Letter*
with Bette Davis in 1940, he turned to character roles,
like his Charles Manning, business associate to Rex
Harrison in *Midnight Lace* – a very palpable red herring
for the villain stakes. Next in order of billing is Natasha
Parry as the girl next to Doris in the bus queue when she
is mysteriously almost pushed under a red double-
decker. She made her début as a Rank Charm School
starlet in the film *Dance Hall* – another of her class in the
film of 1949 was Diana Dors, who went on to international stardom of a sort, while Natasha Parry, despite
striking dark beauty and her marriage to British stage
director Peter Brook, has appeared only spasmodically
on stage and screen since.

Others on the bill make it look like a *Who's Who* of
English character actors: as the friendly pub landlady,
Hermione Baddeley was a top revue star of the London
stage since the Second World War – she and the 'Other
Hermione', Gingold had a reputation for their witty, not
to say waspish, tongues – and after becoming an occasional star of such British films as Graham Greene's
Brighton Rock with the young Richard Attenborough,
now elevated to the peerage, made various appearances
in Hollywood films like *The Unsinkable Molly Brown* and
Mary Poppins. Elspeth March, the talkative woman in
the bus queue with Doris and Natasha Parry, although
mainly famous for having been married to Stewart
Granger, who left her to marry Jean Simmons, was a
distinguished stage actress in her own right. She ap-

peared successfully in the early Eighties revival of *The Last of Mrs Cheyney*, starring Joan Collins at the Chichester Festival Theatre. Richard Ney, American born, but specializing in playing British juveniles, including the son of Greer Garson in *Mrs Miniver*, whom he later married, Welsh character actor Rhys Williams, who made his Hollywood début for John Ford in *How Green Was My Valley*, Terrence DeMarney – Peter Cheyney's Slim Callaghan in the film *Uneasy Terms*, Anthony Dawson, another red-herring sinister presence to frighten Doris, and Doris Lloyd were just a few of the actors imported to give authenticity to the London scene. Not too successfully, it has to be said. Of all this group the doyenne was undoubtedly Doris Lloyd, the Liverpool-born stage actress who emigrated to Hollywood in the silent days, and became a supporting grande dame/working woman/housekeeper until the year before her death in 1968. She even played Mrs Winston Churchill in the 1943 *Mission to Moscow*. In *Midnight Lace* she is Nora, the anxious mother to one of Britain's prime child exports to the States, Roddy McDowell, here acting very queerly indeed as yet another suspect, Malcolm.

Myrna Loy, whose quizzical sense of humour as Aunt Bea is such an asset to the film tells in her autobiography *Being and Becoming* that, despite trying to play the part as a nice, witty and wise woman it all went for nothing because people thought she was working with Rex Harrison to kill her niece. She says, 'That's the danger of being in a mystery. You're all suspect, no matter what you do.' She was delighted that Irene was designing the clothes for the film, having practically discovered her for her personal wardrobe years before she went to MGM as a couturier. It appears that Ross Hunter had lured Irene out of semi-retirement to work on his films: it is fascinating that he modelled his stars on Loy and William Powell: 'I took Doris Day out of the kitchen, put Rock Hudson in tails, after running eight of the Powell–Loy comedies.' He said that he'd never worked with anyone who gave so much to a role, affirming his tenet, 'Once a star, always a star.' He did the same for Constance Bennett in *Madam X* six years later, and, the same year as *Midnight Lace*, Anna May Wong, Hollywood's long-retired exotic oriental star of such films as *Daughter of the Dragon* and *King of Chinatown*, where she was actually born in Los Angeles. She died the year after her come-back in *Portrait in Black*.

Of Doris, Myrna Loy says, 'I have nothing but the best to say. She was wonderful to me, really lovely. She sent flowers when I started, and remained friendly and attentive. As I've said, it's difficult when you start stepping down. You fight so hard to get to the top and then you realize it's time to gracefully give in a little. Doris, who was riding high then, never played the prima donna. I appreciate her attitude enormously.' John Gavin, she found very handsome: Ross Hunter was trying to groom him into another Rock Hudson – but she didn't think he quite had what it takes, and Rex Harrison, grieving for the death of his wife Kay Kendall, seemed to have little time for her or anyone else, but she was always pleased to team up again with her long-time friend Roddy McDowall, who called her 'Fu' referring back to the 1931 *Mask of Fu Manchu* in her oriental days, when she played Boris Karloff's sadistic nymphomaniac daughter.

Natasha Parry, although she did not have a great deal to do with Doris in her role of Harrison's mistress, was also high in her praises when I talked to her after her success in 1989 at Richmond's Orange Tree Theatre in Bernard Shaw's *Mrs Warren's Profession*. Doris was unfailingly kind and courteous – and Natasha was deeply impressed by Doris's meticulous attention to detail. 'She would be in hours before everyone else, and I watched her apply the right shade of make-up to her legs to tone with the stockings she would be wearing in each scene.'

These happy memories aside, the filming was traumatic for Doris, perhaps even more so than *Julie* had been, especially in the scene in which she had to become hysterical. The 'Method' actress in her – her own method – made her relate back to the time Al Jorden had burst into her room, dragged her from bed and hurled her against the wall . . . It was all too real – acting was transformed into reality and she fainted after the take. Director David Miller and Marty attended her in her dressing room and she was sent home for a few days to recuperate. After Doris's hysterics which were uncontrollable and led to her collapse, Myrna Loy stepped in to do an unscheduled scene in one take. 'That's a star!' said Hunter.

After a light dinner in bed Doris listened to Marty singing some of her favourite Christian Science hymns: this was the Marty she had felt such empathy with at the beginning of their marriage, and the religion that had so much power to soothe and tranquillize. She slept soundly that night and did not awaken once until morning, when she felt refreshed enough to return to the set, but with the proviso that she should never attempt another film with the same kind of theme. Marty agreed with her and she was able to get through the ordeal. She says how real the concern was everyone showed for her – even Rex Harrison solicitously escorted her to her car after her fainting spell, and she was grateful for his light British sense of humour, which helped to steady her during the more upsetting scenes in the movie. I worked with Rex on a film and years later met him at the Haymarket theatre; he was charming on both occasions – when he was nice he was very very nice . . .

Director David Miller has often been rated as a highly competent technician, lacking in originality but in this kind of thriller he had few peers. He has been sniped at for keeping Doris in a state of near hysteria which had her screaming for almost two hours. This gives the director no credit for keeping a film about tension on an escalating note of frenzy or the actress for her almost unbearably distressing display of nerves: he had done the same with Joan Crawford in the 1952 *Sudden Fear*, but her more cerebral approach to acting and her almost total lack of vulnerability made her undoubtedly fine display of panic less totally involving than Doris's. Miller also put Crawford effectively through her paces in the best of her pre-Grand Guignol roles, *The Story of Esther Costello*, filmed in Britain in 1957.

The *Midnight Lace* performance was again regarded as a sure bet for a nomination at the Academy Awards, but was bypassed, along with Jean Simmons's inspired portrayal of an evangelist in *Elmer Gantry*, while the Oscar was collected by Elizabeth Taylor for *Butterfield 8*. The tough Louella Parsons was prompted to say, 'It's a rotten shame Doris didn't even get a nomination,' while the object of all this attention was at home in North Crescent Drive concocting ice-cream sundaes and milk-shakes from her own soda fountain. This was the period when her publicity was built on the 'No alcohol – only fruit drinks and the like' tenets – in deference to her and Marty's strict Christian Science creed. Although Sam Weiss believes otherwise and maintains that his attitude as a firm practitioner was only a façade to please his wife, she gives him credit for deep sincerity where his religion was concerned. His devotion to that seems to have been almost as deep-rooted as his dedication to money and the power that could bring.

Apart from occasions like his helping Doris get over her *Midnight Lace* ordeal by hymn singing and meditation, the cracks in their marriage were widening and getting deeper. She had acquiesced in early irritations like Marty making her return a Vlaminck painting of a snow scene around a house in the Valley in Woodland Hills. Jerry Rosenthal, he said, needed every cent for his 'tax shelter programme' and Rosenthal did not approve of paintings, so she had to get back the 400 dollars the painting had cost. She was earning a million dollars for every picture and was not allowed to buy a 400-dollar picture of her own. She did force some kind of a show-down with the lawyer, who assured her that her oil wells were gushing, but his explanations about the tax shelters merely bemused her.

Then there was the small beach house she found great for relaxing, high up in the mountains on Lake Arrow-head, where she could water-ski and take long walks along country roads: in the winter there was snow and in the summer the sun shining on the lake produced a Technicolored picture postcard effect. Doris always felt wonderful there and loved walking the four miles to the village and back, but Marty felt the altitude did not agree with him. She would take Terry and a couple of girl friends and they all had a ball, but in the end she yielded again to his repeated suggestion that she should sell her little dream house, although she was working non-stop at the time and could really do with the change of pace her eyrie in the mountains guaranteed.

Marty's sending Terry to Harvard military academy was the beginning of the end, and something that neither the boy nor his mother was able to forgive. There were more serious family traumas ahead but, in the meantime there was a reunion with Rock Hudson, still for Universal International, as had been her first two for Ross Hunter, while *Please Don't Eat the Daisies* had been made under her contract with MGM. This time the producer was Stanley Shapiro, who wrote the screenplay of *Lover Come Back* with Paul Henning. Marty, of course, was co-producer, with Irene again designing some elegant dresses for Doris to wear in her role as Carol Templeton, advertising executive, who loses an important account with tycoon J. Paxton Miller (Jack Oakie) to Jerry Webster (Rock Hudson) from a rival firm. His method for tipping the balance is a combination of alcohol and girls, especially one of his own particular brand of groupies, chorus girl Rebel Davis (Edie Adams) whom Carol encounters as she enters the building bright and early for a serious day's work: amid scenes of an orgiastic aftermath Rebel is upended in what looks like a giant wedding cake – or was it a violin? After an angry conversation with Jerry over the telephone, in which she accuses him of sharp and unethical practice in finagling away the Miller account from her firm – here the split screen altercation harks back to Rock and Doris's more lengthy crossed lines in *Pillow Talk* – Carol persuades Rebel to testify against him at a meeting of the Advertising Council, but he swings the evidence back to his favour by promising Rebel the lead in a filmed advert for a non-existent product called VIP.

Jerry's neurotic boss, Peter Ramsey (Tony Randall) chooses an unfortunate time to put the commercial on the air, so they hire a Nobel-prize-winning chemist, Linus Tyler (Jack Kruschen) to invent a product to go with the name. Carol visits the laboratory and mistakes Jerry for the chemist, falls lock, stock and barrel for his apparent innocence and beguiling charm, not to mention the fact that he strips well when she teaches him to swim, buys him a new wardrobe and sets him up in a hotel suite, all at her company's expense. Posing as a shy neurotic guy full of doubts and unable to relate to the ladies, she is about to make the supreme sacrifice of her virginity, after singing a little song to herself 'Should I Surrender?' as she takes the champagne out of the fridge and fetches a negligée from her wardrobe, when her bosses phone to inform her that she is indeed entertaining a wolf in sheep's clothing. She drives him thirty miles to the beach on the pretext of a nude swim before the ultimate act of abrogating both their virginities, abandons him and dashes back with her complaint to the Council, as Jerry arrives with the last perfected VIP sweets, tasting delicious, but full of neat alcohol. After an enthusiastic 'tasting' Carol and Jerry wake up in twin beds each wearing half of his pyjamas and with monumental hangovers: beside the bed is their marriage certificate. She rushes out in a frenzy and has the marriage annulled, but nine months later allows herself to be talked into a remarriage in hospital, as she is wheeled into the accouchement ward.

Several critics, among them the *New York Times*, rated this the best of the Shapiro–Day–Hudson scripts to date, but when *That Touch of Mink* was released in 1962, the year after production commenced on *Lover Come Back*, this equally successful comedy with Cary Grant in place of Rock Hudson was voted by a number of film buffs to be not quite up to the high standard set by the second of the trilogy. The theme in all three is who will be the prime mover in the bedding stakes: in the first it is eventually Doris who makes the running, in the second alcohol evens up the score, and in the third, having blown hot and cold on whether to abandon her cherished virginity to the libidinous character played by Cary Grant, she marries him in the end, but finds that the thought of married love brings him out in spots, thus leaving a large question mark over consummation on the honeymoon.

Day and Hudson team ideally, as though they really were destined for each other, and it is only in hindsight that in both *Pillow Talk* and *Lover Come Back* homosexuality may be at the back of his shyness and reticence over sex in the assumed character he's playing.

It says a great deal for his self-confidence as well as for the faith of his public in his unassailable masculinity that he was prepared to go ahead with the charades he was called upon to play. The inspired insecurities portrayed by Tony Randall made an ideal bastion for Rock to pit his contrasting masculinity against and Edie Adams, as his show-cum-callgirl friend has a shape and ingenuous personality any red-blooded macho male might be assumed to get steamed up about. Further, she is a handy catalyst to spark off one of Doris's 'dirty looks', à la Mamie Van Doren and Vikki Dougan.

Jack Kruschen's abrasive eccentricity as the chemist is welcome in his all-too-brief appearances and it is sad to reflect that Jack Oakie's elderly lecher J. Paxton Miller, left over after the executive suite orgy, clutching an empty bottle of champagne, was to be the last film appearance of the eternal overweight slow-witted campus buffoon/chorus boy he played in his Paramount days as a bright new comedy talent. He partnered such disparate lovelies as the screen's most famous vamp and best-dressed woman, ex-Ziegfeld Follies showgirl Lilyan Tashman in *Too Much Harmony* in 1933, the year before her untimely death from cancer at thirty-five, and opera stars Lily Pons in *That Girl from Paris* and Gladys Swarthout in *Champagne Waltz* in the mid-Thirties. Oakie died in 1978, aged seventy-five. The last on the cast list, John Litel, who played a Board Member, visibly turned on by Edie Adams's charms as a witness, had been a dependable, if unexciting leading man to Kay Francis in a couple of her less distinguished films, *My Bill* and *Comet Over Broadway*, the last handed down to her by Bette Davis, her star in the ascendant, who indignantly refused to have anything to do with it. Warner downgraded Kay to decimate her earning power.

Director Delbert Mann's first experience at helming comedies was with *Lover Come Back* and *That Touch of Mink*, and his excellent showing with both makes one wonder why he did not do more romantic glossy pictures. He had won an Academy Award for his first film *Marty* in 1955, and had notable successes during the next two years – *The Bachelor Party* with Don Murray in 1957 and the all-star *Separate Tables* in 1958. Yet he went on to make not always inspired versions of the classics for TV, like *Jane Eyre*, *David Copperfield* and *Kidnapped*, in the early Seventies.

It is not unfair to say that Cary Grant and Doris Day were not an ideal teaming in *That Touch of Mink*. Beautiful people, both, certainly, and the gibes about heavy filters to disguise the advancing age of both stars are unfair and, in the event, pointless. The result is what counts, and, filters or no filters – Christopher Frayling, many years later, came to the conclusion that Doris's cameramen achieved their effects with her by subtle lighting – she, at thirty-eight and he, at fifty-eight, both look in peak condition. That said, whether it was wise to have so much insistence by her flatmate, Connie, (Audrey Meadows) on Doris as Cathy Timberlake's ability to dodge any wolfish advances and preserve her virgin status, which Connie clearly regards as a mite eccentric, is a moot point. Doris herself, logically, realized that what had made her number one world luminary was a script that was witty at a time when people were avid for more comedy in their lives and that she had become a new kind of sex symbol for the Sixties, the self-sufficient working woman, able to maintain her independence and integrity until, in the words of Fanny Brice, 'The Right Man Comes Along' when her attraction and general chic would impel him towards her bed. Only on her terms – i.e. after the benefit of clergy, could he be accepted into connubial bliss. Doris herself defined the character as 'sexy but pure'.

This inevitably led to the games that alternated during those Stanley Shapiro comedies: career woman versus career man, she determined not to be bedded, he adopting various ruses to trick her into giving in, she in the end getting what she really wanted all along. In *That Touch of Mink* the state of play is that Cathy, an unemployed computer operator, is splashed by the car of Philip Shayne (Cary Grant) a bachelor business tycoon, who sends his rebellious aide Roger (Gig Young) to apologize, but Roger manoeuvres her into taking her grievance directly to Philip in person. She falls for him at first sight and agrees readily to accompany him on a platonic one-day business trip from New York to Baltimore and Philadelphia and back, provoking envious sighs and pungent comments from her friend Connie. When Philip suggests a less platonic trip to Bermuda, Cathy is outraged and gives an indignant refusal; later she muses about what she was probably missing – how many similar offers is a mature virgin likely to get? She changes her mind and flies there with him, only to come out in spots at the vital moment before countdown. Medical care at bedtime frustrates any hope of romance, and when they try again, with a second trip to Bermuda, she gets drunk and falls off her balcony. Understandably exasperated, Philip decides to marry her off, so she makes up her mind to reawaken his interest by eloping to a motel with a lustful and highly unattractive employment office clerk, Beasley, (John Astley). Philip gives chase, suddenly mindful of what he has been responsible for, flings her over his shoulder and carries her off to be married: on the honeymoon he comes out in the afore-mentioned rash, the doctor prescribes a quiet night for him and Cathy acquiesces. Is this the end of a fine romance, he laments?

Love will find a way: cut to a baby in a pram, and proud father Philip is out walking with his friend-cum-aide Roger and Cathy. Philip goes off to take a photo of his wife, leaving Roger in charge of the baby and pram. Suddenly he spots his analyst, Dr Gruber (Alan Hewitt) who had misinterpreted Roger's explanation of his relationship with a rich gentleman friend – Philip, no less – and the doctor asks how did that work out?) 'The marriage was last June,' explains Roger, as he proudly lifts the baby from the pram. Fade-out on the doctor's thunderstruck expression.

Hilarious, indeed, for a closing gag – as is the whole film, if you don't stop to think about all the implications, like why is the prospective loss of virginity such a huge joke, and why does every Shapiro-scripted movie have to have intimations, however oblique, that the hero has gay leanings? The best thing to get the full enjoyment is to lie – or sit – back and let it all wash over you as a piece of outrageous fantasy. Apart from Kirk Douglas, Cary Grant is the co-star with whom Doris had least rapport. She found him a very private person, perhaps the most professional and exacting actor she had ever worked with, but devoid of give and take and very distant. When there was a little contretemps over their first close-up – they both preferred to be shot from the right profile – it was resolved by Grant graciously giving in to Doris. This less than total closeness is what comes over in the movie – they are both individually funny and endearing, but collectively the relationship doesn't quite gel. Gig Young and Cary Grant – fine. Gig Young – always on the outside looking in – and Doris – fine. But Grant and Day – not quite.

Interestingly, in *That Touch of Mink* – a title and implication the Doris of today would never countenance, Cary Grant is billed first, as was Rock Hudson in the three movies he and Doris did together. Otherwise, she was always number one in the rest of the films she was to make. Not that there was much competition in star-drawing potential, from her next leading man, Stephen Boyd, in *Billy Rose's Jumbo* – just named after the elephant in Britain, presumably because Billy Rose has never meant a great deal over here. The producer of the 1935 Rodgers and Hart musical, originally a costly failure on Broadway when John Murray Anderson and George Abbott staged it at Broadway's famous Hippodrome Theater with Jimmy Durante and a cast of ninety plus the animals and full panoply of the circus, had it in his contract that his name be featured in any subsequent production. Joe Pasternak and Marty Melcher thought it would be ideal for Doris, and they were right. It was the last of the great MGM musicals, and directed by Charles Walters, who had helmed so many of them, including *Easter Parade*, *The Barkleys of Broadway* and *High Society* – he also choreographed and partnered Joan Crawford in her last dance for the screen in the 1953 *Torch Song*. At the age of fifty she was asked how she had been able to get her legs up so high after such a long lay-off from dancing. 'Only God and Charles Walters could do that!' she answered. Walters had also directed *Please Don't Eat the Daisies*, in which the musical numbers had that little extra *joie de vivre*.

The Rodgers and Hart score for *Jumbo* was magical

and included 'The Most Beautiful Girl in the World' – 'Isn't Garbo, isn't Dietrich, but the Sweet Trick who can make me believe . . .', 'Little Girl Blue', 'This Can't Be Love' and Doris never more radiant, beautiful and young-looking as Kitty Wonder, bareback rider and co-owner of the Wonder Circus with her father Pop Wonder (Jimmy Durante) whose fiancée of many years, Lulu, is so long-sufferingly enamoured she even lets him shoot her out of a cannon. A handsome young stranger, Sam Rawlins (Stephen Boyd), is taken on as odd-job man and doubles as a high-wire stunt man and Kitty falls in love with him, not knowing that he has been sent by his father John Noble (Dean Jagger) of the rival circus to prepare for a takeover bid, aware of the parlous state of the Wonders' finances, which Kitty tries to balance but is constantly undermined by Pop's eternal improvidence. Sam tries to get out of the deal after falling for Kitty, but his father is adamant and his circus absorbs the Wonder troupe including the star attraction, elephant Jumbo. Heart-broken Kitty, together with Pop and Lulu, try to carry on with one-night stands in small venues, but just as they are about to acknowledge defeat, Sam returns, having split with his father and exhorts them to rebuild the circus with the help of Jumbo, who has defected with him. The lovers are all united in a triumphant song and dance spectacle, 'Sawdust, Spangles and Dreams' including a jubilant Martha Raye's Lulu.

There is an air of enchantment over the whole film and the stars are all in top form, Doris superlative as actress and singer, inspired in her rendering of 'This Can't Be Love', 'My Romance' and 'Little Girl Blue' and Stephen Boyd, the handsome young Irishman who achieved stardom as Messala in *Ben Hur* but whom the critics never quite took to their hearts, is manly, hand-some and gives a most moving rendering of 'The Most

Beautiful Girl In the World'. He sadly died in 1977 at the age of forty-nine, having ended his career starring in low-budget foreign movies. Jimmy was never more Durante, Martha never more Raye, he huge-nosed and raucous, she huge-mouthed and entirely lovable, if through cacophony you could hear the big heart beating beneath the large bosom. She had her detractors, including the great English critic S. A. Lejeune, who decided that what was wrong with the early Bob Hope films was Martha Raye, a comedienne she 'could well do without'. Martha also had a resonant singing voice – her *pièce de resistance* being 'Mr Paganini'. Her duet with Doris, 'Why Can't I?', is most affecting.

The flow and kaleidoscopic effect of the musical numbers must have been enhanced by the second unit work of Busby Berkeley, at last given something worthy of his genius to work on. Yet with all this enchantment everywhere, this was the only Doris Day movie in her zenith-of-achievement period that lost money, although it earned her a second nomination from the foreign press, which had awarded her the Golden Globe for *Lover Come Back* as the 'World's Favourite Actress', with Tony Curtis as 'Favourite Actor' in 1958. In the event Rosalind Russell got the Golden Globe in 1962 for *Gypsy*. 1959 was another peak year, when she and Rock Hudson were voted the 'Theatre Owners of America Exhibitor's Laurel Award' as the world's top stars. It seems that *Jumbo*'s financial failure lost her the star parts in both *The Unsinkable Molly Brown*, in which Debbie Reynolds gave an amazingly good account of herself, and *The Sound of Music*, which did for Julie Andrews what *Mary Poppins*, with its Academy Award, had not quite been able to do – and lifted Julie to a pinnacle of achievement which Doris was able to attain with less auspicious vehicles.

1962 held another disappointment of a far more personal nature: on 30 November Marty Melcher moved out of the house on North Crescent Drive and checked in at the Sunset Towers on the Strip. Things at home had been going from bad to worse, with the constant tussle over financial matters, mostly involving Jerry Rosenthal, Marty's ungovernable temper and arguments over Terry's college, which in the end put the kybosh on any hopes he might have had of an academic career. Matters came to a head the day Marty hit Terry in front of Doris. She rounded on her husband and said some of the things that had been raging to come out for so long. She told him of her credo that no human being has the right to strike an animal or another human being, that she had had enough of violence in her early days to last her a lifetime and that she wished to end their marriage.

It seemed an auspicious time to make a break. Marty was about to take a play he was producing called *The Perfect Setup* on the road. He had an understandable ambition to achieve something on his own: not being entirely insensitive he could not have been unaware that all the people with whom he came in contact knew that the power he was so fond of wielding was exercised purely through his relationship with, and the money of, his wife. She divined that the play was a clinker, with inbuilt failure. He agreed to the separation while the tour was on and after a few unhappy weeks on the road it limped onto Broadway. It was on and off in a night, which did not surprise some of the people who had had dealings with Marty. Terry says he couldn't achieve a thing on his own, literally make a penny without Doris. The things he tried on his own were all disasters and Terry thought he probably hated her for that and knew no more about movie producing at the end of his life than he had when he first met her. Under his aegis she had, of course, made some memorable and several entertaining films, but how much of the credit was due to Marty is debatable. Terry is understandably bitter, because during their close relationship he had come upon a twisted and insanely jealous personality, but there were others, like James Garner and Ross Hunter, who were too secure and pragmatic to let Marty's little games upset them; and Sam Weiss, who was convinced that some of the money that disappeared from Doris's account was being stashed away in numbered accounts in Switzerland, and who also saw the way Marty treated Terry when Doris wasn't around. Nobody ever told her, because it would have been very difficult to make the accusations stick and would have upset her needlessly. When matters came to a head she must have regretted she had been shielded from the truth for so long: people have a faculty for going on believing everything in the garden is rosy, even if, at the back of their minds they may have a niggling feeling that something is not quite as bright as it seems.

Their separation did not last much longer than the run of his play *The Perfect Setup*. He asked if he could come round and see her, when he explained that Rosenthal had pointed out that they were so inextricably tied up financially that a divorce was out of the question. All their capital was invested in joint ventures and their ownership of things like oil wells and if they parted company officially they would lose everything. Not only did she recognize that what he was saying was almost certainly the truth, but part of her still loved Marty and she could not help being touched by the sad figure he cut sitting waiting for her verdict in the living room.

After a turn around their swimming pool to get her mind clear she returned to him with some plain speaking she had been bottling up for a very long time. She told him that she no longer felt any sexual attraction for him: what had been comfortable without being ecstatic, now meant nothing, and she was not the kind of woman to pretend over such matters. She found it inexplicable that so many of her female friends went through the motions of enjoying sex, even simulating orgasms when the whole function left them totally cold. She made it clear that, though they would present a united front to the world they would in future lead their own lives; whatever he wanted to do was OK by her, though she asked him to be discreet. As for herself, she was not interested in sex for its own sake, if she was in love that would be different, and, in any case, with a working life that started at 5 a.m. continuing till she left the set at six, and after supper in bed by nine, there was precious little time over for affairs of the heart. The press duly reported a happy reunion for the Melchers.

Terry moved out of the house on Crescent Drive almost as soon as Doris and Marty moved there. In front of Alma Marty turned on his stepson and asked him point blank when he would be getting a place of his own. 'I can't stand the sight of you around here any more,' was his paternal valediction: Terry packed his bags and moved out the next day, despite Alma's anguished entreaties. She had been closer to her grandson than anyone during his formative years and hated to see him go. Within a year he had a respectable job with Columbia Records, producing his own albums and with a top group, the Byrds, under his wing which, at twenty-two was a remarkable achievement. Instead of applauding this proof that Terry could indeed stand on his own two feet, Marty's jealousy came right out in the open. During one visit when he had been invited over for dinner Terry was again ordered out of the house, but by then his confidence had grown sufficiently for him to stand up to his stepfather when he said, 'This time you're going to have to throw me out!' There were tears from Doris, who managed to pour oil on the troubled waters sufficiently for them to finish the meal, but Marty never threatened her son again.

During 1963 and 1964, she made three more excellent and financially successful movies; in the first two James Garner, who became another top favourite of Doris's, was her co-star, and the last was a final reunion with Rock Hudson and Tony Randall. *The Thrill Of It All* with Garner was also her last production for Ross Hunter. All the accustomed gloss and glamour were present, but this time no nonsense about preserving virginity which would indeed have taken some swallowing with such a macho hunk of manhood as James Garner as her husband, Dr Gerald Boyer, a gynaecologist married to suburban mother of two. Doris Day is Beverly Boyer, to whom the eccentric father-in-law (Reginald Owen) of a grateful patient, Mrs Fraleigh (Arlene Francis) takes a fancy. He insists that Beverly take part in a television commercial for his product Happy Soap. Her amateur performance, recounting how she got her children to use *Happy Soap* is so successful that he signs her to replace the sexy starlet who had been used in previous promotions of the product. At first unwilling, Beverly is soon weaned to the idea of earning 80,000 dollars a year and inevitably becoming the star of the Boyer household. This places a strain on the marriage and Gerald adopts various ruses to make his wife jealous, leaving photographs of women about, coming home drunk with lipstick on his collar and so on. They almost reach the parting of the ways, but when Beverly is accidentally present in a car, helping deliver Mrs Fraleigh's baby by telephoned instructions –

a domestic parallel to the situation with the pilotless plane at the end of *Julie* – Beverly realizes that her husband's work is more vital than hers and decides to go back to being just a wife and mother.

Carl Reiner's script is witty and inventive, as is the direction by Norman Jewison at the start of his brilliant career, Doris at her comic best as the housewife fumbling her way to TV stardom though her genuine ineptitude, which delights the nation, and though Garner has reaped more than his share of critical flak for being 'a very heavy-footed comedian' (the English *Monthly Film Bulletin*) he has great charm and suits Doris admirably. Their rapport was total – no wonder, when he considered her 'a very sexy lady who doesn't know how sexy she is'; he didn't think she could have achieved such pre-eminent success, 'if she didn't have this sexy whirlpool frothing around underneath her "All American Girl" exterior'. This is on a par with Ross Hunter's 'One of the wildest asses in Hollywood'. No wonder her appeal was so general, to women as well as men, and the fact that she was unaware of it makes it the more attractive: most sexy stars are all too aware of their attractions, and tend to lay it on with a trowel.

Apart from Arlene Francis who is as heavy-handed as the pregnant Mrs Fraleigh as James Garner was unfairly designated heavy-footed, the cast of seasoned comedians were on top form. They included the homely Alice Pearce, best known for her roles in *On the Town* in 1949 as the classic chronic sneezer and the TV series *Bewitched*. She also appeared with Doris in *The Glass Bottom Boat* in 1966, the year of Alice's death from cancer at fifty-three, British-born Reginald Owen as Old Tom Fraleigh, Edward Andrews, he of the bespectacled moon face as his son Gardiner, and the immortal Zasu Pitts in her penultimate film.

Move Over, Darling, with its catchy Joe Lubin title song — another record hit for Doris — was her second in 1963 and with James Garner, based on the time-honoured D. W. Griffith movie of 1911, *Enoch Arden* which received its inspiration from a poem by Alfred, Lord Tennyson, about a man who returns to his family years after he has been presumed dead. The Irene Dunne–Cary Grant *My Favourite Wife* of 1940, directed by Garson Kanin had charm a-plenty in its leading lady: this time round that commodity is sadly lacking in Doris Day as Ellen Wagstaff Arden, back after years of being shipwrecked on a desert island. Finding her husband Nick (James Garner) has just married again a neurotic young woman called Bianca Steele (Polly Bergen) Ellen's aggression knows no bounds, being sometimes reminiscent of Donald Duck at his most aggrieved. Unable to tell Bianca the truth Nick gets involved in all kinds of shenanigans, Ellen impersonates a Swedish masseuse as part of a ruse to stop Nick consummating his marriage to Bianca. Eventually when the knots are unravelled she is free to marry her psychiatrist, Dr Herman Schlick (Elliot Reid, who was also featured in *The Thrill of It All*), while Nick and Ellen resume their marriage, more or less where it left off five years previously.

Gordon Douglas, of *Pillow Talk*, also directed this one, and he is unable to give the requisite light and shade to what was to be Marilyn's *Something's Gotta Give*, until she sadly fulfilled the promise of the title by dying. One is tempted to wonder what Monroe would have made of the situation: she certainly would have played it more gently than Doris: a sad hangover from the original set up is that the house used in the story was a facsimile of George Cukor, the original director's, own home. He would have had the right gentle touch and almost certainly have prevented Doris from the abrasiveness she uncharacteristically shows in this performance. Chuck Connors assumes the role of the lady's muscle man admirer, a part literally truncated from the Stephen Burkett of the early version, who was played by Randolph Scott at the time he was sharing a bachelor pad with Cary Grant. The underestimated Polly Bergen's Bianca seemed to have had some complexities added to the role from when the supremely beautiful and frosty Gail Patrick was the incumbent. I can recall no psychiatrist in *her* life. Thelma Ritter, as Nick's mother, Grace Arden, lends her unique brand of resigned bafflement to the part, Fred Clark, Don Knotts and Edgar Buchanan add valuable comedy cameos, the latter as the judge trying valiantly to follow the permutations of the plot in the divorce court.

Send Me No Flowers marked Doris's last teaming with Rock Hudson and the end of her peak period of stardom, again directed by Norman Jewison. The stars, including Tony Randall, play together as expertly as ever, after Hudson has managed to convince the audience that, as George Kimball, he is a confirmed hypochondriac, which takes some doing from an actor who was the embodiment of rugged fitness. He overhears his doctor (Edward Andrews) discussing another patient and comes to the conclusion that he has only a few weeks to live. Desolately, George confides in his neighbour and best friend, Arnold (Tony Randall), who seeks relief in the bottle. Together they decide to try and find a new husband for George's wife Judy (Doris Day) and hit upon her schoolgirl crush, Bert (the muscular Clint Walker), which has the reverse effect of making her think her husband is having an affair with a pretty neighbour, Linda (Patricia Barry). In self-defence George tells Judy the truth about his supposed imminent demise. Appalled, she arranges for a second opinion at a specialist clinic, but his doctor assures her there is nothing wrong with George. Furious at what she assumes is his duplicity, she vows to get a divorce, and is only convinced of his veracity when she finds out he has bought a burial plot in the cemetery for himself, herself and a possible third husband. She throws away his pills and potions and they look forward to a healthy future.

The necrophiliac angles of the plot, and the constant harping on the imminence of death, in the case of Rock Hudson now make it difficult to laugh heartily at anything, though I do recall being fairly convulsed the first time round. Doris is again the chic suburban housewife, albeit dressed by Jean Louis, and displays her usual comic inventiveness, especially in the scene where she is preparing breakfast and, after gossiping on the doorstep in her fur bedroom slippers with the milkman (Dave Willock, forever cast in that sort of part) steps on a mixture of broken eggs and leaves, gets her bathrobe caught in the front door and ends by locking herself out. There's a gem of a performance by Paul Lynde as the funeral parlour super salesman of burial plots, and this time Burt Bacharach wrote the title song. It could have been an epitaph to the successful series of films from 1959 to 1964, a Martin Melcher Production which marked the end of his wife's reign as 'Number One Box Office Star'.

From then on it was downhill all the way. 1964 was the year Doris was awarded the Sour Apple Award by the Hollywood Women's Press Club for the second time. It's as though some of the heart had gone out of her – understandably. The constant battles with Marty over scripts, financial dealings of which she wanted no part, but found herself committed to irrevocably, the ceaseless pressure of long hours at the studio – all of these factors made her tired and apprehensive of constantly parrying the same old probing questions.

She insisted she was not anti-press, but had some trenchant things to say about the Sour Apple Award and its instigators. 'Isn't that a dreadful thing? Those poor, suffering sick ladies who do that – still playing little kids' games with apples. Can you imagine? With all the things going on in the world, and there they are at the Beverly Hills Hotel, giving out apples!'

7

❋

Aftermath

After *Send Me No Flowers* there were five films against which Doris fought, but in each case found that Marty had committed her in advance. The sixth, and the last she made, in 1968, *With Six You Get Egg Roll*, was one of which she finally did approve and which she urged him to produce himself. He did so, without having an inkling that it would be literally his own swansong, and the death knell to Doris's film career. The only movie that did passably well at the box office of those last six was the 1966 *Glass Bottom Boat*, which had the advantage of being directed by Frank Tashlin, who tended to visualize scenes graphically, like the cartoonist he was before entering films first as a scriptwriter for Bob Hope and Red Skelton.

Do Not Disturb, made in 1965, was directed by Ralph Levy and co-starred the chunky Australian-born Rod Taylor as Mike Harper, executive for a wool firm, who is transferred to England, where his wife Janet (Doris Day) acquires a rambling house in the country where their landlady is Hermione Baddeley, in the guise of Vanessa Cartwright, dizzy and decked in maribou. Janet also acquires a menagerie – if there was an opportunity to introduce animals into Doris's movies it was seized avidly. When Vanessa espies Mike dining in a London restaurant with his secretary Claire Hackett (Maura McGivney) she loses little time passing on the news and prompts Janet to arouse her husband's jealousy by pretending to flirt with a suave continental antiques dealer Paul Bellasi (Sergio Fantoni), who operates in Paris but has a branch nearby. In Mike's absence in Scotland Paul persuades her to fly to Paris with him to view a Georgian dining-room set to bring back for her forthcoming wedding anniversary. Janet drinks too much French champagne, sings a naughty French chanson in a tavern – 'Au Revoir'; shades of *April in Paris* and 'That's What Makes Paris Paree' – passes out and ends up spending the night with him. Mike unexpectedly turns up, knocks Paul out and announces divorce proceedings. They all meet again that evening at a wool convention party, and after husband and wife are reassured of each other's fidelity she enters the wrong apartment in search of Mike and finds herself in bed with wool buyer Willie Langsdorf (Leon Askin), who gives chase until she makes her way back to the right bed and climbs in with Mike, nicely posed for the happy ending.

The notices for this, and in fact all the succeeding films were not at all bad, on the lines of the *New York Daily News*'s 'a typical Day product'. The British *Monthly Film Bulletin* speaks of Doris, 'getting delightfully drunk, attended part of the time by Hollywood's aging English colony', including, presumably, Hermione Baddeley and Reginald Gardiner as her henchman – clipped moustache and speech well *in situ*, in his last film before a serious fall forced his retirement. He died in 1980.

Repetition, ultimately, was what put paid to Doris Day's career – variations on the same sort of character and the same sort of situation. If she had rung the changes by agreeing, against her principles, to play Mrs

Robinson in *The Graduate* would it indeed have opened up a new career for her in which the familiar Doris Day roles would give way to characterizations of a new depth and maturity? Or would this simply have led to offers of the same kind of part in various permutations of similar themes? In their introduction to the 1980 BFI season 'Move Over Misconceptions – Doris Day Reappraised' when thirty of her movies were shown that December, followed by a seminar on the season, Jane Clarke and Diana Simmonds seem to applaud her decision to turn down *The Graduate* 'because of its exploitive depiction of sexual relations – an acute assessment which many would now share.' Further, on analysing the films on offer, they draw a conclusion directly contrary to the conventional attitude of writing her off as the 'Girl Next Door' or the 'Constant Virgin', seeing many of her roles as particularly relevant today (that is, 1980) in pre-figuring a less repressive, more equal sexuality. Day frequently plays an independent/working woman who confronts the male and forces him to modify his attitudes and behaviour. Moreover, saying 'No' to manipulative sexual situations (a favourite plot device in the sex comedies) is *not* the same as 'clinging to one's virginity'. Tony Randall took the theory a Herculean step forward by saying, 'When you look back it's really she who's after Rock Hudson's virginity'!

It was Rod Taylor again in *The Glass Bottom Boat* as Bruce Templeton, the boss of a space laboratory whose public relations assistant Jennifer Nelson (Doris Day) comes to his notice when he catches his fishing line on the mermaid costume in which, in her other job, she entertains tourists on her father's glass bottom boat. Bruce, to keep her under his eye, sets her to work on his biography, pretending he's developing a rocket to Venus. Various intelligence agents, keeping the laboratory under surveillance with 'bugs' throughout the space centre hear her phoning her dog Vladimir to exercise him by remote control as he runs round the house every time he hears the bell, conclude she is a Russian agent. When she realizes they are all monitoring her every movement she plays her own cloak and dagger game with them at a party at her boss's house, the secret formula is planted on her and a frenetic chase by the master spy ensues. She, of course, wins the day and her boss's hand in marriage into the bargain.

Frank Tashlin's favourite subjects for his razor sharp and hilariously inventive satire include bureaucracy, tourism, the CIA and James Bond – the 'bugged' cocktail olives for example, are a delightful fantasy, and Doris enters into the spirit of all the wild nonsense with joyful abandon and considerable athleticism, with a cast of experienced farceurs hard put to it to keep up with her, including Dom DeLuise, Dick Martin, Paul Lynde in drag, and roped into the extravagant proceedings are Arthur Godfrey as a Scandinavian accessory to the plot, John McGiver, Edward Andrews as General Wallace Bleeker and Eric Fleming as a suavely handsome spy. The director's preoccupation with so-called labour-saving gadgets is outrageously given full rein in an automatic floor-cleaner whose funnel crawls up her trouser leg while she is trying to bake a cake in the oven. Robert Vaughn put in an appearance as Napoleon Solo and Doris's 'sister' from *Young at Heart*, Elisabeth Fraser, was along for the ride with stalwarts George Tobias as Mr Fenimore and Ellen Corby as Rod's housekeeper. Ironically, this film and the next Tashlin vehicle the following year, 1967, *Caprice*, received far more serious appraisal from intellectually minded critics than Doris's vaunted top money-spinning glossy comedies of her 'number one box office' years.

She fought Marty on the subject of *Caprice*, but he had signed a contract on her behalf, and that was that. In fact, during the five years of their 'for business purposes only' marital reunion Doris and Marty enjoyed a happier relationship than she had imagined would be possible. He kept to his side of the bargain over discretion regarding any extra-curricular activities, and Doris said she was never aware of any. But on one subject there was no armistice: lawyer Jerry Rosenthal. She resented the amount of control he had over her career, via her husband, but her hands were tied, as in the matter of *Caprice*. Marty insisted he effected the transaction without worrying her because she was so busy on *The Glass Bottom Boat* – she accused him of making the deal in cahoots with Rosenthal and pointed out that *they* didn't have to go in front of the camera and try to make something out of anything as terrible as she considered this second Tashlin subject. In the event the film emerged as a fast and funny James Bond spoof, and her own work in it as wittily pointed and energetic as ever. From the solid and engagingly blunt charm of Rod Taylor she was now up against the Irish rugby football-type machismo of Richard Harris, whom Marty had put forward enthusiastically as an inducement to interest her in the project. And thereby hangs a tale.

I was still nursing my bewilderment over the 'call a spade a spade' reputation of one of Britain's finest stage and screen actors, ex-hellraiser and imbiber par excellence Harris sending me a message that he could not talk about Doris Day without her 'written permission' when an undercover agent came up with a titbit as intriguing as anything dreamed up by Tashlin in his capacity as scriptwriter. Doris, as Patricia Foster, is a cosmetics firm executive trying to sell the stolen secret formula of something revolutionary in the way of cosmetics to her boss's rival: both firms are hot on the trail of dotty scientist Stuart Clancy (Ray Walston) with a view to getting their hands on his inventions. She becomes involved in the plotting of British double agent Christopher White (Richard Harris) who, for all his ruthlessness is not insensible to her charms as a woman, and one who, moreover, is out to track down the killer of her father, shot on a Swiss ski-slope while on the trail of an international narcotics ring for which the cosmetics outfit is merely a front. Patricia unmasks the villain before being carried off on a runaway helicopter which she manages to land on top of the Eiffel Tower. Christopher is standing by to escort her off on honeymoon.

And here's the pay-off. My mole informs me that originally the script cast Harris as the agent out to avenge the death of his father and Doris as the British double agent who tangles with him: she preferred the hero's role and the parts were accordingly switched, presumably leaving the star of *This Sporting Life* less than happy with his assignment. As an officer and a gentleman, he was not willing to reveal the role reversal without the written permission of his co-star. Q.E.D.

It is understandable that, in the wake of his mesmerizing performance as *Henry IV* and about to embark on his most important film role in years in *The Field* in 1991 he would not wish to evoke the spectre of a film with which neither he nor Doris Day was particularly happy. Under Tashlin's guidance she presented a glorified exaggeration of her mid-Sixties image: platinum hair, huge black glasses, black and white checkered coat, gold dress, hat and handbag, black mesh stockings and gold top boots, with a more than passing resemblance to our own eternal squeaky-voiced eternal *ingénue* Aimi Macdonald. Doris gave a performance of enormous verve and even more physical exertion than in *The Glass Bottom Boat*, falling off balconies, sliding down mountain sides, suspended over precipices, satirizing the invincible heroine, remaining true to herself in the midst of a world of gadgetry and artificiality gone mad. She has a wonderfully funny scene which fully exploits the director's predilection for making comedy out of the use of bugging devices when she finds out that everything on the table where she and Harris are eating is wired for sound and puts the eavesdroppers through hell by crunching potato crisps, banging a glass with her cutlery, slurping Alka Seltzer and so on.

The cast is remarkable, with the very British Edward Mulhare as Sir Jason Fox, who is not at all what he seems to be – like almost everyone else in the film – Ray Walston as the mad chemist with a leaning towards transvestitism, Lilia Scala as Madam Piasco, his mother and the real brains behind the narcotics ring, Michael J. Pollard and Irene Tsu – a distinctly odd couple and Fritz Feld, the archetypal eccentric German waiter, film director, or, as herein, innkeeper.

With all this going for it some of the notices were personally bitchy in the extreme, such as the *Village Voice* 'a long Day's journey into naught', *New York Morning Telegraph* . . . 'another day, another Doris. Only trouble is, it's the same Day and the same Doris' and Judith Crist, 'Miss Day looks like an aging transvestite.' No wonder the heart seems to have gone out of her after this. The last three films of her career to date were shown in 1968 and give the impression that Marty Melcher was trying to give Jerry Rosenthal his money's worth before time ran out. *The Ballad of Josie* directed by Andrew V. McLaglen, son of the actor Victor, Academy Award winner for John Ford's *The Informer* in 1935, is remembered by Doris as resembling a second-rate television Western for which she had to get up at 4.30 every morning.

As Josie Minick she opens the film standing trial for killing her husband with a billiard cue – this was the last film role of Robert Lowery as the drunken Whit Minick. She is acquitted, but her father-in-law (Paul Fix) insists on taking her son Luther (Teddy Quinn) to live with him until she can make a living to support him. She persuades rancher Jason Meredith (Peter Graves) to drive her to her dilapidated ranch at Willow Creek. He laughs at her plan to get the ranch going as a working concern, but, after some unpleasant experiences when she goes to work as a waitress she is determined to set herself up as a sheep farmer. Jason comes to her rescue when Arch Ogden (George Kennedy) leads a group of ranchers to kill her sheep, and when range war threatens to break out the women of Araphoe rise up to support Josie, but such a dispute would put paid to Wyoming's chances of statehood. Attorney Charlie Lord (William Talman) persuades Ogden to a change of heart and he agrees to stock Josie's ranch with cattle. Wyoming becomes a state, Josie gets her son back, burns her masculine appeal in the grate and marries Jason.

After her women's lib stance, fighting the cattlemen rather as she did the railroaders in *It Happened to Jane* this seems rather a climbdown; couldn't she have had a husband and retained the right to dress as she liked? In any case this struck me as the only time Doris seems really dispirited over the material she is expected to rise above, despite an attractive cast headed by the handsome Peter Graves, the always reliable heavy George Kennedy, corn-crake-voiced Andy Devine as a judge and, among the women, Audrey Christie as the proprietor of Annabelle Pettijohn's boarding house for ladies, and Doris's old friend Elisabeth Fraser as one of the supportive townswomen, the Widow Renfrew. The *New York Daily News* summed it up: 'The hot-headed, stubborn, gun-toting, riot-rousing of this Western is no fittin' role for the actress who has successfully alternated between smart career girl and typical housewife of suburbia.' It seems that at this time she just couldn't strike the right chord with the critics and the public seems to have echoed the dissatisfaction. Incidentally, Robert Lowery as the husband dispatched at the start of the film, having failed to graduate from second leads in his youthful days as Twentieth Century-Fox support to ladies like Alice Faye, Gloria Stuart and even Shirley Temple, gained a kind of cult fame as Batman in the 1949 serial, which has been showing during the writing of this book.

Doris has painful memories of her penultimate film *Where Were You When The Lights Went Out?*, directed by Hy Averback, who began his career as an actor in *The Benny Goodman Story*. She called the film 'an alleged comedy' about the New York City power-blackout of November 1965, and it is now mainly of interest that the Broadway star she plays, Maggie Garrison, is headlining in a comedy called *The Constant Virgin*, which really does seem to be pushing her luck as well as flogging a dead horse, to mix a couple of metaphors. Not that she doesn't look as delectable as ever, but what goes on in the blackout is too contrived and witless for even the first-class cast assembled to make more than mildly amusing. Maggie discovers her husband, architect Peter Garrison (Patrick O'Neal), being over-attentive to journalist Roberta Lane (the glamorous Lola Albright) and rushes off to drive to her home in Connecticut, where she accidentally takes some sleeping pills, falls asleep on the sofa. She is discovered by the contrite Peter lying next to an absconding company executive Waldo Zane (Robert Morse), who has taken some of the same pills in the blackout. It is now Peter's turn to be jealous, and in this he is encouraged by Maggie's agent Ladislau Walichek (Terry-Thomas) who hopes that a rift in the marital lute will prevent her carrying out her intention to retire and have a baby. Peter's car is searched by the police when he drives back to New York and is arrested when the money Waldo had stolen is discovered. Several even more incredible plot twists later Maggie and Peter are reconciled and nine months later their first child is born – The Constant Virgin no more.

Apart from the plot, Doris's pain stemmed from the fact that she had to be carried while playing half-drunk, half-sedated across a living room by Patrick O'Neal, who picked her up in a way that resulted in an excruciatingly painful pinched nerve in her back that affected her neck, arms and hand. Marty eventually found a doctor who decreed it would be all right for her to finish the film – already delayed for several painful weeks, as long as she stayed in traction when not actually on the set. She remembers little of the film other than the constant pain, and, in the circumstances, it is astonishing how radiant she contrived to look.

Sadly, Terry-Thomas, one of our most original comedy exports to America, died in 1990, having been unable to work for some years from the wasting effects of Parkinson's disease.

With Six You Get Egg Roll, which Marty Melcher produced himself, at Doris's urging, was directed by Howard Morris, the actor who had turned to directing the year before with the highly entertaining *Who's Minding the Mint?* At last here was a subject with which she was happy, the only one of the last six to which she could relate with confidence. The character, the family situation, all came together in a way that had proved elusive for too long. Doris plays Abby McClure, a widow who is glimpsed at the beginning in her capacity as a steel-helmeted lumberyard proprietress, something which is set aside when the plot gets going. Her sister Maxine (Pat Carroll) makes up her mind that Abby must find a suitable husband and introduces her to Jake Iverson (Brian Keith), the father of a teenage daughter, Stacey (Barbara Hershey), who takes an instant dislike to her father's new interest. Abby's own children, teenage Jason, Mitch and Flip (Richard Steele, Jimmy Bracken and John Findlater) and even their huge sheepdog Calico (Lord Nelson) also resent the romantic attachment between Jake and herself. They fly to Las Vegas for a quick marriage, but on their return the young people do everything in their power to prevent a merger between the two families. Commuting between their two houses presents a highly uncomfortable compromise, and the trailer Jake buys for Abby and himself becomes a further bone of contention. During a furious quarrel Abby tells him to return to his flirtatious next-door neighbour and some-time babysitter, Cleo (Elaine Devry) and sets off in the van to deliver him personally to her door, but Jake falls out of the back and is left raging in his underwear by the roadside. This leads to encounters with hippies and the local police, with Abby still in her nightdress, until eventually the children get together and consent to live amicably.

The situation is a simple one and what binds it together is the reality of the relationship between Doris and Brian Keith: at last, at forty-four she had come to terms with her age and their scenes together show a maturity of passion refreshingly real for a change. Doris never looked lovelier; the hairstyles designed for her by Barbara Lampson *au naturel* have departed from the harsh platinum blonde beehives that prompted one critic of *Move Over, Darling* to comment that she must have had access to an unlimited supply of peroxide on the desert island where she was stranded for so many years.

It was as if the components that had gone to make up the Doris Day persona through the years had finally melded to form an acceptable pattern for future movies: male and female are on equal terms in *With Six You Get Eggroll*, and the magnificent Lord Nelson, the huge shaggy dog giving such an intelligent account of himself as Abby's dog Calico for once seems a genuine member of the family, instead of a cute gimmick as the various dogs in Doris's movie life had tended to be. Among the mere humans it is interesting to compare the teenage Barbara Hershey – now back to her original name after the ill-advised switch to Barbara Seagull – in her first film as Brian Keith's sullen teenage daughter with the mature actress of recent years, and there are delightful cameos by Alice Ghostley as the abrasive housekeeper, and George Carlin as the drive-in movie caterer, who fancies Doris for himself. The one discordant note is the 'humour' of vans crashing into crates of chickens, a frequent scene in those days, and one which today's Doris would surely refuse.

Tragically, at a time when, after years of bitterness, even Terry Melcher seemed to have come to some kind of state of truce with his stepfather, and the companionship between himself and Doris, shorn of conjugal complications was going smoothly, towards the end of the filming Marty began to lose weight noticeably, and took to his bed the day the shooting was wound up. He stayed there for three months and developed chronic diarrhoea: Doris nursed him around the clock and never left the house, acceding to his insistence that no doctors be called and only his Christian Science practitioner, Martin Broones be consulted. However, as he was away on a lecture tour Broones rang daily to tell Marty which

pages and lines of *Science and Health* to study and
concentrate on. Desperately worried as she was she
could not conceive that this illness could have only one
conclusion, in death. Terry was an occasional visitor,
and at the start of the sickness, put Marty's uncharacter-
istic lethargy and sudden drop in body temperature to
the onset of a bad bout of 'flu.

When Terry moved out of his mother's house, his
main ambition was to succeed on his own, spectacularly
enough never to have to go back there, and to prove that
he, too, could earn big money, of the kind that his
stepfather had made his God, and within a few years he
had done so well at Columbia Records that his earnings
were in the region of 250,000 dollars a year. He gave a
large Christmas party at the big and beautiful house in
which he lived with film star Candice Bergen. It had a
swimming pool, a liveried houseman, several acres, and
he led Marty out to show him the view of the city. He
had hoped to make his stepfather proud: 'What do you
think, Dad?' he asked. If he had expected approbation
he was doomed to disappointment. 'It makes me sick,'
Marty snarled, 'a snotty kid to fall into something like
this.' Terry was still publishing through Marty's music
company, both the songs he wrote and the copyrights he
owned, which were making big money for his firm, to the
tune of half a million dollars. During an argument in the
office one day Marty turned on him and told him to take
his copyrights and get out. He called his accountant and
had him write a cheque for every penny owing to Terry –
345,000 dollars. Terry took the cheque, tore it into little
pieces, and threw it in Marty's face, telling him their
account was now square. From then on Marty treated
him like a grown man.

Terry's record albums, produced for RCA, provided
a bizarre addition to the list of lovers with which the

press credited his mother during the period of her marriage 'in name only' with Marty, including the Dodgers shortstop Maury Wills, probably because the Melchers enjoyed going to the Dodger games and knew most of the ball-players. Other reported affairs were with Frank Sinatra, whom she had seen only once since they finished *Young at Heart*, Jimmy Hoffa, the then president of the Teamsters Union, whom she never remembered meeting, and Glen Campbell whom she only met at a dinner when he came up and introduced himself and his wife at a time when the papers were seething with rumours of their torrid romance. Terry rang her one day and informed her she was having a hot affair with Sly of Sly and the Family Stone, whom she had met at Terry's house when he called to play her the recording he planned to make of 'Que Sera, Sera' which he said was one of his favourite songs. While denying all these rumours, Doris admits that during the five years she was making her last six films, she did have emotional crushes on some of her leading men. But as she was no Joan Crawford, who during the time of her heavily publicized 'happy marriages', accepted as standard practice that she would 'relate to' any leading man that took her fancy, in the interests of artistic verisimilitude, in Doris's case the 'affairs' did not proceed further than the film set.

During his illness Marty developed a pathetic dependence on Doris. On one occasion she left the house for half an hour to get some fresh air on her bicycle. When she returned she found him sitting on the pavement outside their house, clad in his dressing gown and bedroom slippers. He complained querulously that she had been away so long. She helped him back to the house and was concerned to find it was all he could do to walk that short distance. Eventually Terry brought in Dick

Dorso, Marty's friend and partner from the Century Artists Agency and it was he who persuaded him to let a doctor see him. The doctor revealed that Marty had an enlarged heart, a condition he had suffered from for a long time, and he called a specialist who ordered him into hospital immediately. He refused to go by ambulance and was driven to Mount Sinai Hospital, where Doris sat by his bed every day from eight until midnight. He was helped into a chair during the daytime, where he did crossword puzzles with Doris's help. One day a nurse brought an elaborate arrangement of flowers: they were from Jerry Rosenthal. Marty asked her to take them out of the room and not to bring them in again. That was when Doris sat beside him and got him to agree that they had to have a talk about Rosenthal and Marty apologized for how hard he had kept her working. They would go on a long vacation when he got out, he promised and he would try and make up to her for all the fun she had been missing. After she helped him into bed she was shocked to find that the crossword he had been working on was just a jumble of words that made no sense.

The next morning early she was called to the hospital: Marty had fallen from his chair in the early hours and had passed into a coma. She phoned Terry, who took her to the hospital and then she called Marty's brother Jack in San Francisco. Terry waited for him and took him into the hospital room, where Marty was undergoing emergency heart surgery, then Terry took her home, much against her will. The hospital rang the next morning at four o'clock to say that Marty was dead. He was 52.

Doris's grief was akin to despair: she had lost a man she had loved for seventeen years, who had controlled everything about her life and now she felt like a fatherless child. After the cremation, which was done without any kind of ceremony, she isolated herself and turned away from the Christian Science that no longer held any consolation for her. She no longer wanted to be part of a formal religion: the Christian Science tenet that God is love and God's love should replace your grief held no meaning for someone like Doris, whose way had always been to express her grief with tears, and she was incapable of putting on an act – possibly her reaction was due to a feeling that Marty's too literal adherence to Christian Science had prevented him from seeing a doctor when there was still time for his heart condition to be treated, as the specialist had said: two months earlier he could have been saved. From then on, although she believed fervently in much of what Mrs Eddy preached, Doris wanted to evolve her own personal religion, one adapted to her own spiritual orientation.

Marty's death was only the first of a series of bitter body blows that began when she went into his room and found two completed television scripts for a *Doris Day Show*. They had discussed television on several occasions, Marty seeing it as the replacement for her kind of films, which were no competition for the explicit treatment of sex that was now so much in vogue but she had been adamant about not undertaking the pressure of having to shoot a complete script in a few days and to keep on churning them out. She had found it difficult to believe that Marty would have committed her to work against which she was diametrically opposed, and asked Terry to investigate. Not only was that the case, but there was worse to come. A cheque that had gone to Terry as executor of the estate and which Rosenthal had urged him to endorse had lifted the cover on a hornet's nest. The lawyer had insisted he needed the cheque made out to Doris for 60,000 dollars immediately; Terry refused, forced a show-down. Over a period of four days he gradually learned the truth – that Doris was left without a penny. The hotels were bankrupt, the oil wells dry and the cattle non-existent. Worse, there were debts, mostly for taxes, amounting to around 450,000 dollars. Dick Dorso was with Terry the day he broke the news; they had been driving round in his car for hours, wondering how to tell her.

At the time the only thing she could think of was whether Marty had been in on this with Rosenthal, or was he the innocent dupe? Rosenthal had covered his tracks with masterly precision. All Marty's files had been cleared out – cabinets and his desk were empty. Neither was there any will to be found. Doris's suggestion that they sell the house to pay the debts – all her life she had made it a principle not to owe anyone – yielded the further revelation that Rosenthal and Marty had borrowed against everything that could be used, including Doris's record contract and the albums she was yet to make. In addition, the large advance from CBS television to Marty for pre-production costs on the *Doris Day Show*, which was planned to be started in the autumn – in fact, half a million dollars – had been spent by Rosenthal and not a penny of it had gone to the two producers, Dick Dorso and Bob Sweeney. When the lawyer refused to answer Terry's questions about where the money had gone, he, as his mother's legal representative, fired him on the spot.

Terry Melcher, pulling no punches about his stepfather, said that just about the best thing Marty did for his mother was to die. At the rate Marty and Rosenthal were going, and the direction they were headed, in another year he didn't believe his mother could ever have recovered. They would have used up all her future television earnings, as well as mortgaging her house and made her bankrupt for the foreseeable future. Rosenthal had evidently foreseen every eventuality, but he hadn't counted on Marty's death. Considering what Rosenthal had in store for the next five years, Terry felt convinced that Marty had reached a hand out of the grave and stabbed his old buddy.

Dick Dorso is one of the few people who believed that Melcher was not basically dishonest, but obsessed with making money so that he could achieve success on his own, which was how he got involved with Jerry Rosenthal. Six months before Marty died, Dick Dorso had pleaded with him to get away from Rosenthal, reminding him that the lawyer had cost several people, including Kirk Douglas and Gordon MacRae, vast sums of money: the latter's lifetime of savings was wiped out when he had to pay the government 480,000 dollars for illegal deductions from his earnings which Rosenthal had taken for the mythical 'tax shelter' Doris had found so incomprehensible every time Marty told her it had to be paid for out of her hard-earned salary. Dorso actually believes that Marty wanted to die and that neglecting his illness, which could have been curable initially, was his way of committing suicide because he knew by then that, through his involvement with Rosenthal he had lost all her money and he could not face telling her. 'Marty simply took the coward's way out,' is his assessment.

Others were harsher, including Les Brown, who said, 'Marty Melcher was an awful man, pushy, grating on the nerves, money-hungry. He lived off Patty Andrews, then Doris.' Only her long-time publicity agent and friend, Warren Cowan, had any kind words to say: 'I think Doris and Marty had a mutual feeling of love and affection; they shared interests and had fun together, and Marty took good care of her . . . In my book Marty was a very direct person, warm, outgoing, with a marvellous sense of humour . . . but he was an inveterate dreamer, and his dream of empire is what did him in . . . his greatest failing was that he was forever changing his mind, hardly the trait of a big executive. Like the time he wanted me to get someone to write Doris's life story. He was on the phone every day about it. I got a freelance writer and set it all up, but when I took the completed project to him he told me it was a bad idea and he wasn't interested. It was as if I originated the idea.' The project was announced in the *Melody Maker* in December 1955. The rest was silence. After that it must be a case of 'Requiescat in pace' for Marty Melcher.

Doris herself, through the numbness of her shock and desolation, found optimism impossible, but the pragmatic side of her induced her to make the adjustments to her life necessary if she was going to carry on with that life, although there were nights when she went to sleep and wished never to wake up. She did not pray to God at that time, because for a whole year she blotted out the thought of His existence. She rented a house in Palm Springs and went there with Alma, her brother-in-law Jack and her close friend Barbara Lampson. Facing up to the fact that she had only six weeks to prepare for her TV series she forced herself up and out of the catatonic trance-like state into which she had fallen when she first arrived in her house in Palm Springs, with its view of mountains and deserts, and tried to eat sensibly: she took up swimming in the pool, a little more each day; by the end of a month she had built her average up to twenty laps a day, besides walking increasingly long distances.

Somehow she started work in good order on the *Doris Day Show* and got through it up to schedule, despite the fact that she was subject to deep depressions which often meant she could do no more shooting that day, and would have to retire to her dressing room to give way to hysterics. It was not until the whole production was in the can that she realized what a godsend having to gear herself up to work had been. The premiere of the CBS TV series was on 24 September 1968, with Doris as a singer, sick of city life, who retires with her two sons Billy and Tony to the country to live at her father's farm. Naturally they become involved in local politics and other small community interests: the setting was one she would never have willingly entered into, but the series proved very popular and lasted through five seasons, with Denver Pyle playing her father in the first two. By the second year Doris insisted on a change of format which took her, although still playing the role of Doris Martin, to work on a magazine in San Francisco, *Today's World*, with Rose Marie as the secretary. Years three and four were the happiest for Doris, as they marked her reunion with Billy De Wolfe, playing her neighbour, Jarvis, and in the last-mentioned she had returned to single girlhood. The fifth and last of the series, in 1972, premiering, like the others, in September provided a new love interest for the star in Peter Lawford, after which she decided the show had nowhere further to go, except perhaps to the bank, and it was time to call a halt.

On 14 March 1971 she was seen in *The Doris Mary Anne Kappelhoff Show* with Rock Hudson and Perry Como as guests: she duetted 'Didn't We?' with Como, besides a medley from *Oliver* and a selection of Beatles and Simon and Garfunkel songs. She bicycled onto the show singing 'Secret Love', included 'Sentimental Journey' and 'It's Magic', giving the viewers a fair old wallow in Doris Day nostalgia, which proved predictably extremely popular. Four years later *Doris Day Today* was even more of a winner, with delightful John Denver, on whose show she had once been a guest, teaming irresistibly with her, and Rich Little providing another stroll down memory lane by impersonating a clutch of her leading men – Clark Gable, Cary Grant, James Stewart, Jack Lemmon, James Cagney, Kirk Douglas and Frank Sinatra.

Between the first and second of the *Doris Day Shows* occurred an event which horrified the world and plunged Terry and Doris into more than a year of intense anxiety and dread. He had effectively to relinquish his career in music to try and unravel her financial disaster as well as to attempt to cope with the problem of his own finances. All his lucrative earnings had, on Marty's advice, been looked after by Rosenthal and of course, vanished into thin air. Terry was named as Executive Producer on the TV series but simply had no time to devote to it, which added to the pressures already weighing him down. Then, in August 1969, the summer after Marty's death, Doris heard the announcement over the airwaves of the Manson murders – ritual killings by followers of the self-styled Jesus-reincarnate of a hippie commune. She was swimming in her pool at the time the news of the murder of the young movie star Sharon Tate at the home of the Polish film director Roman Polanski came over the air. Sharon was eight months pregnant and four other young people were horrendously butchered at 10050 Cielo Drive. The address abruptly stopped Doris's swimming. It was the house which Terry had shared with Candice Bergen – a French farmhouse built for French film star Michèle Morgan when she was fulfilling a Hollywood contract which included the musical *Higher and Higher* with Frank Sinatra. Terry and Candice had sold it to go and live in the beach house on Malibu which had been Doris's but to which she had felt unable to return after Marty's death. Terry was afraid that, if left unoccupied, it would be vandalized. Now, at the time of the murders, he and

Candice had split after several happy years, because he felt he could no longer give her the care and attention she deserved, due to the pressures piling up on him.

They were increased to breaking point when the police told him that according to a witness called Susan Atkins, who was one of the killers, the gang had gone to the house looking for him, and when he was not there they went ahead and butchered everyone who was. Terry had met Manson when he was invited to the commune to listen to his compositions with a view to offering him a recording contract if they were any good. He decided they were not, but went back a second time to where Charles Manson lived with his adoring followers, male and female, in abject poverty, but apparent contentment, to give his music ('below average nothing') the benefit of the doubt by taking with him a friend with a guitar and a recording van. The friend did, in fact, record some of their tribal music and on one of several visits got himself horribly stoned on LSD, from which it took him a year to recover.

Despite the fact that he had treated Manson with courtesy Terry still felt himself menaced when he heard from a prosecutor in the District Attorney's office that there were followers of the cult who were liable to be out to kill him, although Manson and his four devotees who had slaughtered the victims on Cielo Drive were in jail awaiting trial. Terry hired round-the-clock body-guards for his mother and himself: who could tell what kind of action the gang might be prepared to take against either of them to achieve the kind of notoriety they were after? Under all these pressures Terry, whom the police had tried to bludgeon into an admission that he was somehow involved with the Mansons and drug addiction – even that he had fathered babies in the commune – suddenly cracked and withdrew into a twilight world of his own, bolstered by pills and alcohol. Doris was excluded from his existence: he had begun to blame her for all his ills, starting with her introducing Marty into his life. She, at least, had her work to keep her going, and although she was distraught for him in his unhappiness there was little she could do except wait for him to come to terms with himself: she felt that Terry was in God's hands and that something would happen to give him the peace of mind that had been taken from him after Marty's death.

Sometimes 'Divine Intervention' and 'Divine Retribution' are difficult to distinguish from each other: Terry had rented a little house in Idyllwild, a small mountain community on the way to Palm Springs, had set out for a ride on the high-powered motorcycle he had not ridden for two years and had crashed head-on into a car in a bend of the mountain road. He was terribly injured, both legs were shattered and there was a distinct possibility both might have to be amputated. For five nights at the Hemet Valley Hospital, just off the main road to Palm Springs, while Doris waited it was touch and go: twice she was warned he might not make it through the night. She could not pray to God to make him well, because she could conceive of no duality, no God outside Terry. All she could do was to tell Him, 'All right, God, he's Yours. I trust in You.' Her old faith in the precepts of Mary Baker Eddy had been reinforced by the philosophy of Joel Goldsmith in one of his books *The Thunder of Silence*, in which he says that, instead of praying up to God we should be so silent that we can hear the still small voice, which is when He manifests and expresses Himself within us.

Terry was treated by a remarkable man, Dr Howard Lieberman, who was on the staff of the hospital and an expert on leg injuries. After two weeks in the intensive care ward he moved his patient to a private room and began a course of excruciatingly painful reconstitution of the thirty-seven fractures in Terry's legs. During the period of recuperation, with infinite help from the hospital's chief of mental therapy, Dr Charles Head, Doris and her son achieved an understanding more complete than any they had before. She fixed up her guest house for him when he was finally discharged after six months in hospital. At first he was confined to a wheelchair, after four months with his leg in plaster casts, then he graduated to a walking frame; when Doris was out doing her series either her mother or the house-keeper were there to look after him. At thirty years of age, it was the first time he, Alma and Doris had ever lived together under the same roof, and she felt that this was the first time she had actually taken care of him, which she continued to do until he was well enough to go back to his own place – in fact, only a few minutes away, but she felt bereft. At last they had developed a genuine mother–son closeness and she was inordinately proud of the way he had emerged from his traumatic and pro-longed skirmish with death to a new kind of strength and an assurance more positive than ever before.

During the fourth year of her television series Doris had an affair with an actor who had once worked in a film with her. It seems to have been the complete and perfect relationship that eluded her in all her marriages, which is perhaps not entirely strange when she admits that when in love she wants to be with that person all the time, day and night, discussing the complexities of life, sharing the same meals, breathing the same air. An affair conducted at that degree of intensity must surely of necessity be of brief duration, and this one lasted a year, then they parted on friendly terms. Her lover remained married to his wife for the sake of their three children, although he was no longer in love with her. Doris admits she had no qualms about the other person's married life, but how would she have felt, at the time she and Marty were actually living as man and wife, had she learned about his extra-marital activities? Terry would sometimes find dolly ladies in his stepfather's office who were obviously not solely business clients – some distinguished names were bandied about, including Angie Dickinson and even Raquel Welch in her early days as a cocktail bar waitress. Absolute honesty is what Doris insists on, but how absolute can honesty be? Apparently her lover passed through her life without leaving a trace of himself – can that really be love? One love affair that certainly never was, although the film magazines were full of 'revelations' about the inside story, was her mooted liaison with Don Genson, the producer of her TV series – something she neither confirmed nor denied.

Whoever the unnamed actor who illuminated her days and nights for a twelve-month, it was unlikely to be Kirk Douglas who, although Doris says she and Marty were on good terms with him and his wife Anne, has been on record as saying, 'I haven't a clue who Doris Day is. That face she shows the world – smiling, only talking good, tuned into God – as far as I'm concerned, that's just a mask . . . Doris is about the remotest person I know.' For her part she says the film they made together was one of the few utterly joyless experiences she had had in the movies. Kirk was civil and that was about all: she never felt he made much of an effort towards anyone else and that he was exclusively wrapped up in himself. He had, in fact, phoned Marty to warn him about Rosenthal, but, for reasons Doris has never been able to fathom, her husband not only refused to heed Douglas's warnings, but told her that he did not think they should go on seeing Kirk and his wife. 'He's no friend of yours,' he said darkly.

After five years of intensive probing and research Jerome Rosenthal was arraigned to appear before the Superior Court of California. The trial lasted a hundred days and made international headlines: the cost was 250,000 dollars. The trial opened in March 1974 and in September, after a lengthy deposition Judge Lester E. Olsen awarded Doris 22,835,646 dollars – the largest amount ever granted in a civil suit in California. The conduct of the accused, said the judge, 'was sad, malicious and disgraceful.' Among the most distressing aspects of Rosenthal's depredations to emerge was the fact that the suicide of the beautiful Dorothy Dandridge, star of *Carmen Jones* and *Porgy and Bess* was due to the fact that the lawyer had bankrupted her with his worthless investments. Although he had no visible assets, there were six malpractice insurance companies involved, and, with the passage of time, several millions of dollars were recoverable on Doris's behalf, although nothing like the total amount awarded by the court. Her tears of relief as she left the courtroom were mainly over the fact that Rosenthal, her nemesis for so many years, and the scourge of those nearest and dearest to her, had been put to rout . . . 'the hand of Marty reaching up from the grave . . .'

8

———— ❁ ————

Fulfilment

Ever the romantic, when Doris received a letter from a fan about the wedding gown she had worn in *The Doris Day Show* she got together with her costumier and fitter and they made the dress even more glamorous, with yards of tulle and a headpiece covered with lilies of the valley and orange blossoms. They sent it to the bride-to-be and later received an enchanting photograph of her in the gown, which, predictably, had reduced Doris to tears of happiness. There were more tears soon after that when Terry married a beauty called Melissa, at the home of friends of his in Rancho Santa Fe. Doris let her mind dwell on how lovely it would have been had the occasion been a double wedding, although she had gone on record, after Marty's demise, as saying that she could not envisage any plans for a further marriage. So, too, says Elizabeth Taylor, from time to time.

On 14 April 1976, Doris walked down the aisle with husband number four, Barry Comden, handsome and grey-haired, ten years her junior and manager of the Old World Eatery Chain in Beverly Hills, Los Angeles and Palm Springs. *Photoplay* that August headlined an article 'Doris Finds True Love At Last!' Doris herself endorsed the euphoric tone of the piece: 'I just think he's a beautiful person, and we have a marvellous relationship, really better than any relationship I've had before. With Barry, I am romantically fulfilled. We're so happy with each other. I am now a contented, happy, outgoing person.' Everything in the garden, privately and even, retrospectively, career-wise, seemed lovely. Her TV Special *Doris Day Today* – the one in February 1975 in which she and John Denver displayed such a rapport – had been her most successful television show to date. The same year *Film Weekly*'s poll to discover their readers' favourite screen actress found Doris placed directly behind two stars who had films released within the year, Barbra Streisand and Julie Andrews – not a bad placing for a girl who had not made a movie for seven years. Doris said, 'The public wants to see happy pictures about happy people. And I think they still want to see me.'

Doris's marriage to Barry Comden took place in a friend's house in Carmel, the beautiful valley resort she had discovered when on location for *Julie*, so many years before, and to which she moved after her television work came to a halt at her own insistence. After five years' non-stop filming she was tired, and there were so many things she wanted to do, mainly involving the animal kingdom which had always claimed a major portion of her thoughts and affections. At the start of her network TV series she became deeply involved with the organization Actors and Others for Animals started by Richard Basehart and his wife, having already started helping Cleveland Amory's group in New York, the Fund for Animals. During a leave of absence from her work with Actors and Others to look after her mother, who was ill for a period of almost a year, Doris conceived the idea of starting her own Pet Foundation. 'I wanted to do different things from Actors and Others, whose policy doesn't allow for taking in unwanted animals and strays which I find on the street.' Later she acquired her interest in the Cypress Inn and changed their fifty-year 'No Pets' policy: the first to check in were Crisie, a Sheltie and Bo Jangles, a bit of All-sorts, with their owners, Mr and Mrs Eugene Cronin.

Sadly, by 1980 she was telling the *Daily Mail*'s Paul Callan that she and Barry Comden had proved 'just incompatible' and had parted. Terry had said before the marriage that she wanted to get married again but that she didn't really have any idea how to react to a man's attention and would be the last one to know when a man is interested in her. After the break Terry stated flatly, 'Let's just not talk about it.' One of her closest friends, Raquel Rael, a strikingly glamorous interior decorator with jet-black hair and dark skin – the direct antithesis of Doris – told her, 'No wonder you don't have a man; you don't even know when you've got one!' They were staying together at the MGM Grand Hotel in Las Vegas, where a handsome doctor was obviously smitten with her, a fact of which Doris was totally unaware. The occasion was a day-long auction on behalf of the annual Actors and Others Bazaar for the sale of items donated by celebrities. Doris had gone for Tom Jones's pants and Frank Sinatra's pyjamas. She obtained the former without any problem but the latter were never forthcoming, though she attended Sinatra's opening at the Circus Maximus and sat at his personal table with sixty others, including Sonny Bono and Joey Heatherton. Promises, promises, but no pyjamas.

Paul Callan's piece had been written in reply to an article in a colour tabloid which printed a couple of terribly unflattering photos of Doris, taken off-guard and from the worst possible angle, to accompany an article titled 'Why Doris Day has Gone to the Dogs', presenting her as a 'Bitter recluse and pill-popping hypochondriac'.

Doris, looking radiant, met Callan and asked gaily, 'Do I look like some grey-haired hermit in a fortress?' She said the same when Hotchner went to see her to update *Her Own Story*: he found her looking not a day older. She took him over the new quarters she had built for her dogs, where they were divided into groups of three or four, living in separate rooms and taking turns in the exercise yards. Hotchner says that Doris reacted to each separate personality and was always delighted by their eager response to her company. She feels dogs are as vital to her as people. The dogs she lives with are like family to her; and when you are unhappy they give you a loyalty that you cannot find anywhere else. She recognizes a two-way bridge by which she is able to cross freely into dogs' thinking areas and vice-versa. Trees, she finds, have a mystical quality akin to that of the dog.

Doris speaks feelingly about 'the absolute innocence in a dog's eyes' and scathingly on the subject of Elizabeth Taylor's predilection for over-sized diamonds about the time when both stars were riding high in the world's top film-star polls. The idea of such ostentation, said Doris, made her feel physically sick when she thought about how many foster homes the money spent on such jewels could have bought for the world's unwanted dogs. She is much more in accord with three of her other great contemporaries: Audrey Hepburn, who before her death had gradually withdrawn from her film career to devote time to her international work for UNICEF; Brigitte Bardot, who seems to have found a new sense of fulfilment in her espousal of causes for endangered species, which she organizes from her home in the South of France; and Kim Novak, who now concentrates her attentions on animal care at the ranch to which she retired some years ago with a lady friend who helps her manage the business side of the endeavour. These ladies share a bond with Doris Day in having turned to callings that are far more rewarding than transient film fame.

Doris keeps in touch with her fans, answering their many questions on cassettes, through a number of international fan clubs, the Doris Day Society (UK) run by Martyn Daye, The Friends of Doris Day (UK) run by Sue Gökgör and The Australian Doris Day Society run by Alan Moore. Each fan club assists Doris in raising funds for her animal welfare organizations, which now seem to be her main *raison d'être*. However, her love is not for dogs alone, but for all animals. She is bitterly opposed to the wearing of fur coats and has said, 'Killing an animal to make a coat is a sin.'

Apart from animals, Doris's other great joy is her bicycle; she has said recently that every time she goes for a ride it is an adventure, and that after an hour's cycling she has had a workout from head to toe, a philosophy with which the present writer is in total accord. 'I'm happy today with who I am and what I do. I'm living life to the fullest, just the way I want it to be. My philosophy is never to regret the past and to have no anxieties about the future. It's been a wonderful life, but the best is yet to come.'

Always one to speak her mind, Doris's assertion that instead of experimenting on animals scientists might do better to turn their attentions to convicted murderers in the testing of new drugs to combat AIDS has threatened to land her in hot water. 'Why not?' she says. 'They owe society something. Don't stand aghast at that. They're sitting there having three meals a day and we're paying for it. What the hell are they going to do for society to pay us back?' 'Does Doris think they should get a chance at least to volunteer?' asked the *Daily News* on 20 March 1990. She led a group of environmentalists who were up in arms about a proposed bill creating an open-hunting season on coyotes, pointing out that allowing hunters in the woods year-round poses a bigger threat to hikers and the coyotes' distant cousin, the household dog, than the timid predators do to deer. A less controversial subject, which had Doris's full backing, was the campaign to convert ten per cent of the British population to vegetarianism by the year 2000. Madonna joined her in this, an unlikely alliance for Animal Aid, but not as surprising as that with such famous vegetarians of the past as Ovid, Leonardo da Vinci and Pythagoras.

In July 1985, her Cable TV series, *Doris Day's Best Friends*, began its twenty-six-week run starting with a special centred around one of her best friends Rock Hudson, already terminally ill. In Rock Hudson: *His Story* by himself as told to Sara Davidson in the last months of his life and finished by her after his death on 2 October 1985, Doris talks about her last meeting with him. The filming had clearly been a major effort for him, and she was all in favour of calling it off: she had no idea of his condition and he told her he'd had flu, which he was finding difficult to throw off. She recalls, 'When we were walking around out there together, it crossed my mind, it might be the last time. But I didn't really know. I hoped and prayed that it wouldn't be. I didn't know what was wrong with him, but I knew he was determined to do that show if it took his last breath. It was his final thing and I really cherish that.' The last shot of Rock is as his white bus rattles away and Doris softly sings 'My Buddy'. The original choice had been 'Crocodile Rock' by Elton John, but in the circumstances it was all too obviously unsuitable. Rock collapsed on the plane and slept all the way to Los Angeles. When he awoke he said he would go on to Paris: 'Doris is mad at me. There's a doctor in Paris I've got to see, because I guess there's something wrong with me. I don't like it that Doris is mad at me.' She had made him promise her that he would eat more, hoping against hope that lack of proper sustenance was the basis of his gaunt and infinitely weary look.

Those Cable TV shows, running into 1986, were the last appearances Doris made before the Frayling documentary. She has since appeared in another documentary, in 1991 *Doris Day – A Sentimental Journey*, which has not, to date, been seen on British TV.

For Christmas, 1993, *The Love Album* was released – twelve tracks recorded by Doris during May and June 1967. Found by her son Terry in a garage, along with sundry papers and documents, it had been overlooked in the upset at the time of her husband's death. The album, recorded for Doris's company, Arwin, was released by Telstar in Britain and Warner in Australia. Its success brought Doris back to British TV screens in October 1994, with a satellite appearance on *Des O'Connor Tonight* for ITV and in a special Pebble Mill programme on BBC, for which Gloria Hunniford, a confirmed fan of Doris's, who once impersonated her on TV, travelled to Carmel. The rapport between the two was very apparent.

A role suggested for her was the Jessica Fletcher character in the ongoing TV series *Murder, She Wrote*. Doris could have been in her element as the young-at-heart bestseller writer of detective stories who turns amateur sleuth to clear up the mystery in each episode – much as Agatha Christie's Miss Marple used to do. The character is obviously inspired by Mrs Christie's creation, whom Angela Lansbury has played on the screen: Doris declines to discuss the part she might well have excelled in, had she been prepared to devote her time and energies to such a demanding project. Her reluctance to talk about the matter stems from her admiration for Angela, who has overcome considerable family troubles, much as Doris herself did, and gone on to make herself one of the great powers in the television hierarchy.

A particularly intriguing idea mooted for 1983 was a film with Katharine Hepburn in which they would co-star as spinster sisters, one a violinist, the other a pianist – with the title *West Side Waltz* – and the fusion of two such great, though totally dissimilar talents would have been fascinating and would undoubtedly have provided one of the greatest challenges of Doris's entire career.

Mae West delayed her comeback until she was an official seventy-eight going on eighty-two: when it happened she stole the billing, the notices and the glory of the New York Premiere from Raquel Welch as the eponymous heroine/hero Myra Breckinridge. An off-Broadway show, *My Doris Day* (which premiered in London as *Definitely Doris – The Music of Doris Day*) enchanted theatregoers on both sides of the Atlantic from 1996–2002, with sellout dates in London, Boston, Los Angeles and New York. The magical musical and salute to 'Hollywood's greatest legend' was written by Leo P. Carusone and Patty Carver, produced by the Grammy-nominated team of Pierre Patrick, Jerry Goehring and associate producer William Suretté.

There is no doubt that Doris Day could triumph at any age, but it is only fair that the echelons of her animal kingdom, not to mention her two-legged public should be allowed to see her looking as trim and youthful and sounding as mellifluous as she has in her recent appearances – even if the mountain has to go to Muhammad and they have to build a proper studio in Carmel for Doris to continue her recordings under the devoted supervision of her son Terry, who has had that as a pet project for a long time. The Cable filming took place in Doris's own setting, so surely something could be worked out. But, on final analysis, it's all in the lap of the gods – and Doris, so we fade out, perhaps inevitably, on 'Que Sera, Sera'.

AWARDS AND NOMINATIONS

(Compiled by Stephen Munns www.dorisdaytribute.com)

ACADEMY AWARDS/NOMINATIONS

Best Actress in a Leading Role
1959 **Doris Day**
('Jan Morrow' in *Pillow Talk*)

Art Direction
1959 *Pillow Talk*
1962 *That Touch of Mink*

Costume Design
1960 *Midnight Lace*

Music – Song
1948 **It's Magic**
(from *Romance on the High Seas*)
1949 **It's a Great Feeling**
1953 **SECRET LOVE**
(from *Calamity Jane*)
1955 **I'll Never Stop Loving You**
(from *Love Me or Leave Me*)
1956 **QUE SERA, SERA (WHATEVER WILL BE, WILL BE)**
(from *The Man Who Knew Too Much*)
1956 **Julie**

Music – Score
1948 *Romance on the High Seas*
1950 *The West Point Story*

1953 *Calamity Jane*
1955 *Love Me or Leave Me*
1959 *Pillow Talk*
1962 *Billy Rose's Jumbo*

Sound Recording
1953 *Calamity Jane*
1955 *Love Me or Leave Me*
1962 *That Touch of Mink*

Writing – Motion Picture Story
1955 *LOVE ME OR LEAVE ME*

Writing – Screenplay
1955 *Love Me or Leave Me*
1956 *Julie*
1958 *Teacher's Pet*
1959 *PILLOW TALK*
1959 *Lover Come Back*
1962 *That Touch of Mink*

AMERICAN COMEDY AWARDS

Lifetime Achievement Award in Comedy
1991 **DORIS DAY**

COLUMBIA GOLD DISC – PRESENTED FOR OVER 1,000,000 SALES

1956 **QUE SERA, SERA (WHATEVER WILL BE, WILL BE)**
(from *The Man Who Knew Too Much*)

GOLDEN GLOBE AWARDS/NOMINATIONS

Best Actress in a Leading Role – Drama
1961 *Midnight Lace*

Best Actress in a Leading Role – Musical or Comedy
1959 *Tunnel of Love*
1960 *Pillow Talk*

1963 *Billy Rose's Jumbo*
1964 *Move Over, Darling*

Best Performance by an Actress in a TV Series
1969 *The Doris Day Show*

Best Television Series
1969 *The Doris Day Show*

Cecil B. deMille Award – Lifetime Achievement
1989 **DORIS DAY**

Henrietta Award – World Film Favourites
1955 **Doris Day**
1958 **DORIS DAY AND TONY CURTIS**
1960 **DORIS DAY AND ROCK HUDSON**
1963 **DORIS DAY AND ROCK HUDSON**
1966 **Doris Day**

GOLDEN LAUREL AWARDS
Top Female Star
1958 **DORIS DAY**
1959 **DORIS DAY**
1960 **DORIS DAY**
1961 **DORIS DAY**
1963 **DORIS DAY**
1964 **DORIS DAY**

Top Female Comedy Performance
1960 **DORIS DAY**
('Jan Morrow' in *Pillow Talk*)
1962 **DORIS DAY**
('Carol Templeton' in *Lover Come Back*)
1963 **DORIS DAY**
('Cathy Timberlake' in *That Touch of Mink*)
1965 **DORIS DAY**
('Judy Kimball' in *Send Me No Flowers*)

GRAMMY AWARDS/NOMINATIONS

Best Female Recording Artist

1958 **Doris Day**
(for 'Everybody Loves a Lover')

Best Vocal Performance for a Single Female Track

1960 **Doris Day**
(for 'Sound of Music')

Hall of Fame Inductees

1975 **Sentimental Journey**
(Les Brown & His Orchestra; vocal by Doris Day)
1998 **SENTIMENTAL JOURNEY**
(Les Brown & His Orchestra; vocal by Doris Day)
1999 **SECRET LOVE**
(Doris Day)

PHOTOPLAY 'GOLD MEDAL' AWARDS

Most Popular Female Star

1951 **DORIS DAY**
1959 **DORIS DAY**

SPCA USA 'PALLOMA' AWARDS

Significant Contribution to the Welfare of Animals

1993 **DORIS DAY**

NB Awards are in BLOCK CAPITALS and nominations are in Mixed Casing

DISCOGRAPHY

(Compiled by Stephen Munns www.dorisdaytribute.com)

STUDIO ALBUMS

Release Date	Title (Label and Catalogue No.)	Highest US Chart Position
08/1949	**You're My Thrill** (Columbia CL6071)	5
03/1950	**Young Man with a Horn** (Columbia CL6106)	1
09/1950	**Tea for Two** (Columbia CL6149)	-
03/1951	**Lullaby of Broadway** (Columbia CL6168)	1
07/1951	**On Moonlight Bay** (Columbia CL6186)	2
12/1951	**I'll See You in My Dreams** (Columbia CL6198)	1
03/1953	**By the Light of the Silvery Moon** (Columbia CL6248)	3
11/1953	**Calamity Jane** (Columbia CL6273)	2
11/1954	**Young at Heart** (Columbia CL6339)	15
05/1955	**Love Me or Leave Me** (Columbia CL710)	1
12/1956	**Day By Day** (Columbia CL942)	11
08/1957	**The Pajama Game** (Columbia OL5210)	9
11/1957	**Day By Night** (Columbia CS8089)	-
10/1958	**Hooray for Hollywood – Vol 1** (Columbia CS8066)	-
01/1959	**Hooray for Hollywood – Vol 2** (Columbia CS8067)	-
03/1959	**Cuttin' Capers** (Columbia CS8078)	-
03/1960	**Show Time** (Columbia CS261)	-
03/1961	**Bright and Shiny** (Columbia CS8414)	-
08/1961	**I Have Dreamed** (Columbia CS8460)	97
02/1962	**Duet** (Columbia CS8552)	-
09/1962	**You'll Never Walk Alone** (Columbia CS8704)	-
11/1962	**Billy Rose's Jumbo** (Columbia OS2260)	-
02/1963	**Annie Get Your Gun** (Columbia OS2360)	-
12/1963	**Love Him** (Columbia CS8931)	102

NB Mono catalogue numbers (CL/OL) stated only when NO
stereo / *The Love Album* was recorded in 1968 but lost until its
1993 release

UNRELEASED STUDIO ALBUM

09/1986 **Crocodile Rock**
         Daydream
         Disney Girls
         Heaven Tonight
         My Heart
         Octopus' Garden
         Ryan's on His Way to the Round-Up
         Stuval was a Racehorse
         This is the Way I Dreamed It
         Wild Fire
         You are So Beautiful to Me

NB Doris started work on a new studio album with her son
Terry Melcher and his longtime colleague, Bruce Johnston of the
Beach Boys. She recorded the above tracks, a combination of
specially written songs and pop classics. However, due to commitments for her Cable television series, *Doris Day's Best Friends*,
final production work on the album was never completed – the
album remains unreleased!

STUDIO ALBUMS FEATURING DORIS DAY

Release Date	Title (Label and Catalogue No.)	Highest US Chart Position
1974	**Terry Melcher** (Reprise MS2185)	-
	Features *These Days* with Doris on backing vocals	

Release Date	A side b/w B side (Label and Catalogue No.)	Highest US Chart Position
04/1948	**Love Somebody** (Columbia 38174) b/w *Confess*	1
04/1948	**Confess** (Columbia 38174) b/w *Love Somebody*	16
04/1948	**It's Magic** (Columbia 38188) b/w *Put 'Em in a Box, Tie 'Em with a Ribbon*	2
10/1948	**My Darling, My Darling** (Columbia 38353) b/w *That Certain Party*	7
01/1949	**Powder Your Face with Sunshine** (Columbia 38394) b/w *I'll String Along with You*	16
05/1949	**Again** (Columbia 38467) b/w *Everywhere You Go*	2
06/1949	**Now That I Need You** (Columbia 38507) b/w *Blame My Absent-Minded Heart*	20
06/1949	**Let's Take an Old Fashioned Walk** (Columbia 38513) b/w *Unknown*	17
10/1949	**Cuttin' Capers** (Columbia 38595) b/w *It's Better to Conceal than Reveal*	15
11/1949	**Bluebird On Your Windowsill** (Columbia 38611) b/w *The River Seine*	19
11/1949	**Quicksilver** (Columbia 38638) b/w *Crocodile Tears*	20
02/1950	**Bewitched** (Columbia 38698) b/w *Imagination*	9
04/1950	**Hoop-Dee-Do** (Columbia 38771) b/w *Marriage Ties*	17
05/1950	**I Didn't Slip, I Wasn't Pushed, I Fell** (Columbia 38818) b/w *Before I Loved You*	19
11/1950	**A Bushel and a Peck** (Columbia 39008) b/w *The Best Thing for You*	16
01/1951	**Would I Love You** (Columbia 39159) b/w *Lullaby of Broadway*	10
06/1951	**Shanghai** (Columbia 39423) b/w *My Life's Desire*	17

03/1952	**A Guy is a Guy** (Columbia 39673)	I
	b/w Who Who Who	
05/1952	**Sugarbush** (Columbia 39693)	7
	b/w How Lovely Cooks the Meat	
07/1952	**When I Fall in Love** (Columbia 39786)	20
	b/w Take Me in Your Arms	
11/1952	**A Full-Time Job** (Columbia 39898)	20
	b/w Ma Says, Pa Says	
12/1952	**Mister Tap Toe** (Columbia 39906)	10
	b/w Your Mother And Mine	
05/1953	**Candy Lips** (Columbia 40001)	17
	b/w Let's Walk That-A-Way	
06/1953	**Choo Choo Train** (Columbia 40063)	20
	b/w This Too Shall Pass Away	
10/1953	**Secret Love** (Columbia 40108)	I
	b/w The Deadwood Stage	
03/1954	**I Speak to the Stars** (Columbia 40210)	16
	b/w The Blue Bells of Broadway	
08/1954	**If I Give My Heart to You** (Columbia 40300)	3
	b/w Anyone can Fall in Love	
03/1955	**I'll Never Stop Loving You** (Columbia 40505)	13
	b/w Never Look Back	
05/1956	**Que Sera, Sera** (Columbia 40704)	2
	b/w I've Gotta Sing Away these Blues	
06/1958	**Everybody Loves a Lover** (Columbia 41195)	6
	b/w Instant Love	

The following artists are featured on the forementioned A and B side singles, as follows:

  i.   Buddy Clark: *'Love Somebody', 'Confess', 'My Darling, My Darling', 'That Certain Party', 'I'll String Along with You' and 'Powder Your Face with Sunshine'*
 ii.   Frank Sinatra: *'Let's Take an Old Fashioned Walk'*
iii.   Dinah Shore: *'It's Better to Conceal than Reveal'*
 iv.   Frankie Laine: *'Sugarbush' and 'How Lovely Cooks the Meat'*
  v.   Johnnie Ray: *'A Full Time Job', 'Ma Says, Pa Says', 'Candy Lips' and 'Let's Walk That-A-Way'*

FILMOGRAPHY

(Compiled by Stephen Munns www.dorisdaytribute.com)

The order of listing is USA release date, title, film studio, any alternate title *(alt)*, director *(dir)*, producer *(pro)*, scriptwriter *(wri)*, colour process, co-stars, position of Doris's billing when not top.

07/1948   **Romance on the High Seas** (Warner Bros.)
alt UK *It's Magic* / *dir* Michael Curtiz / *pro* Alex Gottlieb and Michael Curtiz / *wri* Julius J. and Philip G. Epstein / Technicolor / Jack Carson, Janis Paige, Don DeFore / Fourth

04/1949   **My Dream is Yours** (Warner Bros.)
dir Michael Curtiz / *pro* Michael Curtiz / *wri* Harry Kurnitz and Dane Lussier [adapted by Allen Rivkin and Laura Kerr from story by Jerry Wald and Paul Moss] / Technicolor / Jack Carson, Lee Bowman / Second

08/1949   **It's a Great Feeling** (Warner Bros.)
dir David Butler / *pro* Alex Gottlieb / *wri* Jack Rose and Mel Shavelson [from story by I. A. L. Diamond] / Technicolor / Dennis Morgan, Jack Carson, guest stars including Joan Crawford, Ronald Reagan, Errol Flynn / Second

03/1950   **Young Man with a Horn** (Warner Bros.)
alt UK *Young Man of Music*, AUS *Young Man with a Trumpet* / *dir* Michael Curtiz / *pro* Jerry Wald / *wri* Carl Foreman and Edmund H. North [from novel by Dorothy Baker] / B&W / Kirk Douglas, Lauren Bacall / Third

09/1950   **Tea for Two** (Warner Bros.)
dir David Butler / *pro* William Jacobs / *wri* Harry
Clork and William Jacobs [from play by Frank
Mandel, Otto Harbach, Vincent Youmans and Emil
Nyitray] / Technicolor / Gordon MacRae, Gene
Nelson

11/1950   **The West Point Story** (Warner Bros.)
alt UK *Fine and Dandy* / *dir* Roy Del Ruth / *pro* Louis
F. Edelman / *wri* John Monks Jr, Charles Hoffman and
Irving Wallace [based on his story] / B&W / James
Cagney, Virginia Mayo, Gordon MacRae, Gene
Nelson / Third

02/1951   **Storm Warning** (Warner Bros.)
dir Stuart Heisler / *pro* Jerry Wald / *wri* Daniel Fuchs
and Richard Brooks / B&W / Ginger Rogers, Ronald
Reagan, Steve Cochran / Third

03/1951   **Lullaby of Broadway** (Warner Bros.)
dir David Butler / *pro* William Jacobs / *wri* Earl
Baldwin / Technicolor / Gene Nelson, S. Z. Sakall,
Billy De Wolfe, Gladys George

07/1951   **On Moonlight Bay** (Warner Bros.)
dir Roy Del Ruth / *pro*William Jacobs / *wri* Jack Rose
and Melville Shavelson [from stories by Booth
Tarkington] / Technicolor / Gordon MacRae

12/1951   **Starlift** (Warner Bros.)
dir Roy Del Ruth / *pro* Robert Arthur / *wri* Karl Kamb
and John Klorer [from his story] / B&W / Cameo
appearances with Gordon MacRae, Virginia Mayo,
Gene Nelson, James Cagney

01/1952   **I'll See You in My Dreams** (Warner Bros.)
dir Michael Curtiz / *pro* Louis F. Edelman / *wri*
Melville Shavelson and Jack Rose [from story by
Grace Kahn and Louis F. Edelman] / B&W / Danny
Thomas, Frank Lovejoy

06/1952   **The Winning Team** (Warner Bros.)
dir Louis Seiler / *pro* Bryan Foy / *wri* Ted Sherdeman,
Seeleg Lester and Merwin Gerard [from their story] /
B&W / Ronald Reagan, Frank Lovejoy

01/1953   **April in Paris** (Warner Bros.)
dir David Butler / *pro* William Jacobs / *wri* Jack Rose
and Melville Shavelson / Technicolor / Ray Bolger,
Claude Dauphin

05/1953   **By The Light of the Silvery Moon** (Warner Bros.)
dir David Butler / *pro* William Jacobs / *wri* Robert
O'Brien and Irving Elinson [from the stories by Booth
Tarkington] / Technicolor / Gordon MacRae

11/1953   **Calamity Jane** (Warner Bros.)
dir David Butler / *pro* William Jacobs / *wri* James
O'Hanlon / Technicolor / Howard Keel

04/1954   **Lucky Me** (Warner Bros.)
dir Jack Donohue / *pro* Henry Blanke / *wri* James
O'Hanlon, Robert O'Brien and Irving Elinson [from
story by James O'Hanlon] / WarnerColor / Robert
Cummings

01/1955   **Young at Heart** (Warner Bros.)
dir Gordon Douglas / *pro* Henry Blanke / *wri* Liam
O'Brien [from screenplay by Julius J. Epstein and
Lenore J. Coffee, original story by Fanny Hurst] /
Technicolor / Frank Sinatra, Gig Young, Ethel
Barrymore

06/1955   **Love Me or Leave Me** (MGM)
dir Charles Vidor / *pro* Joe Pasternak / *wri* Isobel
Lennart and Daniel Fuchs [from his story] /
Eastmancolor / James Cagney, Cameron Mitchell

06/1956   **The Man Who Knew Too Much** (Paramount)
dir Alfred Hitchcock / *wri* John Michael Hayes [from
story by Charles Bennett and D. B. Wyndham-Lewis]
/ Technicolor / James Stewart / Second

11/1956   **Julie** (MGM)
dir Andrew L. Stone / *pro* Martin Melcher / *wri*
Andrew L. Stone [from his original screenplay] / B&W
/ Louis Jourdan, Barry Sullivan, Frank Lovejoy

08/1957   **The Pajama Game** (Warner Bros.)
dir George Abbott and Stanley Donen / *pro* George
Abbott, Stanley Donen and Frederick Brisson / *wri*

Richard Bissell [from his novel] / WarnerColor / John
Raitt, Carol Haney, Eddie Foy Jr

04/1958 **Teacher's Pet** (Paramount)
dir George Seaton / *pro* George Seaton and William
Perlberg / *wri* Fay and Michael Kanin / B&W / Clark
Gable, Gig Young, Mamie Van Doren / Second

11/1958 **Tunnel of Love** (MGM)
dir Gene Kelly / *pro* Joseph Fields and Martin Melcher
/ *wri* Jerome Chodorov and Joseph Fields [based on his
play, with Peter DeVries from his novel] / B&W /
Richard Widmark, Gig Young

06/1959 **It Happened to Jane** (Columbia)
alt USA *Jane from Maine, Twinkle and Shine* / *dir*
Richard Quine / *pro* Richard Quine and Martin
Melcher / *wri* Norman Katkov [from his story with
Max Wilk] / Technicolor / Jack Lemmon, Ernie
Kovacs, Steve Forrest

10/1959 **Pillow Talk** (Universal)
dir Michael Gordon / *pro* Ross Hunter and Martin
Melcher / *wri* Stanley Shapiro and Maurice Richlin
[from story by Russell Rouse and Clarence Greene] /
Eastmancolor / Rock Hudson, Tony Randall, Thelma
Ritter / Second

04/1960 **Please Don't Eat the Daisies** (MGM)
dir Charles Walters / *pro* Joe Pasternak / *wri* Isobel
Lennart [from book by Jean Kerr] / MetroColor /
David Niven, Janis Paige

11/1960 **Midnight Lace** (Universal)
dir David Miller / *pro* Edward Muhl, Ross Hunter and
Martin Melcher / *wri* Ivan Goff and Ben Roberts
[from play by Janet Green] / Eastmancolor / Rex
Harrison, John Gavin, Myrna Loy

03/1962 **Lover Come Back** (Universal)
dir Delbert Mann / *pro* Robert Arthur, Stanley Shapiro
and Martin Melcher / *wri* Stanley Shapiro and Paul
Henning / Eastmancolor / Rock Hudson, Tony
Randall / Second

07/1962 **That Touch of Mink** (Universal)
dir Delbert Mann / *pro* Robert Arthur, Stanley Shapiro and Martin Melcher / *wri* Stanley Shapiro and Nate Monaster / Eastmancolor / Cary Grant, Gig Young / Second

12/1962 **Billy Rose's Jumbo** (MGM)
dir Charles Walters / *pro* Joe Pasternak and Martin Melcher / *wri* Sidney Sheldon [from the play by Ben Hecht and Charles MacArthur] / MetroColor / Stephen Boyd, Jimmy Durante, Martha Raye

08/1963 **The Thrill of it All** (Universal)
dir Norman Jewison / *pro* Ross Hunter and Martin Melcher / *wri* Carl Reiner [from his story with Larry Gelbart] / Eastmancolor / James Garner, Arlene Francis

12/1963 **Move Over, Darling** (20th Century-Fox)
alt Eva Swenson and Eve / *dir* Michael Gordon / *pro* Aaron Rosenberg and Martin Melcher / *wri* Hal Kanter and Jack Sher [from Bella and Samuel Spewack's 1940 screenplay and their own story with Lee McCarey] / De-Luxe Color / James Garner, Polly Bergen, Thelma Ritter

11/1964 **Send Me No Flowers** (Universal)
dir Norman Jewison / *pro* Martin Melcher and Harry Keller / *wri* Julius Epstein [from play by Norman Barasch and Carroll Moore] / Technicolor / Rock Hudson, Tony Randall / Second

12/1965 **Do Not Disturb** (20th Century-Fox)
dir Ralph Levy / *pro* Aaron Rosenberg and Martin Melcher / *wri* Milt Rosen and Richard Breen [from play by William Fairchild] / De-Luxe Color / Rod Taylor, Hermione Baddeley, Sergio Fantoni

07/1966 **The Glass Bottom Boat** (MGM)
alt The Spy in Lace Panties / *dir* Frank Tashlin / *pro* Martin Melcher and Everett Freeman / *wri* Everett Freeman / MetroColor / Rod Taylor, Arthur Godfrey, John McGiver

06/1967   **Caprice** (20th Century-Fox)
dir Frank Tashlin / *pro* Aaron Rosenberg, Martin
Melcher and Barney Rosenzweig / *wri* Frank Tashlin
and Jay Jason [from the story by Martin Hale] / De-
Luxe Color / Richard Harris, Ray Walston, Jack
Kruschen

11/1967   **The Ballad of Josie** (Universal)
dir Andrew V. McLaglen / *pro* Martin Melcher and
Norman MacDonnell / *wri* Harold Swanton / Peter
Graves, George Kennedy, Andy Devine

05/1968   **Where Were You When the Lights Went Out?**
(MGM)
dir Hy Averback / *pro* Robert Vreeland, Everett
Freeman and Martin Melcher / *wri* Everett Freeman
and Karl Runberg [from Claude Magnier's play] /
MetroColor / Robert Morse, Terry Thomas, Patrick
O'Neal, Lola Albright

08/1968   **With Six You Get Eggroll** (Warner–Pathé)
alt A Man in Mommy's Bed / *dir* Howard Morris / *pro*
Martin Melcher / *wri* Gwen Bagni, Paul Dubov,
Harvey Bullock and R. S. Allen / Technicolor / Brian
Keith, Pat Carroll, Barbara Hershey

TELEVISION HIGHLIGHTS

(Compiled by Stephen Munns www.dorisdaytribute.com)

The order of listing is transmission date, title, television network, all other miscellaneous information.

1968–69 **The Doris Day Show, Season One** (CBS TV. USA)
plot: Doris Martin, a recently widowed mother of two sons, Billy and Toby, decides to move in with her father, Buck Webb on his farm / *aired* 24th Sep 1968 to 6th May 1969

1969–70 **The Doris Day Show, Season Two** (CBS TV. USA)
plot: Doris starts a job on a magazine in San Francisco / *aired* 22nd Sep 1969 to 6th Apr 1970

1970–71 **The Doris Day Show, Season Three** (CBS TV. USA)
plot: Doris relocates with family to a new apartment in San Francisco above an Italian restaurant / *aired* 14th Sep 1970 to 15th Mar 1971

1971–72 **The Doris Day Show, Season Four** (CBS TV. USA)
plot: Doris's children return to help their grandfather on his farm and Doris becomes an Associate Editor for the magazine / *aired* 13th Sept 1971 to 6th Mar 1972

1972–73 **The Doris Day Show, Season Five** (CBS TV. USA)
plot: The Palluccis leave and Mr Jarvis buys Doris's apartment building / *aired* 11th Sept 1972 to 12th Mar 1973

The Doris Day Show, regular cast:

Doris Day – *Doris Martin*
Denver Pyle – *Buck Webb* (Season 1–2)

Fran Ryan – *Aggie Thompson* (Season 1)
James Hampton – *Leroy B. Simpson* (Season 1)
Philip Brown – *Billy Martin* (Season 1–3)
Todd Starke – *Toby Martin* (Season 1–3)
Naomi Stevens – *Juanita* (Season 1)
Rose Marie – *Myrna Gibbons* (Season 2–3)
McLean Stevenson – *Michael Nicholson* (Season 2–3)
Paul Smith – *Ron Harvey* (Season 2–3)
Kaye Ballard – *Angie Pallucci* (Season 3–5)
Bernie Kopell – *Louie Pallucci* (Season 3–5)
John Dehner – *Cy Bennett* (Season 4–5)
Jackie Joseph – *Jackie Parker* (Season 4–5)
Billy DeWolfe – *Willard Jarvis* (Season 2–4)
Peter Lawford – *Dr Peter Lawrence* (Season 4–5)
Patrick O'Neal – *Jonathan Rusk* (Season 5)
Lord Nelson – *Nelson (dog)* (Season 1–3)

03/1971 **The Doris Mary Anne Kappelhoff Special** (CBS
TV. USA)
Variety entertainment show, with Perry Como and
guest star Rock Hudson. Features live performances
of: 'Both Sides Now', 'It's Magic', 'Sentimental
Journey', 'Everybody Loves A Lover', 'Quiet Nights',
'If I Had My Life To Live Over' and more

12/1974 **John Denver and Friends** (ABC TV Network. USA)
Guest appearance performing duets with John of 'By
the Light of the Silvery Moon', 'On Moonlight Bay'
and 'I'll See You in My Dreams'

02/1975 **Doris Day Today** (CBS TV. USA)
Variety entertainment show, celebrating the 'now'
world of the Seventies, with John Denver and
comedians Tim Conway and Rich Little. Features live
performances of: 'Day By Day', 'The Way We Were'
and many more

1985–6 **Doris Day's Best Friends** (Christian Broadcast
Network. USA)
Cable television series, total of 26 shows, filmed in
Carmel; featuring guests: Rock Hudson, Les Brown,
Denver Pyle, Joan Fontaine, Ryan Paul Melcher (her
Grandson), Howard Keel, Kaye Ballard, Angie

Dickinson, Robert Wagner, Tony Randall, Lori
Anderson, Jill St John, Tony Bennett and Leslie Neilsen

03/1989   **I Don't Even** Like *Apple Pie* (BBC TV. UK)
Television documentary and interview on the life,
times and career of Doris Day by Christopher
Frayling, written and devised by him / producer
Margaret Sharp / photographed by Dick Rawlings

11/1991   **Sentimental Journey** (PBS. USA)
Public television documentary and interview

10/1993   **Vicky!** (USA)
Interview with Vicki Lawrence, filmed during *Doris
Day's Best Friends* charity event in Carmel, on 9th
October 1993

10/1993   **Good Morning America** (ABC. USA)
Interview with Joan Lunden, again coinciding with
Doris Day's Best Friends charity event

1994   **Don't Pave Main Street: Carmel's Heritage** (USA)
Guest appearance in this documentary film about
Carmel, narrated by Clint Eastwood

10/1994   **Pebble Mill 'Doris Day' Special** (BBC TV. UK)
In depth interview with Gloria Hunniford in Carmel

10/1994   **Des O'Connor Tonight** (ITV TV. UK)
Satellite interview promoting the release of 'The Love
Album' CD

10/1998   **It's Magic** (A&E Biography Channel. USA)
Extensive television biography featuring interviews
with Les Brown, Kaye Ballard, Edie Adams, James
Garner and Terry Melcher

04/2002   **Doris Day – Hollywood Greats** (BBC TV. UK)
Television biography featuring interviews with Andy
Williams, Howard Keel, John Raitt, Kaye Ballard and
Terry Melcher

2003   **Doris Day – E! True Hollywood Story**
(E! Entertainment. USA)
Television biography featuring interviews with Mamie
Van Doren, Jackie Joseph, Kaye Ballard and Rose Marie

BIBLIOGRAPHY

AMORY, CLEVELAND *Parade* magazine. USA (article 'I Even Cry Funny'), 3 August 1986

BAXTER, JOHN *Hollywood in the 'Sixties*. London, International Film Guide Series, Tantivy Press: New York, A. S. Barnes & Co, 1972

BRAUN, ERIC *Deborah Kerr*. London, W. H. Allen, 1977: New York, St Martin's Press, 1978

CAHN, SAMMY *I Should Care*. New York, Arbor House, 1974

CALLAN, PAUL *Radio Times*. London (article 'All in a Day's Work'), 15 October 1980

CLARKE, JANE, DIANA SIMMONDS AND MANDY MERKE BFI Dossier No. 4, 'Move Over Misconceptions'. London, December, 1980

CONSIDINE, SHAUN *Bette and Joan: The Divine Feud*. London, Century Hutchinson, 1989

CRAWFORD, JOAN *My Way Of Life*. With Jane Kesner Ardmore, New York, Doubleday & Company, 1962

DE CAMP, ROSEMARY *Tales From Hollywood: Fifty Years In The Great American Dream Factory*. USA: Cambria Recordings Talking Book, 1990

DIETRICH, MARLENE *My Life*. Translated from the German by Salvator, Attanasio. London, Weidenfeld & Nicolson, 1989

EELS, GEORGE AND STANLEY MUSGROVE *Mae West*. London, Robson Books Ltd, 1984

FRAYLING, CHRISTOPHER *Time Out*. London (article 'A Life in the Day'), 1 March 1989

GELB, ALAN *The Doris Day Scrapbook*. New York, Gresnet & Dunlap, 1977

GOW, GORDON *Hollywood in the 'Fifties*. London, International

Film Guide Series, Tantivy Press: New York, A. S. Barnes & Co, 1971

HALLIWELL, LESLIE *The Filmgoers Companion*. Worcester and London, The Trinity Press: MacGibbon & Kee Ltd, 1967

HASKELL, MOLLY *From Reverence To Rape: The Treatment Of Women In The Movies*. New York: Holt, Rinehart & Winston, Inc, 1974

HOTCHNER, A. E *Doris Day: Her Own Story*. London, W. H. Allen, 1975

HUDSON, ROCK *His Story*. With Sara Davidson. London, Weidenfeld & Nicolson, 1986

JOSEPH, JACKIE *Tolucan Times*. USA (article 'Toluca Lake – Doris Day Revisited'), 21 April 1999

KATZ, EPHRAIM *The International Film Encyclopedia*. London, Macmillan Press Ltd, 1980: Papermac, 1982

KIRK, KRIS *Gay Times*. London (article 'Sugar 'n' Spice – Gay Aspects of Fifties Pop'), May 1990

KOBAL, JOHN *Gotta Sing, Gotta Dance*. London. Hamlyn Publishing Group Ltd, 1970

LAMBERT, GAVIN *Norma Shearer*. London. Hodder & Stoughton, 1990

LATHAM, CAROLINE *Audrey Hepburn*. London, New York, 1984

LOY, MYRNA *Being and Becoming*. With James Kotsilibas-Davis. London, Bloomsbury Publishing Ltd, 1987

LYNN, VERA *Vocal Refrain: An Autobiography*. London, W. H. Allen, 1975

MORRIS, GEORGE *Doris Day*. Pyramid, 1976

MOULES, JOAN *Our Gracie*. London, Robert Hale, 1983

ORDER, DARLENE *Dedicated To Animals*. USA, Standard Buyers Guide/Dog World, 1988

PATRICK, PIERRE *Television Chronicles*. USA (article 'The Doris Day Show'), July 1996

SHIPMAN, DAVID *The Great Movie Stars: The International Years*. London, Angus & Robertson (UK) Ltd, 1972

TAYLOR, ELIZABETH *Elizabeth Takes Off*. With Jane Scovell. Macmillan London, Ltd, 1987 .

TODD, THOMAS *Doris Day*. London, Monarch, 1962

VAN DOREN, MAMIE *Playing The Field – My Story: The Explicit Memoirs Of A Hollywood Sex Goddess*. With Art Aveilke. New York: Headline, First Putnams, 1987

VINSON, JAMES (ED.) *The International Dictionary Of Films And Film Makers: Actors And Actresses.* New York, St James Press, 1986: London, Papermac, 1988

WELSCH, JANICE R. *Film Archetypes: Sisters, Mistresses, Mothers, Daughters.* New York, Arnos Press, 1978

WILLIAMSON, JUDITH *Time Out.* London (article 'Reclaim the Day'), 28 November 1980

YOUNG, CHRISTOPHER *The Films Of Doris Day.* New Jersey, Citadel Press, 1977

INDEX

to Doris's mother and parents –
traumatic fights with her
husband, birth of son Terry, 8
February 1942, husband's
moral cruelty to son and
subsequent eviction from home,
61–9; return to Les Brown and
his Band of Renown, first big
record hit 'Sentimental Journey'
– Pin-up of the Forces, 68–70;
marriage to alto sax player
George Weidler, 72–6; New
York club engagement,
marriage with George unravels,
return to Hollywood party, at
Jules Styne's leads to first film
test and screen début, affair
with Jack Carson, 73–82;
reunion with George Weidler
introduces her to Christian
Science, 86–7; Marty Melcher
takes over Doris's business
affairs, tour with Bob Hope,
second and third films with Jack
Carson, 88–94; film with Kirk
Douglas evokes memories of Al
Jorden, 96–8; Doris triumphs
for seven years at Warners,
98–102; first straight dramatic
part as Ginger Rogers's sister,
102–5; relationship with Ronald
Reagan and with Marty
Melcher (her manager),
109–11; their marriage, his
adoption of Christian Science
and Terry, 112–13; Photoplay
Gold Medal as Number One
female star of 1951, 114; Doris
makes the Top Ten most
popular movie stars after nine
films, 120–1; Doris and the Gay
Community, 125–6; *Calamity
Jane* contrast with Betty
Hutton's Annie Oakley,
128–30; DD's serious illness
and Christian Science, Sour
Apple Award, 131–4; friendship
with Judy Garland, 136; feud
between Marty Melcher and
Frank Sinatra, 138–9; Doris's
most rewarding role as Thirties'
singer Ruth Etting for MGM,
141–4; filming with Hitchcock
and James Stewart, 147–53;
reunion with father at *Julie*
premiere, meets his third wife,
his death, 158–60; empathy
with Gable – most successful
box office for three years,
163–5; two films flop, 167–70;
Ross Hunter changes Doris's
image to glamorous
sophisticate, start of 'Legend of
the Constant Virgin' – teaming
with Rock Hudson leads to
seven years as Number One
Star, 171–92; her last musical
acclaimed by critics, public
indifference, 192–4; Marty's
financial involvement with
lawyer Jerry Rosenthal,
marriage now in name only,
195–6; Terry leaves home,
achieves success on his own,
197–8; Doris's successful
partnership with James Garner,
198–200; beginning of the end
of her film career, 204–17;
Marty's fatal illness and death,
1968, 215–18; DD's
commitment to five-year TV
series, 219–23; Terry's illness
and near-fatal accident after
involvement with Manson gang
killings, Doris's new rapport
with her son, 225–7; trial of
Melcher's partner Jerry
Rosenthal for embezzlement
and misappropriation of DD's
funds – she is awarded damages

John, Elton, 235
Johnson, Van, 149
Jones, Allan, 44
Jones, Carolyn, 152
Jones, Tom, 232
Jorden, Al (first husband), 51–3,
    56, 59–69, 71–2, 77, 87–8, 98,
    154, 183
Jorden, Mr and Mrs, 53, 63, 67
Jourdan, Louis, 154–7
Julie, 64, 154–9, 166, 179, 199,
    231
'Julie' (song), 153–4
Jumbo see *Billy Rose's Jumbo*
'Just One Girl' (song), 116
'Just One of those Things' (song),
    106, 139

Kahn, Grace (Mrs Gus), 119
Kahn, Gus, 119, 141
Kanin, Fay, 165
Kanin, Garson, 200
Kanin, Michael, 165
Kappelhoff, Doris Mary Ann *see*
    Doris Day
Kappelhoff (von), Alma Sophia
    (née Weiz) (mother), 32–44,
    49, 50–2, 59–60, 62–3, 72, 74,
    78, 110–13, 119, 160, 197, 222,
    227, 231
Kappelhoff (von), Frederick
    William (father), 32, 158–60
Kappelhoff, Paul (brother), 29,
    34, 36, 54, 65, 128, 166
Karlin, Miriam, 161
Karloff, Boris, 182
Katz, Ephraim, 144
Keel, Howard, viii, 129–30, 148
Keeler, Ruby, 95, 100
Keith, Brian, 214
Kelly, Gene, 144, 167
Kelly, Grace, 150, 173
Kelly, Patsy, 177
Kendall, Kay, 146, 182
Kennedy, George, 211

Kenton, Stan, 76, 78, 86
Kenyon, Doris, 32, 36, 50
Kerr, Deborah, viii, 25, 35, 138,
    145, 148
Kerr, Jean, 176
King, Alison, vii
Kirk, Kris, 125–6
Klune, Ray, 152
Knotts, Don, 201
Kovacs, Ernie, 169
Krupa, Gene, 53, 56
Kruschen, Jack, 186, 188

Ladd, Alan, 102
Lake, Veronica, 102
Lamour, Dorothy, 88
Lampson, Barbara, 214, 222
Lancaster, Burt, 145
Lane Sisters: Lola, Priscilla,
    Rosemary, 137
Lang, Charles, 139
Langford, Frances, 1, 73–4
Lansbury, Angela, 236–7
Lausche, Frank (Governor), 158
Lawford, Peter, 223
Lawrence, Marjorie, 148
Le Boy, Grace *see* Mrs Gus Khan
Lee, Gypsy Rose, 55–6
Leigh, Vivien, 103
Lemmon, Jack, 169, 170, 172,
    224
Lennart, Isobel, 142, 176
Levant, Oscar, 25, 83, 126
Levine, Lee, 87
Levy, Al, 74–82, 87–8, 154
Levy, Ralph, 204
Lewis, Harry, 57
Lieberman, Dr Howard, 226–7
Lillie, Beatrice (Lady Peel), 45
Lindsay, Margaret, 177
Litel, John, 188–9
Little, Rich, 223
'Little Girl Blue' (song), 193
Livingston, Jay, 149
Lloyd, Doris, 181

266